MIDLIFE QUEER

AUTOBIOGRAPHY OF A DECADE

1971–1981

MARTIN DUBERMAN

SCRIBNER

NEW YORK LONDON TORONTO SYDNEY TOKYO SINGAPORE

SCRIBNER
1230 Avenue of the Americas
New York, NY 10020

Set in Bembo

DESIGNED BY ERICH HOBBING

Manufactured in the United States of America

1   3   5   7   9   10   8   6   4   2

Library of Congress Cataloging-in-Publication Data

Duberman, Martin B.
Midlife queer: autobiography of a decade, 1971–1981/Martin Duberman
p.   cm.
Includes index.
1. Duberman, Martin B. 2. Gay men—United States—Biography. 3. Gay men—United
States—Social conditions. 4. Gay liberation movement—United States—History. 5. United
States—Social conditions—1960–1980. I. Title.
HQ75.8.D82A32   1996
305.38'9664'092—dc20
[B]   95–52738
CIP

ISBN 0-684-81836-1

News From

S C R I B N E R

An Imprint of Simon & Schuster

1230 Avenue of the Americas, New York, New York 10020 fax: 212-632-4957

A **VIACOM** COMPANY

MIDLIFE QUEER
Autobiography of a Decade, 1971-1981
Publication Date: May 6, 1996

Contact: Sharon Dynak
Associate Director of Publicity
212/632-4047

ACKNOWLEDGMENTS

ELI ZAL, MY PARTNER (my soul? my love?—nobody has the words) has long been my best critic. Knowing me so well, and possessing an unparalleled bullshit detector, he has caught a multitude of false or sloppy moments in his several readings of this book, and insisted (while I fought and hollered) that I more deeply re-feel and more cogently re-phrase.

A number of friends have read the manuscript in whole or in part and caught additional errors of fact or judgment. I am deeply grateful to them: John D'Emilio, Jill Dolan, Ronald Gold, Frances Goldin, Esther Katz, Lawrence D. Mass, Matt Rottnek, and Dennis Rubini. For help in locating certain materials, I'm indebted to Robert Ridinger and Polly Thistlewaite. My thanks to Jolanta Benal for her typically skillful copyedit of the manuscript, and to Greer Kessel for her many assists in getting it to press. Leigh Haber edited the book with a graceful congeniality that made it easier for me to acknowledge how irrefutable her suggestions for changes were.

CONTENTS

MIDLIFE QUEER

PREFACE

The recounting of a life is a cheat, of course; I admit the truth of this; even our own stories are obscenely distorted; it is a wonder really that we keep faith with the simple container of our existence.

—Carol Shields, *The Stone Diaries*

I have begun to feel vaguely that all writing is an oddly Buddhistic-Hindu business of cancelling out what has gone before.

—V. S. Naipaul to Paul Theroux, June 8, 1968
(*The New Yorker,* June 26/July 3, 1995)

IN WANTING TO WRITE ABOUT MY LIFE in the seventies, two obvious formats presented themselves. I could do a collection of my essays from the decade, rehearsing and further codifying the views I had published on a variety of contested public topics. Or I could do a volume of excerpts from the detailed diary I kept at the time, focused on private miseries and pleasures.

I wanted to do both. And more besides: I wanted the freedom to weave together and intercut between the public and private, to extract (at the risk of exaggeration) thematic connections—such as the pervasive homophobia I encountered in both arenas; such as my persistent search for new directions to help me reconfigure nagging, ancient issues, professional and personal (perhaps the oldest being the perceived need to "fix" myself). And where the search went barren or became repetitive, I wanted that to show as well, since dead ends and obsessions are also inescapable aspects of a life's story.

I also wanted to find out what experiences from those years still resonated for me in light of all that has intervened; why I was choosing to highlight some aspects of my experience and ignore or downplay others—and wanted, in the process, consciously to lay bare the limits of reliable historical memory. And finally, I wanted to let myself shift tone in tandem with shifting events and subject matter—for I played various roles in the seventies, and in various styles. By ranging in this book from the academic ("The Profession of History") to the novelistic ("Intensive Care"), I wanted deliberately to affront the notion that a coherent life necessarily comprises consistencies of mood, persona, and language.

A diary entry from the beginning of the decade helps to suggest the distrust I felt, and feel, for smoothed-over presentations of the episodic self:

Diary, March 18, 1971

I can't get the "craziness" of my everyday thoughts, fantasies, and, at times, behavior, into this diary. Writing, for me, has always been a process of ordering and clarifying—part of my abysmal apprenticeship in academic nonfiction (more aptly called "making sense out of other people's confusion").

When I started the diary a year ago, I think I dropped some Couéism about it being a "tool for change." Maybe, but if so, as an incidental by-product. I write in here mostly because I enjoy performing, inventing variations on my own experience. It's not simply a matter of finding words to fit my events, or even a matter of recording experience in order to recognize it. Because in fact the recording *is* the experience, intertwining with and shaping the events so pervasively as to transpose them. I think when I began this diary I believed I was "getting it all down accurately." Naive. Only a select number of events and their ingredients even register, and those that do are (consciously and otherwise) instantaneously converted, the chosen words themselves shaping, heightening, foreshortening the experiences described.

It's something of a shock to my residual rationalism. I'm learning that all autobiography, necessarily being a comment on the self rather than the Self (frozen and caught like some specimen on a laboratory slide), is a creation—not a reproduction. Autobiography is the art of creating new experiences out of old memories.

I

THE SETTING

THE SEVENTIES WERE WIDELY REFERRED TO at the time as the "Me" Decade. Sixties activists decried it as complacent, as a sad, careerist-bent falling away from any concern with social justice, a grievous rerun of the "I'm fine, you're fine" fifties. Later, in the eighties, conservatives—themselves luxuriously living out the "Me, Too" (or "II") Decade—would deplore the seventies as *too* residually subject to the utopian pieties of the anti-authoritarian sixties.

Yet the students I taught during the seventies at Lehman College (a campus of the City University of New York) in the Bronx fit none of those stereotypes. Many of them from poor homes, most of them the first members of their families ever to go to college—and to do so, juggling jobs and responsibilities at home with course work—they were neither jaded cynics nor (since their lives often exemplified the tough path of those not born into privilege) unconcerned about social ills. Older than the average undergraduate, struggling to make ends meet and somehow to get the educational credentials they viewed as essential to a better life, they were well aware of—and angry about—the vast disparities of income and opportunity in our country.

In a course I taught on "Radical Protest Movements in the United States," a fair number of the students seemed at least marginally attracted to socialist economic analysis and to feminist values. But (as I described them in an op-ed piece for *The New York Times* in 1978), "the flirtation tends to be intermittent, the commitment sporadic. Not because of callow self-absorption (the standard view of their generation) but from profound wariness. They are neither obtuse nor heartless. They suffer, if anything, from a surfeit of knowledge, a deep revulsion against moralizing, a painful distrust of all prescriptions for social change—even as they profoundly wish it otherwise, wish to end

15

the stalemate between their ethical insights and their political pessimism. They fear to participate and fear not to. They have a canny awareness that corruption is endemic and available solutions shopworn—but in tandem, feel a guilty recognition that the subtlest form of corruption may be resignation."

Many of their left-leaning elders became no less warily disengaged as the country shifted markedly to the right during the seventies. After Nixon's landslide victory in 1972, and with the war in Vietnam winding down (Nixon finally withdrew all American troops in 1973), the glue that held left-wing protest together came unstuck. The call for institutional renovation got renamed by conservatives as "rebellion for its own sake," and the gray acceptance of things as they are gradually re-blanketed the land.

What remained of the once-powerful New Left broke into fragments, frequently at odds and sometimes at war with each other, with differences in strategy denounced as cosmic deviations from Truth. The fragmentation was augmented by developments in Southeast Asia after American troops departed. It was difficult to continue viewing Hanoi's success in the war as the triumph of self-determination over foreign imperialism when so many Vietnamese themselves were forced to become "boat people" in the face of the cruelties of the Vietcong regime—and when it was revealed that Pol Pot's Khmer Rouge in Cambodia was engaged in a massive campaign of terrorism and murder against its own people. (None of these developments, of course, made those of us who had been active in the antiwar movement retroactively change our view that American involvement in Vietnam had been wrong.)

The New American Movement (NAM) represented an effort to draw the scattered antiwar and New Left forces back together, but NAM never took hold, its membership rolls hovering at a few thousand. It was not that a strong left was no longer needed in American life: Ending the war in Vietnam had hardly ended Nixon's obsession (reinforced by Kissinger) with preserving the "free world" from the threat of communism—any more than it had marked their commitment to doing something about racism and poverty at home.

But the passionate moral intensity that had unified a multitude against a patently unjust war could not easily be transferred to organizing against the assorted injustices and growing disparities of wealth which were characteristic of the modern American industrial state—and heightened in the early seventies by the onset of a serious recession.

The time of great mass movements—with the exception of feminism—had passed. I myself—as much of this book recounts—recentered my energy into the struggle for lesbian and gay rights; indeed my own political commitment increased during the seventies. But many left-leaning activists, especially straight white men with no inclination toward the gay or feminist movements and only residually attached to the black struggle, either lost interest entirely in politics or retrenched around mostly local issues that ranged from union-organizing to building food co-ops.

The Watergate exposé in 1973 managed to snatch the country back from the verge of genuine executive tyranny—and (as I wrote in my diary at the time) that "of a puritanical, corporate kind that came close to warranting the label 'fascist.' " But the scandal marked a pause, not a reversal, in the Republican party's domination of political life. The emphasis was now on "law and order"—a chilling climate in which to urge further advances for the have-nots of American society.

When Gerald Ford succeeded Nixon to the presidency in 1974, the only two measures that seemed capable of capturing his attention were the pardoning of Richard Nixon and the prosecution of Daniel Ellsberg and Tony Russo on conspiracy charges for having secured and released the Pentagon Papers to the press. The Carter administration, which followed, marked a presidency with more liberal (if diluted) intentions—but those were largely stymied by a recalcitrantly conservative Congress *and* country. And from Carter, of course, we passed directly to the Reagan years, to the fullest flowering of the "I'm-all-right-Jack" philosophy of corporate greed that proved the most salient characteristic of the American eighties.

I didn't—certainly in retrospect—work nearly enough to help stem the conservative tide. Despite my deepening commitment to the gay movement, I was only peripherally active during the early seventies on the left in general; I continued to work and write for what was a swiftly decreasing number of oppositional outlets—organizations like RESIST, publications like *Liberation* and *WIN*—but most of my time and energy remained focused—as it always had (and like the mainstreamers I criticized) on my own career.

When I was asked to write the introduction to the War Resisters League's 1976 "Peace Calendar" celebrating "creative nonviolence in the American past," I felt flattered and accepted the assignment. But I also felt like something of a charlatan. In the introduction I attacked the mid-seventies retreat to "safer ground" and defended those "troublemakers" who challenged "the *structural* soundness of our institutions or policies (as distinguished from those who wanted the facade of a few buildings repainted or the cornices raised an inch or two)." I even suggested, citing Sartre, that "social protest may well be a concomitant of personal authenticity and not, as the historians have tried to persuade us for so long, a symptom of personal disorder"—the same message I had continued to hammer home year after year in my CUNY course on radical protest movements in the United States.

Yet I remained uncomfortable with how little I was doing along the very lines I was recommending. I remember that discomfort becoming acute one night when Dave McReynolds of the War Resisters League—a man who had remained unwaveringly devoted to fighting for substantive social change—unexpectedly rang my doorbell. (We had recently been corresponding about the pending celebration of WRL's fiftieth anniversary, and I had suggested a drink or dinner sometime.) That evening we talked for nearly three hours—or rather McReynolds, a gifted, compulsive, generous raconteur did, entertaining me with assorted anecdotes about various movement personalities.

It was only when the nascent gay struggle came up that we tangled a bit. McReynolds expressed contempt for the "superficiality" of the gay male lifestyle and claimed to have had little personal trouble accepting his own homosexuality. (For this he credited the good fortune of having met Alvin Ailey in a UCLA men's room in 1949; Ailey, according to McReynolds, was himself so guilt-free about being gay, and so warm a human being, that McReynolds *had* to believe it was okay to love men and lust after them.)

Yet our disagreement about the importance of becoming involved in the gay movement didn't affect my overwhelming admiration for McReynolds's intense, sustained activism in general. After he left, I felt a wave of self-disgust at the comparative indulgence of my own life. As I put it that night in my diary: "As he perched uncomfortably in his shabby clothes on the edge of my glove leather couch, the flames from the fireplace lighting up the luxurious colors of the oriental rugs, casting theatrical shadows on the oil paintings, the suspended ceiling sculpture, I squirmed at the implicit rebuke to my way of life."

The only saving grace, in my eyes, was that I *had* been working actively in the gay movement, serving on the founding boards of Lambda Legal Defense and the National Gay Task Force, and helping to organize the Gay Academic Union. That political work could itself, of course, be characterized as privileged—part and parcel of being a middle-class white man with a secure salary and leisure time, well-positioned and well-protected, despite his sexual orientation, within the larger context of American life.

Indeed, how *as a gay person* one experienced (or today characterizes) the seventies depended very much on who you were and where you found yourself. If you were a young middle or upper-class gay white male living in a big city, doing the latest designer drugs, disco dancing till dawn, taking advantage of the many outlets for casual sex, then you fit the current media image (and subsequent mythology) of the "gloriously indulgent" seventies. But the vast majority of gay men and lesbians did not fit the image. From their vantage point, the seventies was mostly more of the same, more of suffering the various deprivations that had long characterized the lot of any American of the "wrong" gender, skin color, or ethnicity.

Both vocally and in print, I expressed distaste for that segment of the gay male community that seemed to have narrowed its existence to achieving perfectly symmetrical bodies and inscrutably haughty veneers, and to displaying both as often as possible at stylish watering holes and disco palaces (or, alternately, at déclassé meat racks and backroom sex bars). That single-minded concentration of energy seemed fatuous; the "self-absorbed frivolity of the Fire Island/Flamingo [a disco] set," I wrote in an article, lent "credence to the standard homophobic equation of gayness with narcissism and mindlessness."

But I also spoke out against the notion, peddled by gay as well as straight puritans, that physical beauty and bodily pleasure were somehow inherently ignoble, and that sexual "adventuring" (the preferred, sex-positive seventies replacement term for "promiscuity") was, under the guise of pursuing pleasure, in fact a "flight from intimacy"—as the psychoanalytic profession had long insisted.

I was unsympathetic both to the tendency of the harshest critics of the Fire Island–bathhouse–backroom bar scene simplistically to summarize that lifestyle as unbridled, hoggish, male (over)indulgence, *and* to the insistence of its most admiring fans that its participants were heroic spelunkers, plunging into previously unexplored caves of the unconscious, daring to let their fantasies rather than their habits, rule their erotic lives.

It seemed to me that purebred hogs and spelunkers were alike rare (though I suspected there were more overindulgers than psychic pioneers). Most of the gay men I knew moved on and off the Fire Island–backroom bar circuit without wholly committing or succumbing. And often they took away from their adventures something of needed voluptuary value—needed as a counterweight to the injunction of their upbringing to shun and despise the sensual. For many, programmed to view unconventional sexual behavior of any kind as "sin" or "disturbance," the Meat Rack Experience became a genuine seeding ground for liberation.

(Gay men, of course, were not alone in the seventies in challenging earlier formulations of the acceptable boundaries of sexual pleasure. The popularity of such sex guides as David Reuben's *Everything You Always Wanted to Know About Sex*—which was also pervasively homophobic—the gigantic success of Alex Comfort's how-to book *Joy of Sex,* and the semi-respectability of porn films such as *Deep Throat* and *The Devil in Miss Jones,* were strong evidence that a growing segment of the heterosexual population had come to question the long-standing axioms that sexual pleasure required the justifying context of a love relationship and that there was a necessary or organic connection between sexual and emotional fidelity.)

After the onset of AIDS in the early eighties, some in the gay male world were heard loudly to lament their own "foolish" sexual histories; I knew any number of men who rushed to embrace and patriotically to celebrate the "wisdom" of monogamous pair-bonding. Their cheerleader became Larry Kramer, whose 1978 novel *Faggots* had excoriated Fire Island-Flamingo lust and license. Kramer published the novel before the plague erupted; consequently, his jeremiad has been hailed as prescient. But to me *Faggots* represented not uncanny clairvoyance but merely Kramer's own garden-variety sex-negativism. Inactive in the gay movement throughout the seventies ("You just didn't want to get involved," he has said in an interview. "It was not chic"), he still thinks "the baths represented the worst in all areas of what we were all about."

At the time, I hadn't met Kramer, but his unmodulated disdain for the gay male community, and the smug way he distanced himself from it, angered me. When I came to review *Faggots* (in *The New Republic*), I characterized its wooden invective as "no match for the inventive flamboyance of Fire Island hedonism when viewed from an angle wider than primitive moralizing." And I added that the book's "throbbingly self-righteous" tone was in the end "indistinguishable from the most rigid kind of mainstream morality." When Kramer and I did meet soon after, he was polite, even (given my negative review) gracious; and despite his surface over-commotion, I had no trouble at all seeing the warmth in which it lay embedded. But he apparently never forgave me for the review; some ten years later, I found him assaulting me in print for my "misguided" allocation of energy in working to build the field of lesbian and gay studies (rather than working beside him on "the front lines" of the AIDS struggle). A bare civility has since then been our modus operandi.

In bracketing *Faggots* with "the most rigid kind of mainstream morality," I had in mind especially the work of America's favorite sexologists, William Masters and Virginia Johnson. During the seventies they published two best-sellers, *The Pleasure Bond* and *Homosexuality in Perspective,* which, under the guise of "science" essentially reaffirmed standard fifties equations of a long-term relationship with maturity, and sexual nonfidelity with immaturity. In doing so, Masters and Johnson revealed the continuing hold on Americans—even on those like themselves who were practicing the "liberated" new discipline of sexology—of conventional moral values. They reaffirmed in their work the long-sanctified core of American sexual ideology: that the pair-bonded, monogamous heterosexual couple represents the optimal formula for human happiness.

In reviewing both of Masters and Johnson's books, I was reluctant simply to assail them, because their earlier work had been genuinely pioneering in its emphasis on the female ability to achieve multiple orgasms, on the essentially clitoral nature of female sexuality, and on the physiological similarity of male and female sexual responses. Masters and Johnson had provided crucial liberating data for the feminist movement—and for their pains had been widely scorned and snubbed as mere "mechanists" of sex.

Still, the claims they made in *The Pleasure Bond* and *Homosexuality in*

Perspective to a "value-free," "objective" social science were ludicrous, given the insistent ideology that pervaded both books. Among their many value-*loaded* assumptions were that the search for monogamous heterosexual marriage was a constant of human nature, and that "the overwhelming majority of women require an enduring relationship with a man" (in view of their earlier work, a surprisingly anti-feminist judgment).

Instead of evidence to back these assertions, Masters and Johnson gave us a good deal of bland exhortation. The reader was assured in *The Pleasure Bond* that when a marriage ran into trouble, "the commonest cause is simply misinformation." A frank talk, a kind touch, a few easily learned techniques would soon return the partners to the realization that an enduring marriage bond was the most satisfying embodiment of our sexual and spiritual yearnings.

As I wrote in my review of the book, "One need not be overly cynical about the value of talk, information or technique in order to question their sufficiency (let alone infallibility) for cure, or to wonder whether *some* of the widespread discontent with monogamous marriage might not be due to an occasional wish for variety (even anonymity—the appeal of the magical stranger) in our sexual partners."

Viewing monogamous heterosexuality as *the* sign of "maturity," Masters and Johnson were consigning to non-adulthood all those millions—including, to pick a few loaded names at random, Henry David Thoreau, Emily Dickinson, Walt Whitman, and Henry James—who declined such a relationship as the summum bonum of human happiness. When Masters and Johnson further insisted in *The Pleasure Bond* that a marriage without "effective sexual functioning" could survive but would "prove to be a relatively poor one," they were consigning to failure the unions of, among others, Virginia and Leonard Woolf, and Victoria Sackville-West and Harold Nicolson. In the absence of any historical examples of unions they considered "relatively rich," one had to question whether Masters and Johnson had even begun to think through the distinctive nature of, and problematic interconnection between, erotic excitement and domestic contentment.

Indeed, in writing that the measure of a "grown-up" is whether he or she is developing "a long-range relationship rather than concentrating it all on short-term pampering of the individual self," Masters and Johnson (loyal to the values of the culture that produced them) seemed in their books to be placing pleasure and commitment in an oppositional relationship to each other. They confirmed, on the one hand, that sexual pleasure was not contingent on love; yet on the other, claimed it was a misconception that "sex-as-service" ever gave much erotic gratification. To compound the confusion, they further argued that just in case extramarital sex *did* somehow prove pleasurable, that pleasure had to give way to the demands of a long-term relationship—in other words, the erotic needs of the individual had to be subordinated to the needs of the marital unit.

"The search for happiness and personal fulfillment," Masters and Johnson wrote in *The Pleasure Bond,* "sooner or later leads to marriage"—and people eventually do "discover themselves happier to restrict their sexual involvement to just one partner." In insisting on lifetime monogamous heterosexual pair-bonding as the one true path to contentment and maturity, Masters and Johnson were clearly reflecting (and enforcing) mainstream American values. Despite their (and the culture's) rhetoric of concern for "the individual," the books they published in the seventies came down to a set of rigid prescriptions which, if not followed, foretold misery and despair; far from encouraging "different strokes for different folks," Masters and Johnson's work deepened an already profound American intolerance for deviation. And all under the guise of "objective scientific findings." As I wrote in my review, Masters and Johnson "are entitled to their opinion, but we should be clear—even if they are not—that it *is* opnion they are peddling, not science."

A GAP HAS ALWAYS EXISTED, of course, between official prescriptions for contented, virtuous living and actual human behavior—an incongruity between the moralists' words and the citizens' acts. But another corollary is no less true: that the highly publicized "liberated" sexuality of a portion of the citizenry should never be equated with the behavior of all the citizenry. The "hedonistic seventies" did indeed bring us mainstream magazine articles entitled "Bondage as the Last Frontier" and "House Pets as Lovers"; and we did indeed hear a plethora of lurid revelations about congressional pages doing double duty with their employers and about jaded jet-set members purchasing the sexual services of specially reared Great Danes. But excess and experimentation had hardly swept the scene.

Contra Masters and Johnson, I wasn't convinced that a monogamous, lifetime pair-bonded relationship *was* the most satisfying embodiment of human sexual and emotional yearnings—especially when applied as a mandatory blueprint. Don't (shouldn't?) our sexual and emotional yearnings change through time? Perhaps, at least for some people at some points, "happiness" hinges on adventure, risk, surprise, and variety; at other times or for other people, on feelings of safety, familiarity, and permanence. For the young especially, I believed sex had many functions besides the culturally acceptable one of solidifying a couple's "commitment." It could also be an important means for exploring a range of desires, a multiplicity of identities, a variety of roles—for discovering an assortment of buried fantasies and needs.

No, I thought the petted, privileged Fire Island-Flamingo set was shallow not because its sexual explorations were intrinsically "indulgent" or "sick," but because it valorized a lifestyle that seemed so willfully insular. To the apparent contentment of its denizens, Fire Island in the mid-seventies existed outside social reality as most people knew (or were forced to endure) it, and was arrogantly dismissive of those who failed to qualify—meaning the vast majority of gay as well as straight people—for admission to its own white, moneyed, male enclave (to say nothing of being disconnected from unexamined possibilities in their own lives).

If I felt the Fire Island scene should not be automatically adjudged a flight from intimacy, I thought it could with some justice be regarded as a flight from politics. The gay movement in the United States was undoubtedly the strongest in the world in the seventies; indeed, fledgling formations elsewhere looked to the post-Stonewall American movement as the flagship. In continental Europe, where there was a tradition of greater tolerance for same-gender sexuality than in the United States, that comparative tolerance, paradoxically, blunted political organizing; not enough seemed wrong to bother with a full-scale "liberation" movement.

But the tolerance was skin deep at best, and tacitly predicated on gay invisibility, on the acceptance of public nonexistence. Such political formations as came into being tended to reflect the general European view that the formula of "acceptance in exchange for discretion" was a reasonable one. For a time, the French Front Homosexuel d'Action Révolutionnaire militantly challenged so tame a strategy, but that group soon disintegrated and even at its height never approached the popularity of the mainstream French gay movement, Arcadie, which deplored street demonstrations and nonconformist behavior.

(Nor has much changed since; in the early nineties, I got into a protracted argument at a dinner party with an openly gay French novelist who insisted that France, "always liberated on the question of homosexuality," had no need of an American-style gay political movement, while I insisted that the selective tolerance he heralded was based on a polite assimilationism that should never be confused with liberation— a point worth making to many American gay people as well. Neither of us convinced the other.)

But if the American gay movement was the strongest in the world in the mid-seventies, it was not nearly strong enough. The vast majority of gay men and lesbians, if visible at all, were struggling primarily with issues relating to their individual decisions about how best to come out, or how successfully to cover their tracks and remain in the closet; they had scant remaining energy for or interest in political activism. The few who did participate in the fledgling gay movement were sharply divided over agendas and strategies.

In particular, gay men and lesbians found it increasingly difficult to work together politically during the seventies. The reasons were multiple: the waning of gay male militancy, as characterized by the decline of the Gay Liberation Front in the immediate post-Stonewall years, 1969–1972; the indifference of even many activist gay men to feminist politics and values; the emergence instead of a gay male style that aped machismo (even if, marginally and for most unconsciously, it simultaneously parodied that style). To many lesbians, the lives of gay men seemed chiefly devoted to rampaging sexual consumption in bathhouses and backroom bars, to sex disconnected from emotional commitment; this, and their indifference to feminism, seemed to suggest that gay men were much like straight men. Committed to a different (and, some argued, traditionally female) set of values centered on nurturance, sharing, and community-building, many lesbians came to feel increasingly alienated from their purported "brothers" and turned to creating a separatist movement.

I, too, regretted the decline of militance in the organized gay political movement, and the disinclination of its white male leadership to incorporate feminist and nonwhite perspectives. And in print I lambasted the refusal of most gay men, and notably those comfortably ensconced for the summer on Fire Island, to involve themselves in any way politically. But it might be honorable to add that I had never felt much at home in the perfervid disco or Fire Island or backroom bar scenes.

I did go dancing once at the Flamingo, writhing in drug-fueled ecstasy with the rest of the tribe. But once had been enough to convince me that I lacked the stamina, musculature, and attitude to achieve true votary status in that world. I hadn't managed even one trip to what I had often heard were the mouth-watering, mind-bending spectacles on view at the Mine Shaft or Anvil backroom bars.

I'm not sure why I hadn't. I *was* a fan of dancing, sex, and to some extent drugs. But I suppose I was too body-shy to combine them in public and, like most of my generation, too residually guilt-ridden about my deviant desires. Besides, I liked the illusion of being in control of my libido and my time. Often juggling three or more writing projects at once, I didn't need the further unmanageability of juggling a brand-new red-hot sexual scene as well. Much as I had continued to like and to pursue sex (more than somebody in his forties was supposed to), I could no longer easily call up the gladiatorial energy of earlier days. Romance still occasionally ensnared me (and usually still centered on stricken pups in their early twenties or on hard-shelled tough guys in awesome states of denial). But the gorgeous carnal spectacle of the gay male seventies pretty much passed me by. Not even word from a California friend with whom Michel Foucault was staying that the guru had been singing the praises of American gay men for "inventing the first new form of sex in hundreds of years"—fist-fucking—could get me, admirer of Foucault's though I was, down into that particular trench (sorry—sling). Sexual adventure had taken a decided backseat to work.

I joined the sexual revolution in the way scholars have always intersected with life: I wrote about it. Indeed, I decided, in the mid-seventies, to embark on a full-scale "history of sexual behavior." I held out scant faith that in the process I would rejuvenate my loins, but thought I might at least resuscitate my flagging belief in the value of studying the past.

II

THE PROFESSION
OF HISTORY

I HAD LONG FELT AT ODDS with the historical profession's self-regard-
ing claims to "objectivity" and the high-minded pursuit of Truth. During much of the sixties and early seventies, I had rebelled, too, against
the authoritarian rituals of the classroom. Throughout those years, I'd
searched for ways to revivify the study, writing, and teaching of history.
I had tried everything from writing plays with historical themes (*In
White America, Elagabalus, Mother Earth, Visions of Kerouac*), to inserting
my own voice into the historical narrative of my 1972 book, *Black
Mountain,* to doing away with grades and introducing "encounter exercises" in the classroom.

In the heady sixties—the counterculture in full bloom, challenges
to authority everywhere flourishing—I was deeply in sympathy with
the so-called romantics of educational theory: A. S. Neill, Carl Rogers,
Paul Goodman, George Dennison, John Holt, and Edgar Z. Frieden-
berg. Like them, I believed that learning was most effective when it
grew out of what interested the learner, not the teacher. Which was not
to say (as I wrote at the time) "that all formal education was unneces-
sary, or that all children would develop to best advantage if simply
allowed to follow their own instincts and interests. But it *was* to say
that much of what is taught isn't worth knowing, and much of what is
worth knowing can't be taught; that children had to be allowed to
make discoveries; that the young were right to feel helpless in the face
of antiquated rules and bureaucratic manipulation."

In reviewing Charles Silberman's 1970 book, *Crisis in the Classroom,*
for *The New York Times,* I posed the general question "What are schools
for?" "The traditional answer," I wrote, "usually comes in two parts:

schools convey knowledge and skills to the young so that someday they can get good jobs; and schools introduce the young to their cultural heritage so that they can participate in the country's social and political life." But the schools—reflecting the society that produced them—perform neither function adequately. We are no longer sure *what* knowledge and *which* skills prepare young people for the rapidly changing and shrinking job market; "training" is followed by unemployability with terrifying speed.

As for the melting-pot notion of "guaranteeing future carriers of the culture," by the early seventies that goal was already widely discredited among the young themselves. Even among the many white students who never questioned the culture's Eurocentric values, there was widespread awareness of the institutionalized inequities of the system—and hence the dubeity of perpetuating it. The young, I wrote in 1974, "don't want to fill predetermined slots in the society, and they resent the cloistered exercises that in fact keep them quarantined." Besides, I added, "schools devoted chiefly to job preparation and socialization are essentially anti-life, for their secondary effect (sometimes, it seems, their primary intent) is to inculcate docility, suppress curiosity, and atrophy the senses. Most of our schools are joyless. They're preoccupied with order and control, with inculcating chronic dependence while claiming they are busy about the Lord's work of making individuals."

At the beginning of the seventies, I was still teaching at Princeton (I resigned in 1972 to join the City University of New York), and had found there a small—and diminishing—group of students who continued to take their inspiration from sixties radicalism. We would talk fervently together about the need to (along with much else) de-school society, as Ivan Illich put it. We worried about the way a university education emphasized the primary importance of a systematic life, reinforcing the culture's pressure to specialize, to do *one* thing well and forever—an emphasis which in turn bred distrust of the untidy particularity of daily experience and of the many contradictory attractions and impulses we knew we harbored within. We reinforced each other's determination (now viewed as "idealistic" or "utopian") to remain "in process," to guard against (as I put it in a review at the time) "stale vocabularies and categories that render experience safe by reiterating culturally agreed-upon names for it."

In print I defended the radical young against attacks on them by such "wise heads" of the older generation as George Kennan, Jacques Barzun, Norman Podhoretz, and Sidney Hook, men who in my view belied their claim to speak for a tradition of dispassionate, rational discourse in the frenzied, unmodulated way they mounted their assaults on what they liked to call the "barbarism" of the new generation. Of no one was this more true than my old mentor and dissertation adviser, the Harvard historian Oscar Handlin.

In a speech before the American Historical Association in the early 1970s, Handlin railed against radical members of the profession, claiming that their sole interest in the past was as a vehicle for political polemics. I responded to the charges in a review (for *The New York Times*) of Handlin's *Facing Life: Youth and the Family in American History*. I pointed out that his own book, a ranting tirade against the radical young, exemplified precisely that polemical use of history (under the guise of objective analysis), that he had so freely condemned in others.

And I argued widely elsewhere that the very notion of non-political, "objective" history resulted from a naive misunderstanding of what was actually involved in any effort to reclaim past experience. That effort always hinged, I wrote, "on two basic components: the data itself and the individual who interprets it. The former is never sufficiently full, the latter never sufficiently neutral. An episode in the past and the present recording of it merge into a single performance. And if there is to be any hope of keeping the two apart, we have to acknowledge that both are intrinsic to the process of historical reclamation—that a contemporary individual (the historian) is in conversation with certain source materials, mere fragmentary traces, from the past." Like all historians, I thought it was essential to try to contain our biases as much as possible. But that meant admitting them in the first place. Not to admit them was a form of hypocrisy.

A case in point was a book I reviewed in the mid-seventies, *Sex and Marriage in Utopian Communities,* by historian Raymond Lee Muncy. *Because* the subject matter was unusual, the author's hidden biases were all the more vividly highlighted. Muncy's sexism, for example, was as pervasive as it was unexamined. He referred at one point to "woman's natural capacity for jealousy"; at another, he commented that the "zealots" who were bent on changing the oppressive conditions under which women lived "often glossed over the contentment which most wives and mothers had found around their family fire-sides." He characterized Margaret Fuller as "a pathetic creature" and reduced the motives of another remarkable nineteenth-century woman, Frances Wright—who had courageously attempted to establish an interracial community at Nashoba in *pre*–Civil War Tennessee—to a simple desire for "grandeur and glory." Not exactly subtle stuff.

Yet Muncy's book was published by a university press and, in general, respectfully received. He had, after all, followed the rules, long since set, by which the historical profession certified a work as neutral: He had used simple declarative sentences, appended footnotes, bibliography and index, stockpiled details, avoided much overt speculation, and sprinkled his text with "on the other hand"s. But if Muncy decorated his book with the outer panoply of "objective analysis," value judgments disfigured every page. Like so many scholars, he kept his hand gloved, yet it left fingerprints everywhere. "An ideology *is* at work," I wrote in my review, "and because it is never frankly revealed, Muncy need never make the painful effort to examine and contain it—and we cannot be put on guard against the ways it may be contaminating the presentation of evidence. Covert bias is far more insidious than open opinion—simply because its influence on the data is more difficult to trace."

THE RANGE OF PERSONALITY in the ranks of professional historians in the seventies was not as wide as that of the population as a whole, since academia in those years (and to a significant extent still) tended to attract, and to extend its invitations, only to certain kinds of people—meaning relatively few women and almost no people of color. Still, the historical guild in the seventies did contain, among its mostly white male practitioners, a fairly generous spectrum of hotheads and icebergs, child-lovers and dog-haters, authoritarians and anarchists, sexpots and celibates.

The trouble is, you would hardly have known it from reading their books, which were written in such an interchangeably monochromatic style as to seem the product of a single hand. The reigning model was The Monograph—literally translated as "one thing," freely paraphrased as "no style." The more modest members of the profession explained this as a necessary result of their limited literary skill. The larger number of self-satisfied historians insisted that uniformity of product was proof that history had become a science, depersonalized and capable of infinite replication. The equation of homogenization with neutrality was analogous to defining a conforming society as one that had "transcended" the need to hold opinions.

In the seventies, the absence of stylistic idiosyncrasy in a historical work, in combination with the presence of "cliometric" apparatus (that is, the application of statistical methods to the study of history), was widely seen as proof that the historian was a bona fide scholar—and also, more generally, as proof that historians were not in any way a contaminating presence in their own work. This pretense of nonexistence might be thought anachronistic in a culture long priding itself on "individuality." But the gap between our official rhetoric and our actual practice was hardly confined to historical studies; everywhere, in the seventies, it had become more bearable to be seen as an interchangeable part than to be seen. We taught our young to mouth the sacred slogans of individualism, all the while inculcating in them the habits of machine parts.

Moreover, historians—social scientists generally—had long presumed themselves to be immune from vulgar abuses of evidence. They liked to claim that the exploitation of history for polemical purposes was confined to the undereducated and the overambitious—that only the multitude, and their leaders, found in the past what they set out to find. Historians, "trained in the use of evidence" (i.e., possessing an advanced degree) were presumed to be exempt from the common tendency to equate a personal perspective with absolute truth—and from the universal need for self-confirmation.

Yet historians, no less than interventionist presidents, have claimed that studying the past provided proof positive—as shown, say, in the debacle following upon Chamberlain's appeasement of Hitler—of "the need to take a firm stance against foreign aggression." Historians, as well as corporate executives, have "discovered" in the historical evidence ample proof that our free enterprise system has been the chief factor in producing national abundance—just as another group of historians, along with the members of the Socialist Workers Party, have "found" that free enterprise has been solely responsible for the gross maldistribution of national wealth.

Contrary to their preferred self-image, professional historians did not—as they still do not—stand apart from the popular habit of reading contemporary needs into past events, except perhaps in their insistence that they *are* above the fray, that what they write and teach is Truth, not opinion. This attitude, in the late sixties and early seventies, had earned the scorn of the radical, politically minded young. Decreasing interest on the campuses in historical studies was much commented on in the seventies, and the blame usually put on the current student generation itself: It would not accept the discipline needed to master detail; it would not curtail emotion in the name of gaining critical distance.

But I saw the situation differently. I saw radical students in the seventies rejecting historical study as a direct reflection of their search for personal authenticity. As I wrote at the time, "the best of the young reject disguise; they want to know who is responsible; they prefer the personal to the computerized response; they value the distinctive above the typical." And having grown up in the midst of the Vietnam debacle, "they know all about official lies. They want to see the faces behind the masks. And when the mask remains securely in place, they react with contempt."

But professional historians in the seventies were far less preoccupied with uncovering the subjective ways in which they influenced their narratives (even as they hid their personalities) than they were with adopting the new cliometric statistical hardware. Economic historians especially, moved with a rush toward tabulation as the key to the universe. To me, this represented a narrowing, not an expansion, of the historian's preserve. It meant focusing on those limited aspects of human behavior that lent themselves to a chi-square analysis, minimizing human idiosyncrasy in the name of arriving at low-level sociological generalizations. It meant capitulation to the then-popular behaviorist views of B. F. Skinner—what I sardonically referred to in print as "Skinnerism: taking off the hide, and calling it humanity."

The idiosyncrasies passed over, in my view, often told us more about human nature—its gorgeous peculiarity, its plasticity, its variability—than did all the multiple regression analyses stacked end to end. To focus on what was quantifiable in the human experience and to eschew that which was "merely" subjective was to me the equivalent of preserving the shell and throwing away the egg. I saw nothing in t-tests or Z-scores, in non-parametric statistics or Pierson Product Moment

Correlations, that threw any light on those inner needs, emotions, fears, fantasies, drives, and obsessions, which *I* took to be central to human lives through time—as opposed to the lives of computers.

A two-volume study of American slavery, *Time on the Cross* (1974), by Robert Fogel (who in 1993 would share the Nobel Prize in economics) and Stanley Engerman was in the seventies the touchstone of the new cliometric methodology. Though a number of scholars (and notably Herbert Gutman) later published sharp critiques of the work, its initial reception in the mainstream press had been thunderously favorable. The book had been widely hailed as the "masterwork" of the new cliometrics when I decided to undertake a detailed review of it for *The Village Voice.*

I did so with considerable trepidation. The entire second volume of *Time on the Cross* consisted of heavy hardware indeed: statistical tables, data banks, graphs, mathematical formulas, and computer printouts. And like all properly socialized Americans, I viewed such evidences of Hard Science with a mix of deference and fear—the fear a function of my own lack of training in the new techniques.

Besides, Fogel and Engerman had themselves warned against extremists in the cliometric camp who would claim that the writing of history can be reduced to a set of equations. With the authors thus modestly narrowing the claims of quantification, and with all historians except for those who still wrote with quill pens agreeing that the quantifiers had long since established the usefulness of their methodology in answering certain (to my mind, limited) kinds of questions, it would have been pointless to burden Fogel and Engerman with the defense of a position they didn't hold, nor foolishly to denounce all statistical work in the social sciences as misguided.

Yet after reading *Time on the Cross,* I felt convinced that the work—despite its claim to being objective science, and despite the dazzling new technology deployed in support of that claim—was seriously contaminated with Fogel and Engerman's own middle-class, and unexamined, mind-set. The clearest example related to the discussion in *Time on the Cross* of marriage and sexuality in slavery. Summarizing their findings on miscegenation, Fogel and Engerman acknowledged that "many" planters did seek sex "outside the confines of their wives' bed," but then hastened to add that even if all reports of sexual exploitation of slave women were true, the number of cases amounted to "at most a few hundred." But did "a few hundred" refer to the number of sexual acts, or to the number of slaves involved in them? And how did we know that for each reported case there weren't hundreds or thousands that had gone unreported?

One gauge would be the number of mulattoes in the slave population. Fogel and Engerman put the figure at "just" 10.4 percent. "Just"? What "objective criteria" entitled these two middle-class white male scholars to regard 10.4 percent as low? Why wasn't it obvious to them that not every instance of miscegenation resulted in pregnancy, and not every pregnancy produced a live baby? How was it possible to claim mathematical precision about how many slave owners slept with how many slaves, when so few planters (or slaves) had left *any*—let alone detailed—record of their sexual histories?

In lieu of precision Fogel and Engerman offered pseudo-arguments. Planters would have been dissuaded from seeking sexual pleasure in the slave quarters because to do so would have produced "distraught and disgruntled" slaves and would have undermined "the air of mystery and distinction on which so much of the authority of large planters rested." This, in turn, would have compromised what was "obviously" their chief concern: the pursuit of economic gain. Sensible men, the authors presumed, would not have run such risks when they could easily have afforded to keep white mistresses in town. But though it is apparently unthinkable to economic historians, the drive for profit does not always outweigh the dictates of lust.

Fogel and Engerman's treatment of sexuality within the slave quarters themselves was no less suspect. Arguing sternly against the view that "wanton impregnation of very young unmarried" black women took place, Fogel and Engerman offered as counterproof their "discovery" that the average age at which a slave mother first gave birth was 22.5 years. But even should that statistic be accurate, the age at which a woman gives birth should not be equated with the age at which she first has sexual intercourse. Yet Fogel and Engerman concluded from their *birth* data that "the prevailing sexual mores of slaves were not promiscuous but prudish." To conclude further, as Fogel and Engerman did, that in a non-contraceptive-using population "only abstinence" can explain "the relative shortage of births in the late-teen ages" could only mean that the authors were wholly ignorant of folk devices—from the rhythm method to herbs—for avoiding pregnancy or inducing abortion.

Fogel and Engerman proudly announced that their "discovery" of slave prudishness was—along with their additional "finding" that the slave population was a hardworking and not a malingering one—a significant contribution to "the betterment of contemporary race relations." It seemed never to have dawned on them that neither sexual abstemiousness nor an uncomplaining dedication to forced, back-breaking labor is everywhere viewed as signs of virtue or character. Yet Fogel and Engerman felt they had "rescued" black slave culture from denigration—and, by implication, had welcomed contemporary blacks into the human community. This grand feat had been accomplished (as I wrote in my *Voice* piece) by "saddling blacks with those sex-negative, middle-class white values for which they may have more scorn than respect; it congratulates them, with that familiar liberal pat on the back, for being just like us—just as sexually repressed and work-obsessed, just as devoted to the all-American virtues of abstinence, shame and monogamy."

Computers and mathematical models, it was clear, would not diminish dogmatic provincialism in the historical profession—or anywhere else. The new cliometricians, like the "old-fashioned" scholars who preceded them, would continue to discover in the past reflections of their own starting assumptions, however unconsciously held. And those assumptions would continue to be tradition-bound ones. Most historians, after all, are cultural conservatives; the profession, by definition, consists of "conservators," of people willing to devote their lives to preserving the past.

DURING THE UPHEAVALS OF the sixties and early seventies, some of the radicalized, mostly younger members of the profession managed to make their voices heard to a far greater extent than had been usual. (Indeed even later, the Organization of American Historians elected William Appleman Williams, who had held the United States chiefly accountable for the Cold War, its president.) But after Nixon's landslide victory in 1972, there was no missing the shift back toward the safe and the traditional—in the profession no less than in the country.

This became clear to me on a personal level at the 1974 convention of the Organization of American Historians, held that year in Denver. I dislike flying and would ordinarily have avoided the trip, but a panel had been scheduled on "Duberman's *Black Mountain*: The Involved

Self: A New Form of History?", so I forced myself to get on the dreaded plane, plugged the blue plastic tubes in my ears, and heard Beethoven's "Eroica" (or something) four hundred times. I managed *partly* to drown out the whirrs and swoops that ordinarily have me frantically checking the exit signs.

More punishment awaited in Denver. The panel became an occasion to chastise me for having called for a more openly acknowledged subjectivity. I was accused of an antipathy to *all* generalization, and was told that in revealing so much about *myself* in *Black Mountain* I had indulged in "exhibitionism." (As my one *defender* on the panel of three more generally put it, "Too much self-disclosure might end as testimony against ourselves, our meditations revealed as mere dry, withered turds.")

In responding, I was tempted to deconstruct the unlovely self-image of "turds," but didn't want to lose my one (already unsteady) ally. I settled for glancingly referring to it as an index of how we had all been raised to regard our inner lives with contempt, to internalize society's equation of emotion (especially in males) with exhibitionism and immaturity. Those equations had been strongly reinforced, I said, "by a profession that honors us mainly for our industry, occasionally for our opinions, never for our feelings."

Which meant, as a by-product, we were encouraged to detach from our own inescapably subjective response to the data, to mask and deny (rather than to clarify) the way in which our own values and experiences affected our presentation of historical materials. That amounted, I argued, to sanctioning dishonesty. We *are* present in our work—and not just as thinking machines. Our feelings, fantasies, and needs dictate on every page what will be selected and emphasized. The heart of the historical process is not tabulation, but dialogue—one person, living in the present, *engaging in conversation with* certain traces of experience left by people in the past. In emphasizing the reading of history as dialogue, we could thereby (as I said in my response to the panelists) "encourage others to join in it—readers of our books, students in our classes. In letting our voices be heard, our persons seen, we could facilitate the joining of still other voices, other persons. The end product is what is sometimes called 'community.' "

If I had one regret about my book on Black Mountain, I told the audience attending the OAH panel, "it isn't that I revealed too much about myself, but that I revealed too little; that time and again, unconsciously or semiconsciously, I let my training in depersonalization overrule my passion, let normative judgments about propriety, and professional definitions of appropriateness, replace my own sense of what the needs of the narrative required. It isn't conscience that makes cowards of us all—it's graduate school training. I hope that in the future my work will err more on the side of indiscretion—since our profession has so long erred on the side of gentility."

The following year, I reluctantly (because I loathed administrative duties of any kind) agreed to be nominated for the OAH executive committee, yielding to the argument that a number of gay and radical historians had worked hard to get me nominated. But I lost the election by a considerable margin. Two years after that, in 1977, a friend of mine on the OAH nominating committee recounted a strange tale that went far to confirm in my mind the pronounced conservative turn within the profession.

After the nominating committee's first day of deliberations, according to the friend, my name had headed the list of candidates for president of the OAH—with some inconclusive discussion about proposing Oscar Handlin as well. (This was in line with recent precedents of running two candidates for the office.) The chair of the nominating committee had been empowered to call me that night and ask if I would be willing to run.

When the committee reconvened the next morning, the chair reported that he hadn't been able to reach me. At that point in the deliberations, my friend was called away from the meeting. When he returned an hour later, he found that my name had been dropped to third place and ex-liberal right-winger Oscar Handlin and ex-Marxist right-winger Eugene Genovese had been jointly nominated to run for president. According to my friend, the committee chair then announced that if one or both of the nominees declined (in the end both accepted), and I was moved back up to active candidacy, he "would resign as chair rather than place the call to me"—a comment that should have made it obvious that he had never attempted to reach me the night before, when in fact I *had* been home.

The friend who reported all this was convinced that the "gay issue," more than my political views in general, had been salient. Evidence from other quarters suggests he was right.

In 1974 Dennis Rubini (an openly gay historian at Temple University) and I submitted a proposal to the program committee of the American Historical Association's annual convention for a panel to be called "The History of Sexual Behavior." (The AHA includes all American-based historians of whatever specialty, unlike the OAH, whose roster centers on historians of the Americas.) Hearing nothing back and finally inquiring, we were told that the proposal had been "unaccountably lost."

We resubmitted it the following year, and this time the AHA program committee explicitly turned us down. To compound the insult, an article appeared in the *AHA Newsletter* entitled "Undoing History; or, Clio Clobbered," quoting and mocking Dennis and me for having said that "the paucity of gay history offerings throughout the country testifies to the de facto existence of . . . hostility and prejudice generally." The article jovially assured us that the paucity was due instead to the fact "that the history of this and other 'sexual minorities' is unimportant."

Furious, Dennis and I (with Dennis doing most of the work) managed to get a pro–gay studies resolution passed at the AHA's annual business meeting—only to have it subsequently rejected by the AHA Council, the organization's ruling body. The AHA's executive director then asked us to document our charge that discrimination against gay people in hiring and promotion existed.

I tried to explain to the director, in writing, that although some documentation did exist (for example, recent firings at Atlanta's Emory, Boston State, and the University of Delaware), the evidence was hard to come by; even when conscious of their prejudice, most academics were too clever to express it openly and would cite other grounds entirely (the quality of teaching, the extent of publications, departmental "good citizenship," and so on) for voting against an appointment or promotion. And many academics were not even in touch with their homophobia, preferring to believe that as good liberals they were free of prejudice—a form of denial women and people of color had long been familiar with.

I ran into much the same kind of attitude in my own workplace, the City University of New York. When I approached union chair (and history department colleague) Irwin Polishook about getting "sexual orientation" included in the anti-discrimination clause of the university's new labor contract, he himself was supportive. But the effort soon ran afoul of CUNY's vice chancellor. He first proposed changing "orientation" to "predilection" and then, when I reluctantly agreed, withdrew the offer—announcing that "the whole fuss" had only come about because Polishook and I were members of the same history department. (Say what?)

A still more protracted struggle developed with the CUNY graduate school. When I was appointed a Distinguished Professor in the CUNY system in 1972, I had been asked to teach at the Graduate Center at Forty-second Street, where the institution's doctoral work was done. At the time, I declined, saying I'd grown tired in recent years of teaching graduate students—they were too dutiful, in my view, writing my every comment down as if it were Truth—and for a while would prefer to confine my teaching to Lehman College, one of CUNY's undergraduate campuses. But I did agree to sit on Ph.D. oral exam committees and to read doctoral theses for the Graduate Center.

A few years later, as my new interest in the history of sexual behavior grew, I went back to the Graduate Center and said that I would be willing, after all, to teach there—more than willing, eager, for I needed a more academically inclined group of students to bounce things off of. The mere suggestion—and mind, I was proposing a seminar not on gay and lesbian history but on the history of sexual behavior in general—brought a storm of indignation.

I was told that "sexual history" was not history at all, that the subject had been spawned by political polemics not scholarly necessity, and that my involvement in such a non-subject would bring my "objectivity" as a scholar into serious question. Stunned and angry, I told the graduate school history department chair, Gertrude Himmelfarb, that since I was now considered "contaminated," the department would surely no longer want students exposed to me: I refused any longer to sit on Ph.D. orals or read doctoral dissertations. (And I held to that resolve until 1991. By then the climate had changed considerably: I was welcomed back as the founding director of the Center for Lesbian and Gay Studies, and that year offered a course entitled "Reclaiming Gay and Lesbian History, Politics and Culture.")

In 1975 the OAH did approve a resolution affirming "the right of historians and others to engage in research and teaching about all sexual minorities." And by 1977, the AHA finally agreed to schedule our panel "The History of Human Sexuality" (though it turned down our request to change the title and focus to "Sexual Variance in History"). The AHA program committee put the panel in the last time slot on the final day of the convention, when many had already left for home. And they assigned us to a cavernous, unheated ballroom. Nonetheless, some fifty or so brave souls showed up, and it gave me outsized pleasure to say in my gleeful opening remarks as chair of the panel (which included Dennis Rubini, historian of science Elizabeth Fee, and Thomas Szasz), "that the recognition is dawning among historians, despite disavowal and disbelief, that sexual activity *has* been a characteristic of human behavior in the past." The crowd giggled nervously.

By 1978, we had ceased begging for crumbs and had begun to organize our own panels and conferences. A gay and lesbian history study group in New York—which included John D'Emilio, Joan Nestle, Deborah Edel, Lisa Duggan, Jonathan Ned Katz, Bert Hansen, and Judith Schwarz—started holding regular meetings to share information and ideas. And Terry Collins, a brave, openly lesbian graduate student at New York University, put together in the spring of 1978 an ambitious conference entitled "Constructing a History of Power and Sexuality." I remember my excitement as I wandered from session to session during that conference, amazed at how much scholarly activity seemed suddenly about to burst forth. When it came time for me to speak as one of the two "summarizers" of the event, all I could manage was some grinningly incoherent mix of gush and astonishment at how much work seemed finally inaugurated—despite the indifference or hostility of the professional powers that be—and at how gratifying it felt to see *ourselves* mobilized at last to produce accurate scholarship on our own lives.

Indeed, between 1976 and 1980, a number of pioneering books appeared that put the possibility of writing gay and lesbian history beyond cavil, though its legitimacy and importance remains contested within the historical profession down to the present day. Jonathan Ned Katz's *Gay American History* (1976), a massive collection of annotated documents, made it clear that primary source materials *did* exist "out there," awaiting discovery by the diligent. The year 1977 saw the publication of Jeffrey Weeks's *Coming Out: Homosexual Politics in Britain from the Nineteenth Century to the Present,* a work that presented homosexual identity as "socially constructed," not biological—thus providing a conceptual framework for future work (and unending debate).

Soon after came the English translation of the first volume in Michel Foucault's hugely influential *The History of Sexuality*; and then, in 1980, John Boswell's important study *Christianity, Social Tolerance, and Homosexuality*. Reviewing the Boswell book in *The New Republic*, I praised its prodigious erudition and hailed it as "one of the most profound, explosive works of scholarship to appear in recent memory." Though not yet aware of the serious challenges that specialists would later raise about the book's distorting bias in favor of Christianity, I mentioned "the unnerving feeling" I had periodically gotten that at the top of Boswell's own set of priorities "is the wish to hold gay Christians to their religious allegiance." And I predicted that his willingness to deny mountainous evidence that did justify an anticlerical attitude would produce controversy "bound to rage for years."

I had long been arguing, of course, that *every* historian's personal values inescapably colors his or her interpretations ("It's a garden-variety occupational hazard," I wrote in the Boswell review). Ideally, Boswell would have been more self-conscious about the degree to which his personal religious commitment might be influencing his interpretations, would have come clean (in the first instance to himself) about his underlying agenda. Even so, I had no hesitation in praising *Christianity* as "that rare item—a truly ground-breaking study."

A great deal more scholarship was to follow in the eighties and nineties—with a great deal more needed still, and particularly (since most of the work in the seventies was done by, about and for gay men) on female–female relations. By the end of the decade, material on lesbianism could mostly be found not in scholarly books or articles, but in the literature generated by the modern lesbian and gay political movement itself. Books like Kay Tobin and Randy Wicker's *The Gay Crusaders* (1972), Sydney Abbott and Barbara Love's *Sappho Was a Right-on Woman* (1972), and the assorted anthologies edited by Karla Jay and Allen Young were written by movement activists focused on a history of their own times, and could therefore be in spots merely hortatory or sentimental (as well as genuinely, seminally, inspirational). By the end of the seventies, such works had themselves become primary source materials, "historical" in nature. (Which in the United States, to be sure, tends to be defined as anything not on the TV news that night.)

But if scholarship on the gay and lesbian experience was now well inaugurated, not enough had yet accumulated to give viability to the ambitious "history of sexual behavior" that I had embarked on in 1974. In my own travels to manuscript libraries around the country during the seventies, I ran into a variety of roadblocks—from angry disclaimers to cool dissimulations—as I tried first to locate and then to get permission to use additional materials relating to sexuality. The sheer difficulty of finding new primary sources was formidable: In our sex-negative culture, few people recorded the pertinent details of their erotic lives in letters or diaries, even when they had taken care to confine their activities to the prescribed genders and positions.

Moreover, even the largest and most prestigious archival depositories suffered from understaffing, which meant they were years behind in processing their own accessions, let alone in deciding whether to open them for scholarly research. Many archivists were themselves (more so, by far, in the seventies than today) wedded to traditional moral values and were intractably opposed to releasing "sensitive" materials into potentially unreliable (that is, gay) hands. Bound by their own Victorian timidities, they were further hobbled by the restrictions that manuscript donors often place on access to material.

As I would write in *The Radical History Review* at the end of the decade, "To cope with the double jeopardy of archival staffs ignorant of the contents of their own collections or deliberately bent on concealing them, scholars in pursuit of new sources on human sexuality would ideally be equipped with the personality of a Sherlock Holmes: psychic skill in divining clues, fierce tenacity (concealed by elegant surface civility) in running them down. Holmes's easy access to the inspirational white powder would doubtless help, too. Most of us, alas, must make do with less: with a large tolerance for tedious needle-in-the haystack research through pounds of documents 'likely' (family correspondence, say) to yield occasional nuggets; with periodic leads from generous fellow scholars; with the unpredictable surrender of an archivist to our pleas, our perseverance, our prematurely grey hair."

I certainly met with some exceptions. Individual archivists like James R. Glenn of the National Anthropological Archives at the Smithsonian Institution, Stephen T. Riley of the Massachusetts Historical Society, Sandra Taylor of the Lilly Library in Indiana, and Richard J. Wolfe of the Countway Library of Medicine in Boston were people who shared my conviction that research into the history of sexual behavior was overdue and important, and who worked hard to help me locate relevant sources.

Glenn, for example, led me to some ethnographic material never previously made accessible: a set of "depositions," or affidavits, taken between 1914 and 1921 in New Mexico and Arizona, which described varied aspects of Hopi culture and sexuality. But then I came up against the problem of interpreting the material. The Smithsonian documents *seemed* to suggest, for example, that promiscuity, both premarital and extramarital, was commonplace and socially accepted among the Hopi. Yet when I turned to the "expert" anthropological literature on Pueblo culture in the hope of better understanding the affidavits, I found it heavily weighted toward viewing Hopi sexual behavior from the single lens of the ceremonial and symbolic (as "fertility rites designed to bring on rain," and so forth).

I wasn't convinced. "I seen a squaw suck a bucks prick" (as one affidavit read), seemed to me the concrete language of lust, not some metaphorical depiction of a fertility rite. As I wrote when I published some of the Smithsonian documents in 1979 in *The Radical History Review,* "our neo-Platonic penchant in the West for abstracting experience provokes in us a zeal for classification that can nullify what is most special—enrichingly eccentric—in a given event or gesture. Our receding but still deeply ingrained sex-negativism can lead us into performing the most ludicrous intellectual contortions in order to avoid the most obvious evidence of our senses."

In my view, Hopi sexuality (and much else besides) remained puzzling and undertheorized largely because, as I wrote in 1979, our "famously fastidious" social scientists have long preferred to look the other way, eager to avoid material that embarrassed their sense of propriety or that failed to fit neatly into their taxonomy of human behavior. "The professorial experts," I wrote, "are staunch in affirming their respect for 'non-conformist' behavior—but avoid confronting its outer range. Faced with behavior that lends itself least well to traditional categorization and to standard measures of judgment, social science has usually reaffirmed—rather than reexamined—the sufficiency of its categories and measurements. Faced with cultures whose norms challenge the universality of our own values, social science has rhetorically declared for catholicity but refrained from probing implications that might subvert its presumed cultural hegemony." Fortunately, I added, a new generation of social scientists was emerging with "a growing tendency to challenge the entrenched defensive postures of their disciplines; to explore more deeply the evidence and meaning of human diversity; to welcome it as a source of enrichment rather than shun it as a threat."

And my problems with the Hopi affidavits represented one of my strokes of *good* fortune. More typically, I came up empty-handed in my search for material: the card catalogues would be devoid of references to sexuality, or the librarians standing obdurate guard (in the name of "morality" or "a family's good name") over collections that might contain relevant materials, would resolutely refuse to give me access. The week-long trip I made in 1976 to the Kinsey Institute for Sex Research in Bloomington, Indiana, typified the attitudes and obstacles I encountered.

Just before I left on the trip, C. A. Tripp, author of the rich and (especially in its misogynistic passages) flawed *The Homosexual Matrix,* and a man who had worked with Kinsey for nine years at the Institute, invited me to dinner to "prepare" me for what he thought I was about to face in Bloomington. The Institute, he told me, did have a good deal of uncatalogued historical material relating to homosexuality, and he advised me to make a point of letting Paul Gebhardt, its current head, know that I was aware of its existence. Otherwise, Tripp predicted, Gebhardt would be unlikely to volunteer it; though not himself homophobic, Gebhardt was a cautious, bland man who above all wanted to avoid conflict.

And so on my first day at the Institute I repeated Tripp's comment about "a good deal of uncatalogued material" to Gebhardt and mentioned—as Tripp had advised me to—the name of one of the men who had sent Kinsey a long series of candid letters detailing his homosexual adventures as a businessman who traveled the world. Gebhardt visibly blanched, told me he'd "have a look" and would get back to me. Three days later he called me into his office, not to offer historical treasures, but to say how upset he was at Tripp revealing the businessman's real name to me. The Institute, Gebhardt sternly said, considered that a serious breach of confidentiality. (And perhaps it was: when Tripp later gave me his own photocopied set of the businessman's letters to publish in my book *About Time,* he too required that I not use the businessman's actual name.)

44

In any case, Gebhardt was not forthcoming. I was allowed to see precisely *one* uncatalogued collection and restricted to a mere three photocopies; should I wish to take any additional notes, I was told, it would have to be by hand. Tripp had been right: Kinsey's unorthodox, questing spirit no longer reigned at the Institute that bore his name.

This seemed further confirmed in a long talk I had during my stay at Bloomington with Alan Bell, a psychologist on the Institute staff. Rumor had reached me that Bell's soon-to-appear study on the etiology of male homosexuality, in preparation more than ten years, would give renewed respectability to the long dominant but recently challenged psychoanalytic view (associated primarily with the work of Charles Socarides and Irving Bieber) that the parental configuration of absent/hostile/remote father and binding/suffocating/domineering mother was what produced gay sons.

When I put the question directly to Bell, he squirmed uncomfortably and spiraled off into a long-winded, evasive reply. Persisting, I finally got him to say that he had *tentatively* concluded that estrangement from the father (irrespective of the mother's "binding" love or lack of it) *was* likely to produce a homosexual son; and that estrangement from the mother could be directly correlated with a heterosexual outcome for the son. Did that mean, I asked, tongue firmly in cheek, that a male child estranged from both parents would have a natural vocation for celibacy? And would the depth of the double estrangement prove the key indicator of how high the son might rise in the ecclesiastical hierarchy? Bell was not amused.

When his study, *Homosexualities* (written with Martin Weinberg), appeared two years later, it proved a double surprise to me: It avoided the question of etiology, and it was a work of considerable substance. Despite the score of problems I had with its sample techniques and simplistic typologies, I had no hesitation (when reviewing the book for *The New York Times*) in characterizing it as "the most ambitious study" of male homosexuality yet attempted.

But *Homosexualities* did suffer from precisely the same fastidious limitations as its equally "liberal" sponsor, the Kinsey Institute; both the book and the place were part of sexology's mainstream. And I therefore predicted in my *Times* review that while the gay majority would warmly welcome *Homosexualities* for its overall conclusion that most homosexuals do not differ in any essential way from mainstream

Americans, that same conclusion would anger lesbian and gay radicals (of whom I counted myself one).

What many assimilationist gays would see in *Homosexualities,* I wrote, was what many radical blacks saw in the much-heralded study of slavery, *Time on the Cross*: namely, "a sanitized version of their experience offering full membership in the human community on the dubious premise that they are now and have always been devoted adherents of a work-obsessed, sex-negative middle-class culture." I acknowledged that "most homosexuals *are* mainstream Americans— centrist in politics, bourgeois in outlook, eager to be 'let in,' " but added that "this is far less true of lesbian feminists, well aware as they are that the Old Boy network of male power and privilege at the heart of our social system must be transformed, not joined."

I concluded the review with what I took to be certain general principles: "That you cannot adopt (or pretend to adopt) the dominant values of a culture and at the same time hope to reorder those values. That the token adjustments which the power brokers grant from time to time are insufficient to dilute (and—whether by design or otherwise— in the long run strengthen) our society's instinctive distaste for substantive change, its zeal for homogenization and its entrenched suspicion of the very human diversity it rhetorically defends.

"That liberals," I continued—and here I had in mind the Kinsey Institute as well as the authors of *Homosexualities*—"even when they champion 'change,' are conditioned to accept as sacrosanct exactly those propositions about human nature most in need of scrutiny—the 'maternal instinct,' for example, or the equating of erotic adventuring with 'fear of intimacy.' That liberals can therefore never be relied upon as allies in any struggle to break through to a genuinely new socio-sexual order. That indeed they may be less reliable than those 'true' conservatives who have traditionally resisted submerging individual needs in the Common Good." *The New York Times* cut this conclusion from the review on grounds of length.

I had found plenty of confirmation for those concluding propositions during my research in the mid-seventies. Just as I would not have predicted that the "liberal" Kinsey Institute would prove recalcitrant and proprietary, so I would not have foreseen that the staff of the Lilly Library (also in Bloomington), where I had expected rampant Hoosier conservatism, would enthusiastically dig out "forbidden" materials for me. And I had found much the same cooperative attitude in other unlikely places, such as the patrician Massachusetts Historical Society and the august Countway Library of Medicine. Some of that cooperation, to be sure, hinged on the goodwill of individual librarians and was not necessarily reflective of institutional policy.

In any case, after some four years of trying to locate and gain access to manuscript materials relating to the history of sexuality, and despite the fact that secondary literature in the new field *was* beginning to accumulate, I was forced to conclude by 1978 that embarking on a full-scale "history of sexual behavior" had been premature. It would take time, possibly a long time, before attitudes among historians and archivists would change sufficiently and enough information accrue to carry off such an enterprise. In the early eighties, I would use some of the material that I had gathered between 1974 and 1978 for a *New York Native* column on gay and lesbian history. This, in expanded form, became my 1984 book, *About Time: Exploring the Gay Past.*

III

SEXUALITY AND POLITICS[*]

I WAS ONE OF THE FOUNDING MEMBERS in 1973 of the Gay Academic Union, a group that undertook as its tripartite mission protecting the rights of openly lesbian and gay students and faculty on campuses, pinpointing needed areas of research on homosexuality, and originating pilot courses in gay and lesbian studies. We worked for months putting together a two-day inaugural conference, "The Universities and the Gay Experience," for November of that year, sometimes consumed with volatile arguments over feminist values or the nature of bisexual-

[*]This chapter is based almost entirely on materials from my own diaries and my files on GAU and NGLTF, supplemented by some dozen documents Ronald Gold has shared with me from his private papers. Since this material is not in the public domain, specific citations seem pointless. But I have now given my GAU and NGTF files, as part of my collected personal papers, to the New York Public Library, where they are available to other scholars for research and review. Additionally, I want to acknowledge the following works as having been especially useful for the occasional detail and for fact-checking:

Barry D. Adam, *The Rise of a Gay and Lesbian Movement* (Twayne, 1987)
Dennis Altman, *The Homosexualization of America, the Americanization of the Homosexual* (St. Martin's Press, 1982)
Charlotte Bunch, *Passionate Politics* (St. Martin's Press, 1987)
John D'Emilio, *Making Trouble* (Routledge, 1992)
John D'Emilio and Estelle B. Freedman, *Intimate Matters* (Harper & Row, 1988)
Michael Denneny, Charles Ortleb, and Thomas Steele, *The Christopher Street Reader* (Coward-McCann, 1983)
Karla Jay and Allen Young, *After You're Out* (Links, 1975)
Karla Jay and Allen Young, *Lavender Culture* (Harcourt, Brace, 1978)
Eric Marcus, *Making History* (HarperCollins, 1992)
Toby Marotta, *The Politics of Homosexuality* (Houghton Mifflin, 1981)
Leigh W. Rutledge, *The Gay Decades* (Plume, 1992)
Mark Thompson, ed., *Long Road to Freedom* (St. Martin's Press, 1994)
Stuart Timmons, *The Trouble with Harry Hay* (Alyson, 1990)

ity, sometimes frantically trying to stitch together the mundane pieces, from workshop titles to registration forms, that go into creating a conference of any kind.

But this was no run-of-the-mill event, and until the day of the conference itself we were never sure we could pull it off. Most lesbian and gay academics had previously stayed firmly bolted in their closets, understandably fearful of the consequences of coming out in a university setting that despite its purported liberalism was likely to be as pervasively homophobic as society at large. With the modern gay movement still only a few years old, and with lesbian and gay academics never having previously made any effort to band together, we were afraid few would actually risk showing up for the conference.

To our stunned delight, more than three hundred people ended up registering (and another hundred or so milled skittishly about), the atmosphere was a-hum with excitement and enthusiasm, and the plenary sessions and workshops alike proved vividly alive. As I said, happily, in my keynote speech, the conference represented a genuine "rite of passage, that historic point in time when gay women and men decided to organize ourselves around our skills, using them to fight homophobia, to protest the notion that same-gender love and lust affront the laws of nature, to place ourselves in the forefront of the newest and to my mind most far-reaching revolution: the recharacterization of human sexuality."

I expressed the further hope that the conference would mark the beginning of "the long march through those particular academic disciplines and institutions with which we find ourselves affiliated." But marching, I warned, "is notoriously hard work. And institutions are notoriously resistant. Because we challenge the exclusive heterosexual lifestyle by which the majority in this country all at once defines biologic truth, social necessity, and personal essence, our work will be difficult and frustrating."

What I didn't foresee was that infighting among our own ranks would prove at least as frustrating and take as large a toll as would the struggle against homophobia in the outside world. GAU's second conference, in 1974, drew some six hundred people, and by 1975 the organization had broadened from its New York City base to additional chapters in Boston, Philadelphia, and Ann Arbor (and, subsequently, in Chicago, Los Angeles and San Francisco as well). All the standard signs of success were present. Yet within a year of GAU's founding, I had developed a queasy feeling that the victory might be pyrrhic. From the beginning, GAU had drawn many more men than women, and the women, early on and frequently, had expressed disappointment in the lack of feminist consciousness among most of the men.

Some of the GAU men, myself included, self-identified as radicals; we not only agreed with the feminist analysis, but also with the criticism already being sounded by radicals outside the university that the middle-class white male mentality dominant in GAU meant the organization was in danger of replicating rather than challenging the academic world's patriarchal attitudes, hierarchies, and rituals—right down to constructing its conferences around "panels," a format likely to perpetuate already suspect divisions between "experts" and audience, teachers and students, haves and have-nots. Instead of working to broaden standard definitions of what intellectual work *was,* and to break the connections between academic research and established bastions of power, GAU was, so the critique went, in danger of becoming such a bastion itself (or at least it seemed to be earnestly trying to).

Sympathetic to these warnings and complaints, I decided, when asked to give the concluding speech at the second GAU conference, to use the occasion as a vehicle for talking openly about my own fear that the organization was moving in dubious directions.

I expressed disappointment, first of all, that while GAU was largely male, few *tenured* male faculty had affiliated. I suggested that we probably needed to face the fact "that in a very real sense a generation of gay men has largely been lost to us—that they have been superbly, probably irretrievably indoctrinated and cowed by the patriarchal culture. If community *is* to come, the work and rewards alike are going to belong to the young."

What I didn't point out, and probably should have, was that there weren't enough *non*-tenured faculty involved with GAU either. Anyone who wanted to attend a GAU function was welcome—there was no other way to build the organization—so as time went on, GAU became increasingly attractive to well-educated gay white men looking for a congenial environment in which to come out and to find partners and friends. After the first year, these men probably outnumbered the graduate students and junior faculty who actually had university affiliations. Which meant that GAU was handicapped, nearly from the outset, in its specific mission to change the climate on the country's campuses.

In my speech closing the second GAU conference in 1974, I also expressed discomfort over how much of the organization's energy during the previous year had gone into social events and consciousness-raising sessions. I realized how necessary such activities were: "For most people consciousness-raising is a needed prelude to active political commitment. And continuing social contact is a valuable device for keeping that commitment humane—oriented to the needs of people rather than to the dictates of ideology."

But the *amount* of time invested in social events and c-r sessions, I argued, had been excessive to the point of self-indulgence. True, much of the consciousness-raising work had come about in response to criticism from GAU women that many of the gay men were sexist; yet sexism had not been consistently addressed during most of the c-r sessions. And beyond the issue of sexism, I wasn't convinced that we needed as much consciousness-raising as we were lavishing upon ourselves.

Most of us were college-educated, middle-class, and white—in other words, as I pointed out, "already over privileged when compared with the majority of our gay brothers and sisters." And most of us, I added, perhaps overstating, "are in better shape psychologically than we sometimes care to admit to ourselves. The argument that we 'have to get our heads together before we can do any political work' can become a standing rationale for doing nothing: Our psyches are somehow never quite ready, our motors never quite tuned up. I think a lot of this has to do with American perfectionism, and even more to do with male selfishness."

We were in danger of talking too much and doing too little. And talking, moreover, about a limited set of issues. We had heard almost nothing during the second conference—indeed, during the whole second year—about the class and race divisions that characterized the gay community no less than the society at large. It was time to face those divisions, I argued, and to do something about their root causes. As matters currently stood, we were in danger of becoming an organization that gave a conference once a year. "And at that, a conference modeled rather closely on those genteel gatherings we're already familiar with in our respective professional caucuses."

I also voiced concern over the contempt I had heard expressed for those whose style differed from that of the gay mainstream—for bisex-uals, transvestites and transsexuals, and for those involved in S/M. That intolerance, I said, was to me tantamount to playing "a version of the same game the larger society plays with us. Namely: 'Either do it *our* way or be prepared to find yourself ostracized.' It comes down to the same contempt for individual differences that we deplore in the culture as a whole. If we try to humiliate those who deviate from our norms, how do we protest when those who adhere to the heterosexual norm choose to hound and humiliate us? To my mind, we have to oppose *any* prescription for how consenting adults may or must make love."

I strained to conclude the speech on a more upbeat note, praising us for coming together and staying together, for at least beginning the work of combating homophobia in society at large and sexism within ourselves. And I talked glowingly about the potential contribution GAU could make toward the creation of a strong and richly diverse gay and lesbian community.

This closing pat on the head did little to dilute the considerable anger subsequently leveled at me for having stringently criticized the white male contingent that dominated GAU councils. I was surprised at some of it, and particularly at the letter I got from the writer George Whitmore, himself on the left and a friend. George (the author of *The Confessions of Danny Slocum* and *Nebraska,* who died of AIDS in 1989) took me to task for what he characterized as my "ill-advised and over-stated" remarks, and made passing, scornful reference to "bisexual chic." That, I wrote back, struck me as precisely the sort of "reductive phrase for conveniently demeaning the lifestyle of others" that I had been protesting in the first place.

George and I soon patched things up; our politics *were* basically sim-ilar. The larger problem was that our shared vision of a broad-gauged movement devoted to substantive social change, a vision forged during the radical optimism of the sixties, had itself faltered and fragmented in the changed climate of the early seventies. Globally, *the* issue for the vast majority of the world's population was still the one that had engaged socialists for generations: how to ensure freedom from mate-rial want, how to improve the terrible conditions of daily life endured by most people. So little progress had been made toward that goal—and by the early seventies so little will seemed to remain for pursuing it—that (as I wrote in a 1974 essay), "perhaps only a citizen of the

United States could be provincial enough to doubt its continuing centrality. Or arrogant enough to suggest that [what we take to be] a more encompassing vision, the redefinition of sex roles, awaits us."

Richard Nixon may have been forced from power but, as I saw it, his arrogant assumption of our entitlement to dictate the affairs of the globe remained alive and well in national councils, accompanied, as it had long been, by a firm commitment to the "traditional" values of male power, black inferiority, and homosexual pathology. Mean-spirited, vindictive bigotry was flourishing anew in the land by the mid-seventies. Los Angeles police chief Ed Davis showed neither embarrassment nor hesitation in 1973 when he spoke out against law reforms that would extend rights to those "predatory creatures" called "gays." And the *Chicago Daily News* columnist Mike Royko seemed equally assured when, in a 1974 column entitled "Banana Lib," he described how "men in love with monkeys" were winning acceptance by "coming out of the cage."

The picture was hardly all bleak. Even as LA's Davis spewed his anti-gay bile, San Francisco's police chief signed an order prohibiting *his* officers from using the words "fruit," "queer," "faggot," or "fairy." Even as Royko mocked homosexuality, the American Bar Association adopted a resolution urging states to repeal their anti–gay sex laws, Governor Milton Shapp of Pennsylvania issued the first state executive order banning employment discrimination against gays, and a national Council of Churches of Christ conference concluded that antigay discrimination was "immoral."

Despite these seesaw political developments, overall the conservative trend had become ever more pronounced by the mid-seventies. And GAU was not immune to that trend. A growing number of men with less than progressive views became more visible and active in the New York GAU, with the result that most of the men (myself included) who self-defined as radical and who had founded the organization began to drift away. Almost all the women—who from the first had thrown in their lot with GAU uneasily and tentatively—became disaffected (as, with the growth of lesbian separatism, they were simultaneously withdrawing from other co-gender gay organizations as well).

Probably the best-known of the conservative men who moved into prominence in GAU was Wayne Dynes, a professor of art history at

Hunter College. He was surely among the most vocal. As early as the second GAU conference in 1974, Dynes had locked horns with Charlotte Bunch, a leading lesbian-feminist writer and organizer. (She was a founder of D.C. Women's Liberation, of the Furies collective, and of *Quest: A Feminist Quarterly*.) In her speech to the conference that year, Charlotte had expressed the view that gay men insufficiently acknowledged the rights and needs of women, and she spoke movingly of the value of the burgeoning separatist movement in providing lesbians with respite from being constantly on the offensive, and with the needed time and space to build a community congenial to their needs. To end separatism, Bunch said, we had to end the reasons that had made separatism necessary: the failure of the gay movement to fight male supremacy.

Dynes indignantly replied that this was nothing more or less than an invitation to male self-flagellation. He was tired of being told what was wrong with him, he said, tired of "obligatory therapy" that at bottom undermined the self-esteem of gay men; and, he added ominously, he rejected any purported self-examination that came at the "expense of mind"—whatever that meant. Dynes insisted that GAU's proper mission was simple and straightforward: to pursue cases of anti-gay discrimination in academia and to increase the amount of reliable scholarship on gay lives.

Barbara Gittings, the longtime lesbian activist, also took issue with Charlotte, though the cordial tone of her criticism and her underlying wish to build bridges were light-years away from Dynes's sardonic divisiveness. Gittings deplored the growing mystique about "vast differences" between gay men and lesbians, fearing it would minimize our very real commonalities and thereby our ability to join forces against shared oppression. "Nothing would suit anti-homosexual bigots more," Gittings said, "than that we fragment." Separatism, she added, "seems to me uncomfortably close to the notion that anatomy is destiny."

Though I basically agreed with Charlotte, I shared some of Barbara's fears. In particular, I felt that Charlotte had failed to acknowledge that some gay men—not enough, certainly, and obviously not including Wayne Dynes and his growing cohort—had been trying to incorporate feminist values in their lives and work; almost certainly more gay men than straight men.

Yet basically I believed, with Charlotte, that fighting sexism had to become central to our movement work. Gay men and all women *were,* I had become convinced, natural allies in the struggle against an emotionally constricted machismo that the culture had long enthroned as the noblest form of humanity. Only an infusion of radical feminist insights, I believed, could keep the gay male movement from edging ever closer to a narrowly gauged agenda that would simply allow gay white men to take their place beside straight white men at the apex of privilege. Hearing me espouse these views led another anti-feminist man in GAU to write Howard Brown, when he was helping to put together the first National Gay Task Force board in October 1973, *not* to include either me or Bert Hansen (another outspokenly pro-feminist gay man). Our antagonist wrote Brown that Bert and I were, of course, "real gems" and he was "personally fond" of us. But our "ideological posturing and consistent moralizing" at GAU meetings had led to "incessant debate about the role of women," which in turn accounted for GAU's "dissipated vigor of late."

The gulf between Bunch and Dynes, and the positions they espoused, continued to widen. In a letter to me in 1975, Dynes characterized feminism as "a rickety ideology with an astonishing affinity for mythos. . . . I believe it to be playing a parasitic and negative role in the gay movement." Two years after that, he launched a public assault on Bunch. In a letter to the national gay publication, *The Advocate,* Dynes characterized her as "virulently homophobic and man-hating," insisted she had a "considerable history of anti-male thinking," and even suggested that "her activities would make a good subject for investigation."

This seemed to me cranky even for Dynes. I decided his misogynistic outburst needed a response, and I wrote a letter of my own to *The Advocate*. I suggested that instead of "investigating" Bunch, Dynes might try investigating her writings. If he could "get beyond his own prejudgments," I wrote, he would find a wise and humane attempt "to point out how much *all* of us still adhere, at some semi-conscious level (to put it in the most favorable light) to patriarchal and hierarchical values—the very values that stand in the way of the psycho/sexual 'revolution' we call for out of the other side of our mouths. I suppose it's predictable that such insights would prove threatening to many. But the fault, dear Horatio (Dynes) is not in the stars but in ourselves."

Wayne Dynes was not one to be silenced, then or since. (In more recent years he has denounced me as a "communist.") He promptly wrote a second letter to *The Advocate*. It was rip-snorting, and not without wit. Asking whether he should refer to me henceforth as "Duberperson," Dynes claimed he *had* read Bunch's writing and had found it a "melange of sloppy thinking, utopian visions and grudge-gathering." Only a man like Duberman, Dynes continued—"middle-class and muddle-headed"—could be misguided enough to think Bunch's writings trenchant or convincing.

Just to be sure the message had gotten through, Dynes wrote me privately to say I had defended "poor wronged Charlotte" because I had internalized "the pedestal theory"—because I viewed women as unsullied saints. In the limited sense that I decidedly trusted women more than I did men, Dynes had a point; but I was unwilling to accept it from a man who equated support for feminism with "pedestalization." For good measure, Dynes signed the letter "Your former friend." I had been marked as a gender traitor.

(Dynes has gone on to make some real contributions to lesbian and gay studies, notably as editor of the *Encyclopedia of Homosexuality,* a compilation as valuable as it is bizarre. One of its few "female" contributors, "Evelyn Gettone," credited with some two dozen articles, was later revealed to be a pseudonym for one or several of the volume's male editors. This, when publicly disclosed in 1995, led the publisher to fire Dynes as editor of a planned new edition of the encyclopedia.)

Vitriol has always, it seems, been a staple of movement politics (gay and otherwise), and I grew pretty adept myself at take-no-prisoners rhetoric. How to account for the endemic cut-and-slash style of movement work, the penchant for converting *each other* into the Enemy, is an ongoing puzzle, even as it takes an ongoing toll on movement strength. Does it reflect accumulated anger (and even psychic damage) resulting from entrenched oppression and from frustration over the failure to win long-overdue substantive change? And is the anger "safely" (if inappropriately) discharged against one's own, much as an abused child's rage will often turn not toward the offending relative directly but toward some infinitely more benign adult authority figure in their lives?

I've never been sure what is at the root of the penchant for movement infighting and invective. Nor have I (or apparently anyone else) figured out how constructively to rechannel such vehemence. Though I see myself as a skilled conciliator in some situations, I know perfectly well that in others I can be thin-skinned and defensive—which usually surprises those who confuse a controlled exterior with internal serenity. If someone comes at me with what I take to be an unfair accusation, I go right back at them, punch for punch. It wasn't always that way. Earlier in my life, I "made nice" when assaulted. But that, I painfully learned, only incites the bullies of the world to pummel you more. Yet if I've found self-assertion to be necessary self-protection, it can sometimes get triggered too quickly or expressed too fiercely, bringing it regrettably close to that very machismo I theoretically deplore. My defenses, alas, were developed long before my ideology—and have proven far more intractable.

ALTHOUGH INTENSIVELY INVOLVED in the first two formative years of GAU, by the time the third annual conference came around in 1975, I had moved myself to the sidelines. Indeed, along with almost all the women and radical-minded men, I was more than halfway out the door, distressed at the increasingly mainstream (male) tone and goals of the organization. Perhaps those of us who dissented from that trend should have stayed and fought the good fight longer. But the odds seemed poor, our energy limited, and the need to get on with other work compelling.

I did attend the first day of the 1975 conference. I even thought the surprising diversity of the crowd might bode well for a revitalization. But as the choice of keynote speaker made clear, that optimism was misplaced: The conference organizers had chosen Air Force Sergeant Leonard ("I love the military") Matlovich. Recently relieved of his duties after coming out as a homosexual, Matlovich had been much in the news (including the cover of *Time*) of late.

I had recently had some personal experience of him when covering his preliminary discharge hearings at Langley Air Force Base for *The New York Times*. Though I had found him likable and decent, his right-wing politics decidedly turned me off. Matlovich had voted for Goldwater, had erected an eighteen-foot flagpole in his front yard, and had volunteered for three tours of duty in Vietnam because "that was where my nation needed me." Later, in the mid-eighties, he would join other gay conservatives, including the publicly anti-gay Terry

Dolan (the cofounder of the National Conservative Political Action Committee who, like Matlovich, died of AIDS) and Robert Bauman (the Republican congressman who was "outed" and subsequently defeated for reelection), in forming Concerned Americans for Individual Rights (CAIR). The group was designed to oppose the virulent anti-gay stereotyping of fellow conservative Republicans like Jesse Helms and William Dannemeyer, without requiring its members to separate themselves from the Helms/Dannemeyer public philosophy they otherwise found congenial. But CAIR was short-lived; few gay Republicans proved willing to write checks, let alone stick so much as a toe outside the closet door.

By no stretch of the imagination could Matlovich be described as an intellectual, let alone an academic. Yet neither those disqualifications nor his right-wing politics had outweighed his "star" appeal in leading GAU to choose him as keynoter. The choice seemed further alarming evidence of the conservative drift of the organization. (Ironically, Matlovich failed at the last minute to show up for his speech.)

Illness kept me away from the last two days of the 1975 conference, and thereafter my ties to GAU pretty much evaporated. As late as 1978 I still felt an obligation to serve on the jury that selected the first GAU scholarship awards, but by then the national office had shifted to Los Angeles, and Wayne Dynes had become one of six—all white male—directors of the New York chapter. That was less disheartening than it might have been because vital gay and lesbian caucuses had by then taken root within other academic professional organizations. The process had begun with the formation of the Gay Caucus of the Modern Language Association in 1973 and had spread rapidly thereafter to the other disciplines. GAU deserved some credit as the seedbed for those caucuses, but those of us who had left the "parent" organization were relieved that GAU, ever narrower in its dimensions, was now being outflanked in importance.

My OWN MOVEMENT WORK had by then relocated to the National Gay Task Force.

NGTF emerged as an offshoot of the growing dissatisfaction some of the leading figures in the Gay Activists Alliance (GAA) felt with that organization. GAA had become the dominant gay political group in New York City in the early seventies (superseding the Gay Liberation

Front); its creative "zaps"—militant street confrontations—on behalf of gay civil rights, fair housing, and job equity had managed to draw considerable media attention, and even some public policy changes.

Despite these achievements, GAA's practical-minded emphasis on "changing laws" had drawn fire as "mere reformism," especially from those who measured the organization's "limited" agenda against the earlier attempt by the Gay Liberation Front (GLF) to treat gay issues in conjunction with those relating to racism and sexism. From the radical GLF perspective, the goal of getting sodomy statutes off the books, or putting anti-discrimination laws on them, could never end the oppression of gay people; homophobia was embedded in the minds and hearts of mainstream Americans, and anti-gay statutes and court opinions merely reflected the negative national bias. What had to be ended, the radicals argued, was the mind-set that equated heterosexuality with "normalcy," the nuclear family with optimal human happiness, and dichotomous gender roles with divine intention.

But the radical-minded had no clear-cut strategy of their own for ending the institutionalized heterosexism to which they rightly called attention. And even less apparent in those years—to radicals and reformers alike—was the understanding that there might not be one strategy, one path, one kind of politics or temperament that would put an end to what we now call heterosexism.

Even today not enough people (in my view) seem willing to acknowledge that our movement needs to make room for—and applaud—diverse contributions on a variety of fronts. Social transformation requires a range of efforts and a plethora of skills: lawyers, lobbyists, media experts, scholars, cultural workers, youth advocates, sexual liberationists, community organizers, mainstream politicians, and so on. "Let each contribute according to his or her abilities" rings like stale Marxism; yet the sentiment, at its heart, serves a goal at the opposite pole from sectarian rigidity. A bit less insistence on the absolute rightness of *this* path, and a bit more openness to the possibilities of *that* one, might cushion (although it could not obliterate, since diversity does require expression) some of the more bruising divisions, past and present, that have diluted the strength of the gay movement.

None of the three principal figures who put NGTF together—Nathalie Rockhill, Ronald Gold, and Bruce Voeller—were ideologues; they prided themselves on being (in Gold's words), "incremental pragmatists." Which is not to say that they were devoid of strong convictions, or had feather-duster personalities. Hardly—of the three, only Rockhill was able to hold firmly to a position without becoming abrasive. Indeed, her even-tempered good sense, her ability really to *listen* to opposing views without defensively flaring up, made her, in the eyes of many, something of a movement saint. Rockhill had worked in publishing and been a GAA vice president; once NGTF got off the ground, she would serve as its national coordinator and then legislative director; still later, she became a lawyer, and a central figure in the Lambda Legal Defense Fund.

Bruce Voeller, a handsome thirty-eight-year-old once-married father of three, held a doctorate in biochemistry and had until recently been on the staff of Rockefeller University. He thought of himself as a tough-minded, efficient professional with enough accumulated experience in a variety of worlds to play a leading role in the burgeoning gay movement. Articulate, smooth-tongued, and shrewd, he knew how to cut through, co-opt—or if need be, circumvent—opposition; though when it persisted, he could become testy and authoritarian.

Ronald Gold, roughly the same age as Voeller, had been an antiwar protester and a member of the *Congress of Racial Equality (CORE),* the civil rights organization. A Brooklyn native of independent means who had also been a reporter for *Variety* and a longtime editor at *TV Guide,* the outspoken, opinionated Gold was both admired and feared for his sharp intelligence, his rapid-fire speech, and his caustic, sometimes overbearing manner. All of these were made more palatable by Gold's modesty, nearly unique among movement leaders. His capacity for hard work was matched by a willingness to let others take credit for it. He preferred to remain in the background; building the movement, not his own celebrity, was what fired him.

Gold, Voeller, and Rockhill had all been active in GAA; in 1973 Voeller was serving as its president and Gold as chair of its media committee. In the opinion of many, GAA had by then lost its steam; more time was going to protracted argument than to organizational work, and much of the energy that did remain had shifted from planning zaps to ensuring that the hugely popular Saturday night dances held at the Firehouse, GAA's SoHo headquarters, continued to feed the organization's coffers. Which is not to say that zaps ceased, or that they no longer succeeded in bringing media attention to gay issues. But to the growing number of GAA's detractors, the organization had become too much of a social agency for middle-class gay white men who—boys being boys—turned meetings into interminable rumbles and put gleeful jockeying for position above the need to set a comprehensive agenda and see to its execution.

Voeller and Gold were themselves middle-class gay white men. But they were older than most of GAA's members and had become increasingly fed up with what they characterized as GAA's self-indulgent, sophomoric talkathons, endless counter-cultural chatter about peace and love, and tedious "consensus-building"—all of which in their view had turned GAA into an obstacle course impeding the ability to get concrete tasks successfully completed. In an article Voeller wrote at the end of the decade for *The Advocate,* he further complained, in looking back, about the "Blue Denim Elitism," the countercultural snobbery, that he felt had characterized GAA; a woman in a dress, or a man in slacks and a sport shirt (instead of the de rigueur "long hair, beads and blue jeans") was likely, according to Voeller, to be scorned or "coolly tolerated."

Yet neither Voeller nor Gold could be accurately characterized as establishment squares or over-the-hill spoilsports. In that same *Advocate* piece, for example, Voeller—sounding for all the world like one of those countercultural radicals he was purportedly at odds with—insisted that "we gays have some unique contributions to make to the world *from our experience of being gay.*" And among those contributions, Voeller gave high priority to the way gays and lesbians had pioneered non-traditional families, and egalitarian, nonmonogamous relationships. This was not the standard we're-just-folks argument favored by gay establishmentarians.

Gold, too, had some decidedly radical views. Preferring to work behind the scenes (and he worked indefatigably, churning out the bulk of NGTF's written material in the early years, including many of the speeches given by the organization's officers), Gold saved some of his strongest views for his private correspondence. "Let's not be afraid to be angry at the immorality of the 'establishment' we face," he wrote in one memo. "I think we ought to be saying it *is* a moral question. . . . We must push the parallels with Jews . . . and with blacks, who said, 'We demand your acceptance, but we don't need your approval . . . [and] we must be prepared to say that *without question* there WILL be more gay people if children are permitted to know the truth that people they know and love and respect are gay."

At the same time, Gold believed in the importance of *talking to* the straight world—of "getting the word out." For which willingness he (and the Task Force in general) would be labeled "merely reformist," eager (as one critic put it) to "suck up to the establishment." When Gold agreed to discuss with William Safire a column Safire was writing on a pending New York City gay-rights bill, and the column turned out to be more homophobic than not, Gold was crucified for "dealing with the oppressor." "What should I have done," he bellowed, "tell Safire to get his ideas from the firemen and the Catholic Archdiocese? . . . Call this 'reformist' if you like. . . . But I think it's the only way to prepare the ground for revolution. What are our alternatives? Consciousness-raising sessions with our friends? Letters to the converted in *The Advocate*? I don't think so—there's a world to be changed!"

What Voeller and Gold despised about GAA was not its militant zaps, but the organization's seeming inability to get anything—or to get *enough*—done. For a time, they tried to push through a variety of organizational reforms, including the establishment of a board of directors with the decision-making power to circumvent or conclude the marathon discussions by the full membership. Both men believed the gay movement had to professionalize its operations, support a salaried staff, and develop a streamlined organizational structure that would curtail the tendency of participatory democracy to talk itself into impotence. They wanted greater *results*—and wanted them on a national scale. And to get them, they were willing and eager to seek allies among liberal elements in the straight establishment.

In 1973, Voeller and Gold initially felt confident they could turn GAA around: the two men saw themselves as skilled infighters able to push through their own agenda. But their views ran into sharp and sustained opposition within GAA, and they were personally denounced as more interested in assimilation than in liberation, and as having "too much power." When the two proposed a change in the governing rules that would have limited participatory democracy, a leaflet appeared denouncing them as "homofascists," and a resolution was introduced to impeach Voeller. During a stormy and ultimately climactic general meeting, Voeller, realizing he might well be forced out, upped and quit.

Gold's initial response was to try to get Voeller to reconsider, but

Nath Rockhill suggested instead that they just "forget it—let's start something else." Along with Tom Smith (the African-American former social and operations director of GAA, who would end up running NGTF's community services) and Greg Dawson (former political action chair of GAA, who would be reluctantly persuaded to take on the thankless job of NGTF's director of finances), the five began to meet in Voeller's kitchen to plan the outlines of a new organization.

They soon agreed that Voeller would be the executive director, and that it would be a big plus for the organization if they could persuade Howard Brown (the city's onetime commissioner of health and a behind-the-scenes GAA financial supporter, whose recent coming-out had been featured on the front page of *The New York Times*), to serve as chair of the new organization's board of directors. Howard immediately said yes.

He and I having recently become friends, Howard himself approached me about joining the board. I agreed at once, and a week later, on October 15, 1973, participated—along with some half-dozen others, including Rockhill, Voeller, Gold, Howard Brown, Barbara Gittings, and Frank Kameny—in a press conference at the Ballroom Restaurant (Voeller and Greg Dawson were part owners of it) that formally announced the birth of the National Gay Task Force. If my memory serves, there were more of us at the podium than reporters in the audience. Howard spoke movingly of his hope that the new organization, "focused on national issues and employing a full-time professional staff," represented "the next logical step in the development of the Gay Liberation movement." The Task Force, he said, aimed at nothing less than "ending all discrimination and prejudice against gay people." It was a speech redolent with Howard's trademark brand of ardent, even naive, optimism—precisely what was needed for undertaking the formidable project he had outlined.

Initially the Task Force conducted its business out of Voeller's Spring Street house, and for a time (despite Howard's brave words at the press conference) no one was salaried. Gradually, NGTF (in the mid-eighties, it belatedly became NGLTF) was able to move to a small office on lower Fifth Avenue and to gather a tiny, wildly overworked staff of men and women (whose average pay was seventy-five dollars a week) dedicated to professionalizing the movement and to combating homophobia on a national level. The staff had minds—and track records—of their own, were not rubber stamps for Voeller, and sometimes grew irritable with his occasionally high-handed ways.

Greg Dawson, burnt out over helping to get the Task Force on its feet, soon handed over the job of fund-raising to Bob Herrick. An openly gay Episcopal priest, Herrick had earlier been part of a group of clergy supportive of gay rights; Voeller managed to persuade him that taking on the difficult task of managing NGTF's never-sufficient finances could be seen as a legitimate function of his ministry, an argument that apparently proved persuasive to Herrick's superiors as well.

Ginny Vida, initially a member of the board of directors, became another important staff member. Like Nath Rockhill, Vida had earlier been a GAA vice president and had been active on its Lesbian Liberation Committee (which in 1973 transmogrified into the independent organization Lesbian Feminist Liberation, LFL). Eventually Vida would replace Gold as communications director of the Task Force.

Jean O'Leary, an ex-nun, also joined the staff. Like Vida, O'Leary had played a leadership role in LFL and, with pronounced gifts as a strategist and communicator, would in 1976 become Voeller's co–executive director (a move he would initially oppose but, being a canny man, then embrace). Like Rockhill and Vida, O'Leary was committed to a work-within-the-system political approach, did not see herself as a lesbian separatist, and had not despaired of working politically with gay men—though all three women insisted on the need for greater lesbian visibility within the organized movement and had periodic doubts about the level of feminist consciousness among their male cohorts.

O'Leary, for one, had denounced Voeller while they were both still in GAA, for his insensitivity to lesbian concerns. And at NGTF, distrust over the depth of Voeller's commitment to feminist principles and practice would occasionally resurface. Yet the distrust was not always proportionate or deserved. At one point, for example, Voeller (spurred by Rockhill) rejected the suggestion that two male board members represent NGTF on the popular Jack Paar television show. Paar refused to substitute a woman for one of the men, and the appearance was canceled, hungry though NGTF was for visibility. Voeller could sometimes be *so* responsive to lesbian issues that Gold would berate him for being "entirely too willing to back down and agree with any woman who claimed to be speaking in the voice of feminism"—in contrast to his own tendency (as he himself put it) to "tell them they were full of shit when I thought they were."

THOUGH I HAD IMMEDIATELY and enthusiastically agreed to serve on the Task Force board, from the start I felt more ambivalent about the new organization than my instant acceptance suggested. The very night of our inaugural press conference at the Ballroom, I wrote in my diary that I feared NGTF was too much "in the liberal, reformist mode: 'let us in' rather than let us show you new possibilities.' " Not knowing the full range of views held by some of NGTF's founders, I judged—perhaps misjudged—on the basis of their public rhetoric. In his speech at the Ballroom, for instance, Howard had made a special point of noting the "distinguished people, successful in such fields as politics, education, religion, medicine, business and the law," who had agreed to serve on the Task Force board. I feared that the new organization might prove too tamely accepting of the country's social and economic inequities. I feared, too, that the stated emphasis on "professionalism"—which I recognized as necessary to building a movement—might strike those lacking in the requisite legal, media, and lobbying skills as representing a deliberately exclusionary attitude.

NGTF's limited frame of reference and practical-minded emphases offended my utopian side, that part of my politics shaped in the sixties and devoted to the possibility of a revolution far more encompassing than the limited though important right to engage in genital sex with members of one's own gender. Even if NGTF proved successful in its political strategy, I feared that the net effect might be to win recognition of gay people as a legitimate minority, but a minority wedded to dominant mainstream cultural values. A new world would not be ushered in, but the old world reaffirmed—with the addition of a few prosperous, well-educated, middle-class, white queers.

But if my utopian side made me wary, other elements in the mix drew me in. I felt flattered at being included on a board with such pioneer activists as Gittings and Kameny and such current stalwarts as Charlotte Bunch, Marc Rubin, Pete Fisher, Meryl Friedman, Barbara Love, and Sydney Abbott. The willingness of such people, many of whom shared my leftist politics, to serve on the board helped quiet my fear that the Task Force could prove a top-down organization lacking any legitimizing constituency.

Besides, I saw few other available political options. GAA became somewhat reinvigorated after the dedicated, energetic Morty Manford assumed its presidency, but factionalism and political lethargy—the latter a growing *national* phenomenon in the Nixon/Ford years—continued to sap the organization's strength; after a fire of suspicious origin gutted its headquarters in October 1974, GAA was reduced to a shadow organization. Minuscule gay socialist and anarchist groups did exist, and I felt closer to them philosophically than to the Task Force, but they were confined to a few dozen people, barely made a blip on the political screen, and seemed doomed to ineffectuality.

But it wasn't simply for lack of options that I joined the Task Force board. I did have a strong practical side that coexisted with my utopianism, and it attracted me to NGTF's can-do agenda. Had I not been able and willing to play the game from "inside the beast" (as we loved to say in the sixties), I could never have had the career success in academia that I had achieved. That success had often been taken as presumptive proof that I had to be comfortably committed to "things as they are." My boy-next-door good looks worked to the same end: I was in the dominant mold, I couldn't possibly have a radical thought in my head (and indeed I hadn't had, until the upheavals of the sixties educated me).

But now, in the mid-seventies, it rankled when my institutional success and standard-American looks were taken as the sum of who I was. When Arthur Bell, one of the founders of GAA and a waspish, witty *Village Voice* columnist, wrote an article in 1974 entitled "Has the Gay Movement Gone Establishment?" my presence on the Task Force board was adduced as part of the proof that the organization was merely "safe." That hurt, since I prided myself on holding political views to the left of the Task Force—and of Bell. (Two years later, curiously, when Jean O'Leary and I appeared on the *Today* show to talk about the gay movement, Bell wrote me privately to say how wonderfully he thought we had done and how he for once felt able to "rejoice" in having "a gay leader" represent *him*. Well, none of us is consistent.)

In any case, by the mid-seventies, with the country again heading into a right-wing deep-freeze, utopianism of any kind had scant chance of winning converts or making gains. Probably the most that gay activism could hope to accomplish in these years would be to win some limited (and desirable) legislative and judicial victories, and to expand its own subcultural institutions.

By the end of the seventies these institutions would range from gay male discos, bars, and bathhouses to lesbian-separatist communes, women's festivals, recording companies, and publishing houses; from the gay Metropolitan Community Church to Integrity (Episcopalian), Dignity (Roman Catholic), and lesbian and gay synagogues; from gay and lesbian businesspeople's groups such as the Los Angeles Business Guild and New York's Greater Gotham Business Council to gay and lesbian Democratic and Republican clubs helping to finance the campaigns of allies and to elect the first openly lesbian and gay candidates (Elaine Noble in Massachusetts, Allan Spear in Minnesota).

This cumulative set of accomplishments did seem to be having some effect in slowly, very slowly, changing entrenched mainstream views that equated homosexuality with pathology or with what the pope in 1976 described as "a serious depravity." But if any number of gains in mainstream acceptance could be pointed to, they were often paralleled by demonstrable losses, making it difficult to draw an accounting that confidently pointed to a positive balance.

Thus 1974 saw the introduction into Congress of a federal gay civil rights bill for the first time—a moment of real symbolic importance—but the legislation had few sponsors and no chance of passage. And although by 1976 sixteen states had repealed their sodomy laws (and by 1979 twenty-five had), the repeals mostly came about as the result of a general overhaul of penal codes—the result, that is, of a legal mind-set changing in advance of public opinion. Similarly, two states and some forty cities had, by 1979, legislated job protection for gays and lesbians, but in most cases this was confined to municipal and state employees.

Similarly, the U.S. Civil Service Commission ruled in 1975 that homosexual applicants would no longer be *automatically* disqualified from employment, and a State Department directive in 1977 instituted a policy of considering gay job applicants on a case-by-case basis. But neither ruling could guarantee that such cases would be objectively evaluated and that an actual shift in hiring policy would result.

Not, that is, when the dominant climate in 1977 still allowed the City Council of New York to (once again) defeat a gay rights bill; let the national columnist George Will condemn gay rights ordinances as "part of the moral disarmament of society"; enabled the Toronto police to raid the offices of Canada's leading gay publication, *The Body Politic*;

and allowed Florida governor Reubin Askew—who had a *liberal* reputation—to announce that he would not want "a known homosexual"
teaching *his* children.

Not when vandals could ransack the feminist Diana Press in Oak-
land, California, filling its printing presses and typesetting machinery
with paint, chemicals, and Comet cleanser, destroying plates, soaking
with solvent (and ruining) five thousand copies of Rita Mae Brown's *A
Plain Brown Rapper* and three thousand of *Lesbian Lives*. (When a few of
us set up a drive to raise money for the press, Wayne Dynes sent us a
denunciatory letter insisting we should be raising money instead for
GAU's journal, *Gai Saber*).

Not when *The New York Times* could publish a virulently anti-gay
op-ed piece, and then, when I protested it in a private letter to the edi-
torial-page editor (whom I knew slightly), have her justify it to me as
part of the paper's standing policy of trying "to give the full range of
ideas a chance." Indeed, she added in her letter to me, the *Times* had
the "obligation" to publish pieces "most thinking people" might not
agree with. I acerbically replied that the "full range" was represented in
the *Times* in regard to certain issues only, and that it was hypocritical to
claim comprehensiveness as a general policy: "You have given ample
space," I wrote her, "to what someone has called 'Hitler's viewpoint'
on homosexuality, but not on, say, blacks, Chicanos, women, et al.
When was the last piece you ran arguing that the cranial size of blacks
is on average smaller than that of whites? When the last piece debating
whether Jewish greed is congenital or merely cultural? These views *are*
held by a large number of Americans—probably at least as many as
think gays are diseased or demented—but their opinions, *that* segment
of the 'range,' has been carefully excluded." This time I got no reply.

The seventies saw real gains—we had an openly lesbian state repre-
sentative, a gay synagogue, a political action committee, and so on—
but the gains remained tentative, incomplete, and—especially to those
who were not white, did not live in big cities, did not hold secure jobs
or salaries—of marginal significance or none at all.

No, heterosexuality remained decidedly the national measure of
health, the sum of well-being. Even in liberal straight circles, homosexuality could be accommodated only when seen as a pale shadow of
the superior heterosexual way. Any suggestion that homosexuals, with
their special historical experience, had a unique and valuable perspec-

tive to contribute—especially in regard to nonconformist gender roles—was perceived (accurately) as a threat to the established psychosexual order and treated, at best, with uneasy, patronizing scorn. To insist, as GLF once had, that "we must release the homosexuality in heterosexuals and the heterosexuality in homosexuals" would be, in the mid-seventies, to talk into the wind.

Like so many others, I longed for less-qualified progress, a more sweeping mitigation of straight bigotry and gay self-hatred. But to achieve that, my radical lobe insisted, required an across-the-board assault on the country's manifold inequities. To fight for anything less—to try to win rights within a profoundly corrupted system—was mere tinkering around the edges. Worse, to focus on a limited civil rights agenda that left institutionalized heterosexism and racism in place would simultaneously guarantee that such rights would never amount to more than superficial toleration *and* create a false expectation of full acceptance that would shore up the very system needing demolition. But the pragmatist (and optimist) in me kept responding, "To hold out for a full-scale revolution that, in this conservative, conformist country, is unlikely ever to come, is to surrender the chance of making at least *some* lives better now."

It was a debate—within me, within the country—that has never had a satisfying resolution. Did the effort to end the slave trade, by raising the value of those already enslaved, in fact rejuvenate the institution? Did the movement to win the right to vote for women come at the expense of a more encompassing assault on gender roles? Did the nineteenth-century movement for an eight-hour workday sap—and thus ultimately betray—the Socialist effort to destroy a capitalist system in which the brutalized many worked for the exorbitant profits and pleasures of the few?

In the face of immediate suffering, it is difficult *not* to want and to work for piecemeal change. Where misery is rampant, visible, and concrete, Revolution can seem a distant, even heartless abstraction.

No, the Task Force, with its limited civil rights agenda, its just-folks veneer, its willingness to play ball with the heterosexual powers that be, was never going to usher in a libidinal revolution that featured androgyny and polymorphous perversity as its starring attractions. Nor was it going to do much if anything about racism, sexism and classism. But if NGTF could achieve some legislative and judicial victories, that would at least shrink the legitimate boundaries of public homophobic expression (which is all civil rights legislation can ever do), and thereby reduce to *some* extent the daily toll that hatred and violence took on gay and lesbian lives. Even more, perhaps, it would encourage gays and lesbians to feel better about themselves, to band together for mutual support, and to work for a more hopeful future. That was surely not everything—but, just as surely, it was something. As I wrote in my diary several years after joining the Task Force board, "For all NGTF's 'reformism,' it *is* at least reforming."

The list of the Task Force's accomplishments became fairly impressive, even if the press releases sometimes outdistanced reality and the claims for success sometimes proved more ardent than the follow-through needed to assure it. But in saying that, one must remember the difficulty of the obstacles faced, the entrenched homophobia that continued to circumscribe even the most dedicated efforts. Nor should one fail to remember that most gay men and lesbians were "otherwise engaged" in the seventies—the men with their pleasure domes, the women with building separatist institutions. An organization like the Task Force, which held to the vision (even though sometimes failing to implement it in practice) of gay men and lesbians continuing to work together, did so in the face of a divided community largely indifferent to politics.

That the Task Force made mistakes, could be all at once overambitious and underefficient, had blind spots—some of them huge and egregious—was riven with internal tensions (between director, staff, and board), inflated some of its victories and failed to capitalize on others—all this is less surprising than that it had so many real victories to celebrate.

Early on in its existence, NGTF—and Ronald Gold in particular—helped conclude the negotiations (begun under GAA's auspices) that led the American Psychiatric Association in December 1973 to drop homosexuality from its list of pathological disorders, rounded up support in Congress for the introduction of a federal gay civil rights bill, and helped to form the Gay Rights National Lobbying Office (GRNL) in Washington, D.C., to work for progay legislation. (I was one of thirty elected to serve on GRNL's first, mostly window-dressing board.)

The Task Force also formed the Gay Veterans Committee to assist gay people fighting military discharges, and in 1976 got the U.S. Job Corps to reverse its long-standing policy of excluding "sexual deviates." By the end of that year, NGTF had also lent strategic support to local forces pressuring for the repeal of sodomy laws (and the passage of antidiscrimination ones) in sixteen states and thirty-six cities.

A caucus formed by lesbian staff and board members of the Task Force became active in a variety of national coalitions with women's rights groups, and in 1977 helped to organize the lesbian caucus for the National Women's Conference that succeeded in getting a sexual preference plank added to the conference's "National Plan of Action." The NGTF lesbian caucus also played a role in promoting lesbian visibility during International Women's Year in 1975 and in getting the mainstream feminist movement to more openly embrace its lesbian members.

And throughout the mid-seventies, the Task Force worked hard to exert pressure on large corporations to examine their antigay bias in hiring—and got such giants as IBM, American Airlines, and Citicorp to put anti-discrimination policies into writing. The Task Force also created a Gay Media Alert Network (a listing of local gay organizations paired with local television stations in more than a hundred cities) to protest negative media representations of gay life; the Network won an especially notable victory in pressuring ABC to soften an episode in the popular *Marcus Welby* television series that stereotypically portrayed gay men as child molesters.

The achievement that received the most press—and from within the gay world, the most criticism—was the 1977 meeting, brokered between NGTF and lesbian presidential aide Midge Costanza (who was not publicly out at the time), with Carter White House officials. Bruce Voeller and Jean O'Leary chose twelve gay and lesbian leaders from around the country to join them at the meeting. That alone produced wounded outcries from those who had been omitted, and (from radical gays) loud denunciation of those who had been included. (Radicals characterized them as unrepresentative, well-scrubbed types all too eager to sell out their less-fortunate brethren for a chance to share in dirty-tricks politics as usual.)

Other critics objected to meeting with the aides of a President—Carter himself went off to Camp David—who seemed at best ambivalent about homosexuality and whose sister, the evangelist Ruth Stapleton Carter, denounced it as a sin. These critics pointed out that although Carter, during his 1976 campaign, had said that he opposed discrimination based on sexual orientation and would support and sign a federal civil rights bill to that effect, he had then withdrawn his support for a gay rights plank in the 1976 Democratic party platform (the plank was adopted at the 1980 convention), and had admitted on television that homosexuality "puzzled" and "troubled" him. Not a bad state of mind, to be sure, when measured against the overt, unapologetic homophobia of the Republican party's leaders. But not exactly a clarion call to end antigay discrimination, either.

Despite the assorted objections, the White House meeting went forward. It generated considerable press, some subsequent meetings with various departments and agencies (especially with the U.S. Civil Rights Commission), and few concrete results—that is, beyond the undoubted symbolic importance of having gained direct access for the first time to the Oval Office. Some commentators—including the influential gay reporter Larry Bush—insisted that results would have been greater if NGTF, more adept at getting the spotlight than holding it, had not itself failed at vigorous follow-through. But Jean O'Leary and Ronald Gold have both retrospectively insisted that NGTF did make considerable effort; it foundered (in Gold's explanation) on a combination of changes in NGTF personnel and the easing out of Midge Costanza by administration homophobes. In any case, those who believed Carter was *not* basically homophobic could later cite his 1978 advice to California voters to vote no on the notorious Proposition 6 (designed to bar gay and lesbian teachers from the classroom), and his 1979 appointment of openly lesbian Jill Schropp to the National Advisory Council on Women.

PLUSES AND MINUSES, criticism and praise, self-recrimination and self-exculpation—these are the standard ingredients of organizational work, gay or otherwise. Not the least that can be said on the positive side of the Task Force's ledger was the mere fact of its survival. A national gay and lesbian political organization with a paid professional staff had demonstrated, by virtue of continuing to stay the course, that a certain level of visibility had been achieved and could be built on— and that gay people could no longer be *entirely* ignored.

By 1978, five years after its inception, the Task Force could boast eight thousand members (though not even a third were women) scattered in all fifty states, a steady rise in revenues (though still not suffi-cient to establish hoped-for regional offices, let alone to provide the staff a decent wage), and a board, initially reliant on East Coasters, that now included representatives from around the country.

Which isn't to say that the initial doubts I and others had had about the Task Force had been laid to rest. We would still involuntarily twitch at the periodic charge that NGTF was an "elitist" organization out of touch with the needs of ordinary lesbians and gays and their grassroots communities, and unwilling or unable to embrace nonwhite or work-ing-class cultures. In this regard, nothing made us more uneasy than the favorable opinion West Coast millionaire David Goodstein (who had purchased *The Advocate* in 1974) expressed about the Task Force, and his solidifying friendship with Bruce Voeller.

Goodstein was widely distrusted as a *merely* ambitious man intent on becoming a power broker. He shared Voeller's talent for skillful media manipulation, and his belief in the primary importance of working within the system to produce change. But Goodstein did not share Voeller's intermittent sympathy for left-leaning analysis and action—which Goodstein's influence, we feared, might make more intermittent still. His insistence that well-placed "professionals" lead the movement threatened to narrow its base, and its agenda, still fur-ther. And Goodstein used *The Advocate* as a personal sounding board for his conservative views.

In a 1976 editorial, for example, he deplored radical gay "obstruc-tionists" who might conceivably derail or delay our acceptance into the American mainstream—a theme Goodstein continued to pound home through the years in his *Advocate* columns. Middle-class respectability was his totem; he wanted those of us who might qualify (namely affluent white men) to take their place on the assembly line of the American Dream, and those of us who couldn't qualify, to get out of the (his) way. By 1979 Goodstein was claiming that "moderates" were responsible for all the movement's successes to date, and the "left-wing radicals" responsible for nothing but "noise . . . an enor-mous amount of friction in the gay community and a lot of unhappi-ness."

The election of another gay conservative, Charles Brydon, to the NGTF board—a choice urged by Voeller—caused additional alarm among its left-leaning contingent. Brydon was the founder of Seattle's

Dorian Group, an organization of gay and lesbian professionals and businesspeople, and he had done important work in pushing for anti-discrimination ordinances. He was also known for his close connections with the local and state power structure, and obviously relished his role as an insider. Indeed, he seemed mystified as to why getting ahead in the system wasn't everybody's goal.

Brydon liked to claim that he was more liberal than his detractors thought. Yet if so, not by much—as his own reaction (recorded by Eric Marcus in *Making History*) to his first Task Force board meeting attests: "It was like a trip back into the sixties counterculture era. . . . By and large, people involved in the movement at that time were not your mainstream persons. They were individuals who did not have to worry about risking their careers to do this kind of work because they didn't have professional careers. . . . Very utopian kinds of ideas or solutions to problems would be expressed . . . unrealistic, usually idelogically skewed points of view."

In 1979, after I had resigned from NGTF, Brydon became its executive director, the board apparently feeling that his financial expertise and connections could carry the organization through a difficult time. But he became outraged early on when the board elected a female co-director, Lucia Valeska, and wholly alienated when she insisted on participating in all decision-making. (Though it should be added, in fairness, that Valeska, too, had her detractors; some thought she seemed indecisive and unwilling to carry her share of the load.)

Brydon was committed to the "right to privacy" strategy and insistent that conservatives like Ronald Reagan would respond favorably to a gay rights campaign based on that principle. (This was a view also shared at the time by the pioneering and powerful California gay leader Jim Foster, who baldly told the *Body Politic* that "money buys you access to the political process.") Brydon, in any case, quickly alienated the board majority; it came to see him as a man who equated affluence with acceptability, and possibly even with morality. For his part, he came to see the board as pie-in-the-sky romantics. He was soon eased out.

Friction within the organization was in fact a constant—friction between Voeller and certain staff members, between the staff (which often felt underappreciated) and the board (which usually felt under-consulted). The Task Force's real accomplishments always seemed to be accompanied by serious personality conflicts, turf wars, and angry divisions based on gender, race, and—less, or less visibly—on class. (After all, most of us were squarely—in both senses—"middle.")

The Task Force had been barely three months old when board member Frank Kameny—who in the pre-Stonewall years had played a heroic, militant role—shot off a furious letter to the staff and board declaring himself "dismayed and, in fact, appalled" at the lack of leadership and systematic planning thus far apparent. Frank wanted a formal constitution, a firm statement of purpose, and a clear-cut demarcation of lines of authority between board, staff, and executive director. He wanted the board to govern NGTF "rather closely and in considerable detail," and believed the role of the membership, no matter how large it eventually became, "should be close to, if not actually nil."

Frank's view that the board should set policy and priorities and not be (as some boards are) simply a high-profile, fund-raising body was shared by most of us and, after considerable debate, this was established as a guiding principle. But in practice, during most of the seventies, policy decisions were primarily made by the staff; and to maintain that control, the executive directors usually presented the board with only a carefully limited set of agenda items to debate. The board, however, had more than its fair share of tough and independent-minded characters; it frequently rebelled against playing a secondary role and insisted on reasserting its policymaking power, even as the executive directors tried, with minimal success, to get the board to take on more fund-raising responsibilities instead. All of which produced frequently fractious board debate, with Kameny usually the most fractious of the lot.

Anyone who had known Frank earlier in the movement had grown familiar with his penchant for emphatic, and sometimes throbbingly self-righteous, diktats. In the face of one of his repetitive tirades, most of us on the board would try to keep our eyes on the floor and our tempers cool, repeating over and over a silent mantra: that only someone with Frank's truculent personality could have had the guts to take on the federal government and the psychiatric profession in the sixties, at a time when the gay movement was little more than a gleam in the eye. And so we tended to let Frank vent, to think of ourselves as high-minded for doing so, and to resign ourselves to the interminable discussions of structure that made us almost as irritable as they did him.

★   ★   ★

IT BECAME APPARENT EARLY ON that others on the board were even more uneasy than I over the Task Force's (mostly) reformist orientation. Two board members defected almost as soon as they were elected: The writer Arthur Bell sniffed the establishment air for a meeting or two, then thunderously denounced our mealy-mouthed ways as he headed for the door. Bebe Scarpi, a pre-op transsexual schoolteacher, lasted a bit longer, but she, too, departed—though not (as rumor had it) because Voeller suggested she might want to "rethink" her decision to wear drag to an NGTF benefit at the Eagle, a leather bar.

Several other resignations hinged on racial issues. The first African-American member of the Task Force board, Jon L. Clayborne, stayed but a short time, making clear his dissatisfaction with efforts to involve Third World gays in the official movement and insisting that the elimination of racism in the gay world "should be as much a consideration" as the elimination of sexism. And Clayborne was certainly right that it was not. As Thomas Dotton, another African American, wrote in an angry 1975 article, "Nigger in the Woodpile" (for the anthology *After You're Out*), after five years of working in the movement he still found racism "unseen" and had become fed up with "the endless apologies and excuses." (Or, as the black lesbian writer Pat Parker put it in her poem "Have You Ever Tried to Hide?", the white lesbian's foot might well be smaller than the white man's, "but it's still on my neck.")

Just as in the early feminist movement, the gay movement could not seem to focus its attention on issues relating to race and class. Its *in*attention kept most nonwhites (and most nonurban working-class whites as well) unwilling to set aside their own agendas and their sense of multiple identities and loyalties, in favor of a single-issue political movement. Even a radical publication like *Gay Community News* (which began in Boston in 1973), though devoted to broad analyses and alliances, and with a substantial readership of eight thousand by the mid-seventies, proved unable to attract more than the occasional non-white staff person or even subscriber.

Besides Clayborne, who stayed just briefly, the only other African American on a Task Force board that by 1976 had thirty members, was Betty Powell, an instructor at the Brooklyn College school of education; she was soon elected co-chair. And before the end of the decade, the board had implemented as formal goals that a minimum of twenty percent of the body should consist of minority members and that the ratio between men and women should be fifty–fifty. But the awareness that such goals were desirable was not tantamount to meeting them; as regards minority inclusion, especially, the accomplishment was (and in most gay organizations remains) woefully incomplete.

Zulma Rivera, the one Latina voted onto the board in the mid-seventies, never even took her seat; no sooner had she been elected than she resigned in outrage at a letter Bruce Voeller had sent to the entire board. In it, Voeller criticized us for failing "to obtain for our Board a substantial group of people of means or influence," and for refusing in general to discharge the traditional board function of fund-raising. "If NGTF is to survive," Voeller angrily informed us, "it cannot be a kind of Gay Legion of Honor for movement leaders."

Rivera, at least as angry as Voeller, immediately sent in her resignation and scorchingly told him off: "It is not the time to question my value as a Board member *after* I have been elected and *before* I have had a chance to demonstrate my abilities. . . . As a lesbian I experience enough abuse in my everyday life. I don't have to be subjected to it among my own people."

Frances Doughty, in her role as board co-chair, sent us all a diplomatic letter asking us to "stay out of the unproductive cycle of blame, responsibility-shifting, and finger-pointing"; she urged us to redirect our energies toward the goal of ensuring "the survival and growth of the Task Force." But when, following Frances's lead, we did try to reconfigure the organization, a whole new series of disagreements ensued, mostly centered on gender issues.

By then I had already formed friendships and a loose political alliance with several of the women on the board, especially Betty Powell and Charlotte Bunch. (Years later, expressing my admiration for Charlotte, I would say, "Whenever I was in doubt how to vote on an issue, I would wait for Charlotte's hand to go up and then follow with mine.") Our alliance was based on the shared perception that NGTF's continuing focus on winning powerful mainstream allies in order to foster a civil rights agenda was insufficient.

A weekend-long meeting of the Task Force board in June 1976 exemplified much of what was bothering us. The site alone was troubling. The painter Larry Rivers (whose sexual affairs with men, including Frank O'Hara, were not then widely known) had lent us his loft on Fourteenth Street for the meeting. But it turned out he had a quid pro quo in mind: to film and tape our sessions for a documentary he said he was making. I had already had one unpleasant experience with Rivers's documentary filmmaking, and was wary of risking a second. During an antiwar demonstration in Washington, D.C., a few years earlier, Rivers had out-rabble-roused everyone else on the eve of the march—but then, instead of going to jail the next day with the rest of us, *filmed* our arrest.

Several of us expressed strenuous objections to allowing Rivers to record closed discussions on basic policy matters, and possibly releasing them in circumstances over which we had no control. After a typically lengthy argument (some board members were obviously gratified that a "straight" artist of Rivers's renown was at all interested in us), a compromise was reached: We agreed to let Rivers film us (sound turned off) for a few minutes at the end of our discussions and left it up to individuals to decide when and if they wanted to give him separate interviews. Several did; I didn't.

There were a number of newly elected board members at the weekend-long retreat (Charles Brydon was one of them); meeting them confirmed my already well-entrenched view that the women of NGTF were far more impressive, politically and humanly, than the men. I was especially taken with Pokey Anderson from Houston, Jean Crosby from San Francisco, and Dorothy Riddle from Tucson; all three, I felt (as I wrote in my diary), had "a forceful grasp of the larger political context, the radical commitment that should underlie our reformist activities"—precisely what I felt was lacking in a number of the men. But as I was told at the time (and since), I have a way—a deplorably "essentialist" way—of overcategorizing and overcriticizing "middle-class white men" (that is, people like myself) and, in contrast, overgeneralizing about the superior political insight and all-around wisdom of lesbians. I persist in this, I am told, even while well aware that the lesbian community has itself been racked with factionalism and ideological warfare through time. And so I try, like a good analysand, to work on my bias about the superior virtue of lesbians—of women in general. Yet it stubbornly holds.

By the mid-seventies, the women on the Task Force board had formed a women's caucus and had made it clear that the organization would henceforth function on a coalition ("women *plus* men") not a unity ("people") model. That might not represent the optimal hopes some of us—including some of the women—had, but it did represent the current reality of how gay men and lesbians could best work together.

The fact was that by then a significant portion of the lesbian community had concluded that the male-dominated gay political movement could not represent their needs. They were disgusted at the lack of feminist consciousness among gay men; were convinced most of them were merely reformist; were repelled by gay male rhetoric about the "wonders of promiscuity" and the "absurdity of monogamy"; and—at a time when cultural feminism, with its insistence on the fundamental differences between women and men, had eclipsed radical feminism within the women's movement—considered the "lurid" gay male style (which they sometimes exaggeratedly attributed to all gay men) as at odds with their own values. This did not mean (as many younger lesbians today assume) that the lesbian-feminists of the mid-seventies were antisex prudes. But it is true that they defined lesbianism less as a *sexual* identity (in contrast to the way most gay men regarded themselves) and more as one centered on their gender interests as women.

The women of NGTF were somewhat unusual in the mid-seventies in their continued willingness to work with gay men, but they were not willing to keep letting lesbian-feminist issues take a backseat to gay male ones. This was notably true of Charlotte Bunch. Herself a key figure earlier in the lesbian separatist movement, she had not, when deciding to join the Task Force board and work again politically with gay men, left her feminist values at the door. As Bunch put it in a 1976 essay in *Christopher Street,* "Lesbian-feminists assert that homosexual oppression is intricately connected to women's oppression through the patriarchal institutions of male supremacy and heterosexuality, and therefore heterosexism and sexism must be fought together."

This outraged Frank Kameny above all others. By the time of the June 1976 retreat, Frank had already exploded several times in board meetings over the "intrusion" of feminist values. At Larry Rivers's loft, the heat went up several notches. As I wrote in my diary afterward, "Every time one of the women talked of the need to end lesbian invisibility or insisted upon the semantic propriety of 'gay men and lesbians,' Frank, leaping to apoplectic cue, would either shake his head with vigorous displeasure, mumble something about the 'fanaticism of revolutionaries,' or do some of his furious (and infuriating) speechifying about the need to maintain a clear separation between the feminist and gay movements."

When it came time at the end of the first day of the retreat to elect board officers, much of this antagonism came to a head. Charlotte and Betty took me aside to say that the women on the board trusted, among the men, only me and Bert Hansen (an assistant professor of history at the Binghamton campus of the State University of New York, and a staunch feminist). They wanted one of us to agree to run with Betty for co-chair of the board. Neither of us wanted the job. I tried to persuade Bert to take it on, *assuring* him that he had the higher feminist consciousness. But he was adamant: He was on leave the following term to get some writing done and feared embarking on additional political work.

That left me. Flattered at having the women's confidence, and already convinced that NGTF had to move in the direction of a radical feminist perspective, I was reluctant to give a flat-out no. I told Charlotte and Betty that I strongly preferred not to run but that if they couldn't persuade Bert to change his mind, I would leave the final decision up to them.

When nominations began the following day, I was startled to hear Betty put up Gary Van Ooteghem as the male co-chair, and even more startled to have Dorothy Riddle then nominate me. Van Ooteghem was a recently elected board member who had been fired from his job as assistant controller for Harris County, Texas, after coming out as a gay man. (A U.S. District Court judge later ordered him reinstated with back pay on the grounds that his free speech had been unreasonably curtailed.) Though I admired Gary's courage, I disliked his air of hard-edged certitude, and some of the women, too, viewed him as a kind of Kameny-in-training. Failing to catch Betty's eye, I asked for a five-minute adjournment.

Betty and I then huddled and she explained what had happened. She had had a long talk with Gary and had concluded that she could work with him, even though she distrusted his instincts and worried about his close ties to Voeller. (Voeller had been strongly urging Gary's selection as male co-chair.) Better, Betty felt, to let Bruce's choice go through than to have a major showdown over what she felt was finally a minor matter. Besides, she added, "Gary desperately wants the job and you desperately don't."

I completely agreed—but Dorothy Riddle didn't. She found Gary "too unreliable politically" and insisted that she was going ahead with her plan to put my name on the ballot. I finally prevented that by agreeing to run for the eight-member executive committee, which met monthly (whereas the board met only four times a year). Since Dorothy, Charlotte, Betty, and Meryl Friedman (co-spokesperson of the Gay Teachers Association) would also be on the executive committee, we expected henceforth to have a strong voice in setting NGTF policy.

(In the end, Van Ooteghem had a stormy and brief tenure. After sending an unauthorized letter in NGTF's name to President-elect Jimmy Carter asking for a meeting with him, Van Ooteghem was reprimanded by NGTF's officers and within the year had resigned from the board. He later denounced the organization for "biting off more than it can chew.")

At the close of the June 1976 board retreat, I felt full of optimism about the Task Force's future. As I put it in my diary, "I think there's now a good chance (and there wasn't before) that NGTF will begin to think through a political stance that offers something beyond immediate survival issues (crucial though those are), that in the process of working for desperately needed reforms, we will hold in mind a more encompassing social transformation as our ultimate goal."

Such sentiments were precisely what a Charles Brydon scorned as "utopian" (and by his lights, with reason). But I have never seen any cause to apologize for "utopianism." Why drive through a tunnel if there's no expectation or hope of passing straight through to the light? I have always thought a strain of utopianism essential to any political project worthy of the name. Utopianism even makes strategic sense; in concluding my keynote speech at GAU's inaugural conference in 1973, I had put it this way: "The goal is utopian, and must partly fail. But only utopian goals, I believe, will allow us partly to succeed."

The *height* of "realism," I've often argued, is to recognize that what does not yet exist, what has never been tried, is nonetheless possible; to reject so-called "historical necessity" in the name of what is not yet known. In a real sense, that has been, and remains, the sum of my political philosophy.

In any case, the hoped-for transformation of the Task Force proved tough sledding. And probably because, at bottom, transformation—personal or social—was not what most gay Americans (any more than most straight ones) have in mind. Voeller's we-want-in politics were (and still are) far closer to what the majority of gays and lesbians desire than are the policies of us self-styled radicals. Most gays, after all, see themselves—and want others to see them—as good mainstream Americans, believers in the essential "rightness" (indeed superiority) of Our Way; and Voeller's strategy of working through established channels for piecemeal change was, and is, entirely consonant with their own views. Thus it was in the seventies that tens of thousands read David Goodstein's *Advocate,* and far fewer the radical *Gay Community News.*

I got a strong taste of the dominant mind-set within two weeks of the board retreat. At the June 1976 Gay Pride March, I noticed for the first time that the largest contingents were marching under the banners of religious groups—Gay Presbyterians; Dignity; the Metropolitan Community Church, and so on. As I wrote in my diary, "It filled me with disgust. I felt like Ralph Ingersoll, sniffing the fundamentalist air, fearful of contamination. To me these religious affiliations are simply another example of gay imitation of the worst of straight culture, pious posturings that seem increasingly to dominate the movement." (Though my adamant secularism hasn't diminished over time, in the nineties I increasingly hear it characterized as a "lamentable lack of spirituality.")

I got further confirmation of what seemed to me the movement's growing devotion to dead-center politics when attending a panel that same month of June 1976 entitled "Where is the Gay Movement Headed?" Most of the speakers were impressive, particularly Allen Young and John D'Emilio. Young, the co-editor with Karla Jay of several important early anthologies of gay liberation writing, spoke eloquently about the need to proclaim our sex-positive traditions—so needed in the culture at large, so in danger of being buried under what he (and I) viewed as a misguided effort, growing ever stronger in the movement, to win acceptance from straight America by denying the full range of experience and behavior in our own communities.

John D'Emilio, then working on his doctoral thesis in history at Columbia (it would be published a few years later as the pathbreaking *Sexual Politics, Sexual Communities*), gave a lucid plea for organizing ourselves around a more extended range of issues—for example, abortion—than those relating solely to our sexual orientation. Along with demonstrating that we were more than sexual beings, this strategy would also serve to reach out to our natural—and needed—allies among other marginalized and minority groups.

But if the panelists were exhilarating, the audience response was depressing—a series of self-enclosed little speeches irrelevant to the issues Young and D'Emilio had raised. Instead of grappling with assimilationism and insularity, we were treated to a heated debate that night between two members of the audience as to whether we ought to accept a march permit for Sixth Avenue, the one insisting that it was "a second-class street," the other replying indignantly that "Sixth Avenue is *not* a second-class street! After all, Radio City Music Hall is on Sixth Avenue!"

Beset on the one side by lesbian separatism and on the other by the mounting gay male conviction that discoing till dawn was certainly more fun, and infinitely more chic, than politics, the organized gay movement seemed badly positioned for the onslaught from the religious right that swiftly gathered momentum in the mid-seventies. The bell in the night sounded in 1976, when the Supreme Court, refusing even to hear oral argument, voted six to three in "Doe v. Commonwealth" to let stand a Virginia statute (and by implication laws on the books in thirty-four other states) punishing sodomy between consenting adults; that law, the Court declared, was not an unconstitutional invasion of privacy.

Signs of a backlash had been evident for at least a year: The New York City Council had again defeated a gay civil rights bill, with the Archdiocese of New York proudly leading the fight against what it liked to call the "sexually disoriented." City Council member Matt Troy had, during a television show, scornfully referred to gay people as "lepers." William F. Buckley, Jr., had written a vicious "let's face it, they're *sick*" column. And the psychiatrist Charles Socarides had been pressing hard for the American Psychiatric Association to repudiate its 1973 vote dropping homosexuality from the category of illness.

I had tried, in my optimistic way, to put the best face on the building backlash. Perhaps, I'd written in my diary, it would serve to "activate some of those complacent gays who choose to equate their individual success with general toleration, who will not understand that selective toleration is itself a convenient blind for passionate distaste. It will also be less easy now for well-disposed straights to dismiss talk of homophobia ('Oh, Iowa yes; but Manhattan?—never!') as hysterical exaggeration."

But the sweeping 1976 Supreme Court "Doe" decision made it much more difficult to see the bright side. It felt (as I put it in my diary) "like a snake breaking suddenly, hungrily, through the crust of the earth." And what could we do about it? One friend urged a public statement saying "we are not now and never will abide by any 'law' which in essence denies our right to sexual expression." But how many would sign such a statement? Wouldn't mainstream gays themselves reject it as confirming the image of gay people as outlaws?

Was any other response more tactically promising? Should we try to organize a mass rally in protest? That would at least provide an outlet for anger, but low attendance could prove an embarrassment. Should we have a teach-in on homophobia? But wouldn't we end up preaching to the already converted? How about tax refusal, like that practiced by a segment of the opposition to the Vietnam War on the grounds it would not support a government that denied basic rights? Would even a handful support a measure so unorthodox? Should we put our energy into lobbying for the gay civil rights bill recently introduced into Congress? But was there even the remotest chance we could mobilize the needed votes to enact such legislation when the Court had just announced that it was constitutional to discriminate? In fact every tactic we could think of, from militant zap to quiet plea, had already been tried, and none seemed able to touch the country's entrenched—and seemingly deepening—homophobia.

Attempting to remain at least marginally optimistic—for how else does one remain political?—I managed to find *a* bright side: The Supreme Court opinion (I wrote in my diary) "does make clear—and most gays need to see this, too—that we're not struggling against a phantom oppression or overstating the obstacles in the path of acceptance. Despite the backlash, I find it hard to believe we'll be thrown back (in New York at least) to the days of widespread police entrapment. Indeed, the establishment clampdown is an almost infallible sign that a certain level of change *has* been achieved."

And I tried remembering two other things as well: That movements for social change are always subject to fluctuating fortunes; the graph never traces linear upward progress but rather peaks and valleys of varying, maddening, unpredictable duration. And that for all the "one step forward, one step back" nature of the gay (or any) advance in the United States, progress here seemed infinitely greater than elsewhere in the world. In Barcelona in 1977, the police fired rubber bullets into a gay pride march; in London that same year, the editor of *Gay News* was convicted on charges of blasphemy. In 1978, when Australia finally managed to field a gay rights march of two thousand people (more than a quarter million turned out that year in San Francisco), the police moved in and made arrests for "indecent behavior." And in Iran in 1978, six men were executed by firing squad for the crime of homosexuality—with thousands of additional executions to follow under the Khomeini regime.

With those chilling images in mind, the fact that NGTF's application for membership in the liberal Leadership Conference on Civil Rights was turned down in 1977 (it was later accepted), did seem less than catastrophic, especially since other liberal organizations, like the American Civil Liberties Union, the National Organization for Women, Americans for Democratic Action, and the National Council of Churches remained supportive of gay rights. Still, an awareness of relative well-being can carry one just so far; finally, spirits sag or lift in response to developments within one's immediate environment.

And sag they did in 1977, when Anita Bryant announced her Save Our Children campaign to repeal the recently passed Dade County, Florida law that forbade discrimination in jobs and housing based on sexual orientation. The Dade County law was one of some three dozen such ordinances that the outraged singer (and Florida citrus pitchwoman) characterized as protecting the rights of "human garbage." By the following year, California legislator John Briggs had introduced a state bill—for which he had collected some half-million signatures—calling for the expulsion from the classroom of not only gay and lesbian teachers but also any other teacher who presented homosexuality in a positive light.

The hard-fought Briggs amendment ultimately went down to defeat by the considerable (and unexpected) margin of 59 to 41 percent. But Anita Bryant's forces, after a vicious campaign that portrayed gays as recruiting and molesting children—and aided by a pro-Bryant letter from Archbishop Coleman Carroll, read aloud in Catholic churches on the Sunday preceding the referendum—succeeded in rescinding the Dade County ordinance by a vote of more than two to one. The readers of *Good Housekeeping* that year named Anita Bryant "The Most Admired Woman in America."

The coalition that defeated the Dade bill was bound together by opposition to a host of other progressive measures: busing, the Equal Rights Amendment, abortion rights, the ban on official prayers in public-schools, and liberalized marijuana laws. Those who voted against gay rights abhorred nonconformity of any kind, believed women's place was in the home, and were "patriotic" to the point of xenophobia. A score of preachers, of whom Jerry Falwell became the best-known, took to their pulpits and to the airwaves to denounce homosexuality as a threat to the nation's "moral fiber" (translation: to "traditional family values" that upheld a strict gender division and the undisputed hegemony of the patriarchal father).

The rising tide of social conservatism in the late seventies saw the defeat of the Equal Rights Amendment, attacks on affirmative-action programs and social welfare legislation, and the popularity of "right-to-work" laws aimed at diluting the strength of labor unions. Not surprisingly, gay rights—the newest kid on the block—suffered its own share of setbacks. In 1978 alone, gay civil rights ordinances went down to crushing defeat in St. Paul, Minnesota; Eugene, Oregon; and (by a three-to-one margin) Wichita, Kansas.

Though a substantial backlash was at work, *some* comforting signs of progress continued to appear. New York City mayor Ed Koch (who in 1972 had called the Department of Defense's policy of dishonorably discharging homosexuals "cruelly out of date") issued an executive order forbidding anti-gay discrimination in municipal government; in Seattle, voters retained a gay civil rights bill by a wide margin; representatives from fourteen European countries joined forces to set up the International Lesbian and Gay Association (ILGA) to work globally for lesbian and gay rights; a comprehensive gay rights ordinance passed the Los Angeles City Council in 1979; and, in that same year, the ACLU set up its National Gay Rights Project.

Such comfort as these occasional upbeat signs provided was more than offset when, within weeks of the Seattle vote that seemed to stem the tide of anti-gay reaction, Harvey Milk, the only openly gay member of the San Francisco Board of Supervisors, was assassinated (along with Mayor George Moscone) by ex-supervisor Dan White. Brought to trial in 1979, White was convicted—by a jury from which gay people had been excluded—of two counts of voluntary manslaughter. (He was ultimately released after serving a five-year term, and was later a suicide.)

Enraged at the jury verdict, thousands marched on San Francisco City Hall—and then exploded into what became known as the White Night riot. Police cars were overturned and burned: several hundred people were injured; a million dollars' worth of property was damaged. And the message was delivered loud and clear that those who thought an appropriate response to the murder of a gay hero was a slight tap on the wrist, could not rely forever on the formidably gentle nature of the gay people they so blatantly abused.

The tide of social conservatism had far from run its course by the late seventies. And such fledgling gay organizations as existed were not, it became more than apparent, likely to prove equal to the ongoing threat. Their councils were too divided, their staffs and revenues too small. Those limitations, in turn, reflected the inability of the organized movement to repair the political breach between lesbians and gay men, and to reach out to a non-white, non-middle-class constituency. But the weakness of the movement reflected, too, the essential lack of political will in the gay world. Too many gay men had, after coming out, headed directly into the arms of commercialized pleasure; too many lesbians had headed for the woods.

Several years later, with the religious right and Jerry Falwell's Moral Majority flourishing and the gay world still under-politicized and over-factionalized, I was invited to speak at a Lambda Legal Defense Fund dinner (I was on the organization's largely inactive advisory board). I tried to use the occasion to analyze our current plight.

Reviewing the history of the post-Stonewall gay movement, I argued that at its inception it "had spoken and acted boldly against entrenched privilege based on gender, racial, ethnic, and class discrimination." But in the mid-seventies had come an influx of many more prosperous white males into a movement they had previously disdained as composed of noisome hippies and impractical visionaries. "The more those who earlier eschewed the gay movement have now joined it, the more their bland deportment and narrow social perspectives have come to dominate. The gay movement," I said, "is currently characterized by skilled lobbyists pressing for narrow assimilationist goals through traditional political channels."

Working within the system *had*, I acknowledged, produced some important gains; we *had*, overall, achieved greater visibility and more legal protection. But the gains had come at no small cost: We had taken to downplaying our differences from the mainstream (differences we had once proudly affirmed), to discarding radical social analysis, soft-pedaling our distinctiveness, discouraging and denying the very diversity of behavior and lifestyle our conformist society stood most in need of."

And in the process, I concluded, we had pretty much abandoned any effort "to address the plight of *all* gay people: the invisibility of lesbians, the discrimination against non-whites, the scornful disregard of the rural poor." The shift was all too typical of how protest movements in this country have always unfolded: "Originating in fierce anger and initially marked by broad-gauged demands for social change, they rapidly evolve into well-behaved self-protective associations, and in the process abandon demands for challenging the vast inequities endemic to our social system." To build a movement of larger numbers and impact, we needed to demonstrate to a diverse and mostly still closeted gay population that the movement was concerned enough with the difficult realities of their daily lives to be worth joining. And beyond all that was *the* problem: how to build and sustain a collective struggle in a country that emphasizes radical individualism. We (especially the already privileged) are constantly reinforced in the notion that the cultivation of one's own precious personality is more important than binding oneself in common cause to others.

It is true that political involvement requires some detachment from self-obsession. But the process is paradoxical. Participation in a common struggle with others opens up opportunities that feed the self in unexpected ways. Though political work *does* demand that we concentrate on the public purpose at hand, it simultaneously provides the individual with the comfort of community and a newfound security and confidence. That, in turn, can lead those long suffering from the corrosive effects of oppression to self-discoveries and assertions that previously felt too "dangerous" to experience or express. And these discoveries often (for the individual) transcend in value any of the public gains won by the political struggle itself.

*　　　　*　　　　*

WHEN, EARLY IN 1977, I received a bulky packet of materials to read through for yet another upcoming, talk-laden meeting of the NGTF board, I knew I had come to a divide. As I wrote Betty Powell, then serving as co-chair, the planned agenda "seems to me so top-heavy with organizational matters and so little concerned with substantive issues that I simply can't face sitting through the meetings anymore." This was not to say, I added, "that I no longer value the work of NGTF. It *is* to say that my own association with it feels increasingly lifeless, perfunctory." It was, I wrote Betty, time for me to resign.

Perhaps, at bottom, my perfectionist temperament gave a certain inevitability to that resignation. I had a lifelong malcontent's way of overemphasizing what was wrong, and losing sight of or undervaluing what was right. Perhaps that's what "burnout" comes down to: that not all expectations have been met; not all old wounds magically healed; not all hopes—such as complete transformation of the world—realized; not all secondary gains—like finding a bevy of intimate new friends or one mate—secured.

But oh, how soon I missed that imperfect world of gay politics once I had moved myself to its margins. When a graduate student from New York University came by one day to interview me for a paper he was doing on the early days of GAU, I was astonished by the amount of emotion the conversation uncorked. As I summarized it that night in my diary, "When he arrived I was irritable with overwork, lack of time. When he left two hours later, I was bathed in tears and thanking him for helping me to relive a series of events and see for the first time how much they had meant to me—and how deeply I feel their loss. . . . I don't know what-all he opened up—or how. I'm numb, exhausted. It's the loss he opened up: those years of intense commitment to each other and to our sense of a mission. . . . We're strangers now, or distant friends, or enemies. And gay politics itself yet another impotent talk-fest to add to the slag pile of promises. The movement was supposed to change the world—it hasn't even saved my life. I know—my expectations are always too high, and the fall proportionate. . . . That doesn't diminish the loss; it merely describes my contribution to it."

For a few months I tried to fill the void by sitting in on meetings of the small Committee of Lesbian and Gay Male Socialists. I considered myself a socialist in the sense that I believed the amount of suffering in

90

the world could and must be reduced, that neither "human nature," as conservatives claimed, nor the "mysterious intentions of the Deity" mandated its continuance. I was a socialist of ends, not means. Priority had to be given to the needs of the *least* fortunate; how we established that priority was unclear. I wavered as to whether it could be best accomplished through the state, through a compassionately educated populace working locally, or by some combination thereof. I often felt more the anarchist, deploring the state's potential for tyranny, bureaucratic and political, and its disregard for individual rights—which meant I was not a traditional socialist who viewed state monopoly of the means of production and distribution as *necessary* preconditions to a classless society.

In any case, the protracted and fractious doctrinal debates that preoccupied the Committee of Lesbian and Gay Male Socialists very quickly grated on my activist nerves. Was the "patriarchal capitalist system" responsible for *all* our ills—and would a socialist revolution automatically cure them? Would bringing an admittedly needed "working-class perspective" to the gay movement really prove sufficient to reinvigorate it? What of the fact that large segments of the American working class held to an ingrained conservatism on cultural issues like feminism and gay rights? Wasn't a "working-class perspective" in fact rife with homophobia? And wasn't the record of socialist countries (or those claiming to be) a good deal *worse* on gay rights than that of capitalistic ones?

In a long introductory essay to the published version of Hans Magnus Enzensberger's 1970 play *The Havana Inquiry*, I raised and explored some of these issues, specifically in regard to the Cuban revolution, as a microcosmic way of trying to sort out some of my encompassing ambivalence about ends and means. I proceeded from several givens: that our country's historical imperialism in Latin America ran deep and continued to the present day; and that the Cuban revolution *had* eased the vast gap earlier separating rich and poor, white and black, urban and rural Cubans in income, job opportunities, health services, diet, and education. I went so far as to write that "no one would want to claim that the United States, proportionate to its resources, has made comparable strides."

But I did take issue with the notion (central to Enzensberger's play, and to the ideology of the Lesbian and Gay Male Socialists group) that our country's imperial pursuits inexorably, exclusively pivot on matters of profit, trade, and markets. That kind of orthodox Marxism, which tends to see values and ideas as having no authentic or independent life apart from the material relationships that brought them into being, seemed to me too narrow. Among other things, it failed (as I wrote in the *Havana Inquiry* piece) "to take account of the missionary zeal to spread (or defend) 'democracy' and 'Christianity' that has always been a significant element in the American character and has always encompassed passions beyond the monetary."

"Missionary zeal," to be sure, has sometimes, perhaps even usually, been no more than a convenient cover for greed. But I thought it was a dangerous oversimplification to assume that the vocabulary of "anticommunism" our leaders used to justify their murderous policies in Southeast Asia, for example, was *merely* a cynical smokescreen designed to conceal their real aim of protecting American markets and investments.

Johnson, Kennedy, Nixon, and their ilk, I wrote, have unquestionably been sympathetic to the view that what's good for American business is good for the world, and their policies have reflected that sympathy. But to say that much was not to summarize their ideology, nor to unravel its several complex strands. Like most of us, our leaders are capable of sustaining varied loyalties: in their case, to "free enterprise," American profits, God, "individualism," and parliamentary democracy. That these loyalties have in general been mutually reinforcing does not justify the assumption that they are interchangeable. To recognize, moreover, that the Johnsons, Kennedys, and Nixons have certain *non*-material commitments is not to soften the indictment against them but to clarify it.

Nor were Castro's values as easily gauged as orthodox socialists in the early seventies claimed. Castro was surely right in characterizing elections and political parties in pre-revolutionary Cuba as designed to legitimize and preserve the interests of the privileged, but the exploitative purposes for which those political institutions had been used under an oligarchy did not automatically discredit their potential value under socialism. As Salvador Allende had shown in Chile, parties could serve as authentic alternatives to, rather than mere echoes of, privilege. The same was true of the institution of a "free press." Yes, it was often the handmaiden and alter ego of the power elite—an argument Castro had used in suspending publication of the avant-garde *Lunes* and in forcing the poet Heberto Padilla publicly to confess his "sins." But as *The New York Times* had demonstrated in releasing the Pentagon Papers, and *The Washington Post* in exposing the Watergate scandal, a free press, far from being an impediment to justice, could sometimes (if not often enough) be its agent.

The perspectives of the feminist and gay movements had additionally complicated my views, sharpening my ability to see some central contradictions in Castro's revolution (and in left-wing male rhetoric generally). Castro had, after all—as I pointed out in the *Havana Inquiry* piece—rounded up homosexuals and put them in prison, a repression that had recently given way to subtler but still real forms of coercion and ostracism. From a radical feminist/gay perspective, moreover, the older utopian goal of "freedom from material want"—still so elusive, still so central to building a more decent world—should perhaps no longer be regarded (could it ever be achieved) as the final stopping point on the utopian continuum.

Beyond it, one could now envision a psychosexual transformation in which "male" and "female" became outmoded differentiations, individual human beings instead combining in their persons the qualities previously thought the preserve of one sex or the other. Such fluidity of being and behavior would transgress previously static notions of the self. Those of us who had caught sight of this latest vision and who saw the redefinition of gender and sexuality as the newest cutting edge of change tended (I wrote in the *Havana Inquiry* essay) "to regard the contours of Castro's 'new man' as distressingly old: 'Honor' and *Machismo* on the one hand, and Statism and Authority on the other."

Perhaps, I wrote, Castro had no choice, doubly beset as he was by "the ingrained aggression of our country and the ingrained stereotyping of his." Perhaps he thought it neither wise nor possible to push the revolution into still further areas of innovation. Perhaps he was a willing prisoner of the Marxist paradigm that sees changes in material relationships necessarily preceding changes in cultural outlook. But perhaps, too, I concluded, Castro—and, by extension, most traditional heterosexual male leftists—have neither sympathy for nor interest in the gender and sexual transformation which feminist and gay perspectives offered.

In the two decades since I wrote my *Havana Inquiry* essay, little additional evidence of such sympathy has accumulated, even (I wrote in 1974) as psychosexual revolutionaries have found, like "so many visionaries before, that ultimate goals forever recede as they forever approach."

WHEN I RESIGNED from the Task Force board in 1977, my disillusion with the current political posture of the organized gay movement was a—perhaps even *the*—salient reason. But it was certainly not the only one. I didn't pretend in my letter of resignation to NGTF, or to myself, that I was acting solely from high-minded political principle. I wasn't, and I knew I wasn't. Just as I've never believed the conservative cant that social activism derives solely, or even primarily, from the need to work through some private grievance or heartache (under the guise of championing some "cause"), similarly I have never trusted the claim of those *dis*affiliating from political work that their dashed hopes are wholly unrelated to other requiems tolling in their lives.

Much more had been going wrong with my life than the slippage in vision of a political organization I happened to be affiliated with. I was depressed at the breakup of a love affair, and at my inability to fall back for solace on habitual hard work. After having given up my plan to write a broad history of sexual behavior, I seemed unable to find a substitute project sufficiently ambitious to absorb my energies (though I did continue to produce assorted articles and reviews).

Just as my work was going stale, leaving me unanchored, my mother discovered that she had malignant melanoma. (I had lost my father some fifteen years before to a heart attack). After a year and a half of shifting diagnoses and treatment, of hopes raised only to be dashed, my mother died in September 1977. Her death had a deep and lingering effect on me, not least, I suspect, because our entangled relationship had never gotten worked through; the emotional bond remained powerful but subterranean, felt but avoided.

My mother was one of those women, typical of her generation, who had never had much of a chance. Beautiful, smart, dynamic, she had gone to work at thirteen, finishing high school at night. She had then made a mostly prudential marriage, pouring her prodigious energy first into housewifely routines, and, when the marriage turned loveless, into contentious altercations with friends and driven devotions to grandchildren—leavened, happily, by a resilient, openhearted ability to make fun of her own feisty obsessions.

Growing up, I had never had reason to doubt her love for me; she had been my rock, the omnipotent guardian angel who could magically make everything come right. Her shamanistic power had remained with me even after my teen years, when I had stopped telling her anything important about myself. I didn't want to risk getting near the subject of my homosexuality and, more encompassingly, had grown to resent her intrusive, engulfing ways; to her onslaught of questions, I had returned monosyllabic replies. Though I credit the fact that I survived—despite having internalized so much of the culture's homophobia—to my mother's unconditional love, I had sensed early on that it was a love embedded in control.

The strong bond and the equally strong discomfort between us never got sorted out. As an adult, I felt perpetually annoyed with her, even as I felt perpetually guilty about my own fortified, withholding behavior toward her. A defensive strategy constructed in childhood to hold her smothering attentions at bay seemed never thereafter able to soften, let alone dissolve—much as I wished for it to. When I knew she was dying, I kept thinking we would, we must, have that final talk that would erase the long-standing tension and leave the love, uncontaminated, intact. But as is so often the way, that final talk never took place. And part, doubtless the largest part, of my intractable grief at her death was that so much had been left unexpressed and unresolved between us.

IV

ALTERNATIVE THERAPIES I

A FRIEND OF MINE, Pete, a devotee of countercultural nostrums and alternative therapies, told me I needed to be "dynamited." There was no other way, he said, to end my depressed stalemate, to begin a new cycle. The "talking cure," of course, was out of the question; I had had too many negative experiences in psychotherapy and besides (according to Pete), "my defenses were too entrenched to yield to any rational, verbal approach." No, a direct assault had to be made. What he had in mind was his latest discovery: LSD therapy.

The instant Pete made this suggestion, I thought of a line of Kerouac's (I had been trying to write a play about the Beats) that had stayed in my head since I first read it: "We're seeking derangement to bring us landward back." Yes, I thought, exactly—Pete must be right. The staleness I had been experiencing needed to be blown, not talked, away, my cautious, ambivalent intellectualism bypassed. I had to bust loose, push towards excess. There was no other way to free myself from all the baggage of an entrenched, prudent life.

So, anyway, said the initial rush of bravado. When Pete told me more details about what an LSD "intensive" involved—he had done his first the previous month and had found it "miraculous"—I had some frightened second thoughts. It seemed that Dr. Martino (as I'll call him), the theoretician and leader of the sessions, operated on the assumption that what most people called a "bad" LSD trip was in fact the preferred one: It put you in touch with precisely those buried, negative experiences that most needed airing. The whole point of the intensive was to produce a bad trip, to see to it that people did indeed "go crazy"—the better to confront their demons.

It all reminded me of the theories of R. D. Laing, which had been popular in the sixties: the schizophrenic break as a form of revelation and a guidepost to true sanity. For someone like me, who still regarded the sixties as a magical time of renewal and hope, the overtones were not unattractive. (It was only much later that the extent of the damage done by Laingian therapy was more fully revealed.)

But even in the mid-seventies I had doubts about the efficacy of the cataclysmic approach to personality change. The experience sounded potentially transcendent—*and* dangerous. When Pete told me that the sessions took place in various rented farmhouses in New Hampshire, my uneasiness increased; I associated the city, not the country, with safety. And when he revealed that Martino allowed people to bring their own LSD, I felt downright alarmed. What if they brought lousy street stuff, thus contaminating the experience? Was Martino interested in scientific controls, or was this some kind of party game for advanced freaks?

Seeing me back off, Pete suggested an "in-between" step. He was due to try his second trip in just a few days. He could arrange for me—as he already had for his girlfriend, Robin—to come along as an "observer-assistant." Robin and I would not take LSD. We would serve essentially as hospital orderlies—"cleaning up the shit and vomit, keeping an eye out for violence, seeing that the shrieks and terrors ran their course unabated and were not aborted on false grounds of 'concern.' "

After Pete finished *that* description, I felt certain that actually taking part in the experiment would be more than I could handle. But "derangement," even from a distance, still held its appeal. I gave Pete the okay to put in a call to Martino and ask if there was room for another assistant that weekend. He said there was, but told Pete to warn me that "no one remains as uninvolved as the title 'assistant' implies." On balance, I decided to go ahead.

I FLEW TO BOSTON early that Sunday morning—entirely free of my usual fear when on a plane. As I said to Pete later: "If I had felt that way *after* the two-day session, I would have been convinced it had indeed worked miracles."

Pete and Robin, who lived in Boston, met me at the airport and we set out in their car for New Hampshire. It was a spectacularly clear day, the ripe beauty of the late-summer landscape underscoring my sense that "all was well," that this passage would be as snug and untroubled as the serene New England towns we were driving through. At some point during the ride, the notion, with uncommon nonchalance, entered my head that perhaps, after all, I should participate in the experiment rather than observe it from a safe outpost. Pete enthusiastically seconded the impulse. Pleased at my own daring, I let the idea take hold, perhaps because I didn't believe Martino would let me make a switch at the last minute.

But when we arrived at the farmhouse and I put the question to him, Martino said they could "accommodate" me—though I would have to make a final decision immediately. Pete, standing at my side, urged me on: "You're being offered a great and rare opportunity—seize it."

Swallowing hard, I said yes, I would participate. My hands instantly got cold. I told Martino that I had already eaten breakfast, which participants were not supposed to do; I suspected that might well disqualify me from the trip. "No," he responded coolly, "you might vomit, but that doesn't matter."

I took to telling everyone in sight that I was terrified of not coming back, of ending up as a vegetable in a state hospital. The standard response was along the lines of "Dr. Martino has done nine hundred sessions and never lost anyone." I rushed up to Martino to say that "everyone else seems to have had multiple experiences with hallucinogens, but I've never done acid and can't believe it's wise deliberately to embark on a 'bad' trip before having experienced a 'good' one." To which Martino replied, "Those are your defenses speaking."

Along with the other two dozen participants, I was put to work writing a required autobiography and filling out a Hartman Personality Test. I confessed in the autobiography to varied discomforts—like the disparity between my radical politics and my middle-class lifestyle—and elaborated in detail every physical symptom I'd ever had (translation: "This is a sensitive flower; *be careful with him*"). I also made a point of listing my assorted credentials, as if to say, "You can't afford to let anything happen to this Distinguished Man—the news would hit the papers and ruin you!" Warning delivered, I began to calm down *somewhat*.

For the next six hours we milled aimlessly around, waiting, waiting—and watching the assistants, as our own hunger grew, conspicuously gorge themselves with food. The impatient (a category that did *not* include me) were told that "the Room has to be prepared"—we were not allowed any advance look inside—and that the assistants, one of whom was Robin, "had to be briefed." The long delay may also have

been part of the trip, intended to build anxiety and allow the participants to get to know each other a little, at least visually, so that projec-
tional images positive and negative ("She looks like my sister") could
accumulate. As we waited, there was some polite, wary talk between
us, some desultory banter.

At about six P.M. we were finally taken into the Room. It was dark
when we entered, the windows had been sealed and covered with
black masking tape, and it was airless. Mattresses and pillows were
scattered over the floor. Audiovisual equipment was everywhere. We
had been told to leave shoes, sharp objects, and watches outside, but
were temporarily allowed to keep on our eyeglasses—only, we were
told, until "the slide projections" had been completed. White sheets
covered the front wall; the Hartman Personality Test scores had been
taped to them.

Dr. Martino spent the first two hours going over our Hartman
scores, my distrust mounting throughout. Up to that point I had spotted little or nothing about Martino that suggested an obvious faker, but
I now nervously felt he was placing far too much emphasis on a test
that seemed to me simplistic and value-laden. While filling out the
Hartman form, I had had no trouble guessing in advance how our
rankings would be established; a stated preference for "baby" or
"nature" over, say "a tidy operation" (too anal) would doubtless be
equated with a high degree of mental health. Though I have no great
attraction to either babies or nature, I had put both a notch or two *lower*
in my rankings than I ordinarily might have, out of pique at the seeming transparency of the choices.

Whether for that reason or some other, my test results were analyzed (out loud) as among the "worst" in the group. Martino
announced that I had the highest score by far in "rebelliousness in rela-
tion to authority." Given the authorities in this culture, from the
Catholic church to the Republican party, I thought that might be taken
as a sign of perspicacity. But Dr. Martino thought otherwise; he labeled
rebelliousness one of my "problem areas." Doubtless questioning his
authority in these matters would have further been indication of my
"problem."

I was at least as suspicious of the purported "positive" findings in
my Hartman results. I had "no significant blockage," Martino
announced, in the area of "loving, relating with fellow beings." In the

category of "how realistic you are with yourself," I also had "no problem"; yet in a seemingly related area, "knowing oneself," I scored
"badly." Similarly, I supposedly revealed all at once both a "lack of
security" and "good bottom"—the latter defined as "calm, sensitive
equilibrium." To be described as "calm" should have been signal
enough for me to dash to the door.

Indeed, I came close. At the end of the two hours, with the slides
about to begin, I cornered Martino. "If the test scores *are* accurate," I
blurted out, "I could destroy the successful equilibrium I've managed—apparently against all odds—to achieve!"

"You are exactly the kind of person who can benefit most from the
trip," Martino replied without elaboration, and promptly disappeared.
A spasm of terrified ambivalence coursed through me. Then I sank
down on a mattress next to Pete.

The lights went out. Multiple, overlapping slide projections came
on, covering the white-sheeted wall with mandalas, cartoons, scenes of
mutilation and violence, flowers, mountains, lakes, various depictions
(comic and sensual) of sexuality (there were two female-female slides,
no male-male ones). As the slides were being projected, "Warren
Mark," a lovable, dippy, garrulous man in his mid-seventies (who I
later learned was a professor of the psychology of religion, the author
of a book on "chemical ecstasy," and an associate of Timothy Leary),
passed among the mattresses telling people that it was "time to take the
material you have brought with you," and wishing them a good trip.
Mark, it turned out, was Martino's chief academic sponsor in this
country (Martino was based in Mexico); and Mark had carefully chosen his words with a eye to establishing, should problems arise, some
basis for legality.

In fact almost everyone took not their own "material" but the blot-
ter acid provided. Each individual was asked to suggest a dosage for
him or herself. I was relieved to hear Martino tell many people to take
less, in no case raising the amount the person suggested. Some asked
for one tab of (I think) seventy-five to a hundred milligrams; no one
wanted more than two. I asked for one. Two of the younger guys
received Martino's permission to take peyote buttons (ten each) that
they had with them. I'm pretty sure Warren Mark was the only person
who took acid that he had himself brought; I was later told it was some
new lab creation still legal because not yet widely known.

About an hour into the slides, we were told to take the acid. An hour after that, just as the slides were ending, somebody abruptly clamped headphones over my ears and a mask over my eyes. "Come this way, Martin," a disembodied voice ordered.

I was deposited on a mattress somewhere in the room—I had lost my bearings. Then, as the music coming through my earphones began to build in intensity, I started to get frightened. Robin later told me that I seemed *so* frightened, she could hardly bear to look at me; as she saw it, I was making a furious effort not to let go, not to give in to the drug. It turned out that only five of us, those who had been diagnosed as having the "greatest resistance," had been given headphones. (The other four, I later learned, had had so many acid trips that it was felt they could predict and abort the anguished reactions Martino considered essential.)

According to Robin, I barely moved for hours; then, my stomach began mildly to convulse and my hands started weaving subtle, weird motions in the air. What was going on in my head was far more dramatic than my movements. Remembering Pete's injunction to "go with it"—whether "it" was joy or terror—I was trying to let the sound from the earphones wash over me. I thought my whole body was contorting wildly to the drums and rattles coming through the headset. I "knew" some of the music was by Maria Sabina (Where did I come up with that name? Did such a person exist?), and one of the few times I opened my mouth was to say her name out loud. Ah, I thought, that will impress them. ("He's been touched directly by her spirit. He knows her name. His body moves as if at one with the sound. He is clearly a chosen vessel, a special one. We will not harm him.")

Animal noises now replaced the drumbeats; pig grunts, jungle screeching, came in louder and louder on the earphones. Frightened, I tried to calm myself: "These noises are meant to scare me—I know that—but I'll keep listening to the beautiful mambo band I hear in the background." I said "beautiful mambo band" out loud, timidly, as if afraid to be too overtly defiant. But locked away behind my mask and headset, I had no idea if anyone heard me.

Then suddenly there were screams and laughter, loud enough to pierce the noise from the earphones. I couldn't see anything, but could feel people stepping around my mattress, occasionally bumping into me. I thought someone might kick me in the groin or fall on my head.

The prospect didn't overly frighten me, but now and then I curled fetus-like on my side to prevent a direct assault.

I reached out with my hand to try to find if anyone was nearby. I touched an arm, hairy, not young, responsive. When I asked who it was, he said "Sam." Sam!—who I had earlier decided was a nice, warm man. I needed him; the panic was rising. I held on tight to his arm, yelled above the din that I was scared, didn't know what was happening, didn't think I could hang on. He comforted me, said he was there. That helped, momentarily. But soon I was fighting panic again, terrified something nameless would engulf me.

Then I abruptly hit on the idea of trying to get to a bathroom. Would they let me off the floor, out of the room? All I can next remember is being taken by the hand, being told I could *briefly* remove the headphones and mask, and being led to a bathroom. My head was swimming, yet I realized—with the headphones off and the bombardment of music, screams, and laughter stilled—that I wasn't as spaced out as I had thought, that I could cope.

Reassured, I was able to let go more after being returned to the room, especially since I was told to put only the mask back on, not the headset. I found myself—maybe I was put—in the arms of none other than Warren Mark. He talked nonstop at me about Martino's "genius," about "the integrity of these people." It soothed and comforted me, blather though it may have been. But then Mark started repeating exactly the same phrase about "the integrity of these people" over and over. I decided he was comforting himself more than me.

Suddenly, in the middle of his praise for Martino, Mark nervously said, "Even the best can make mistakes." Or I thought I had heard that; maybe I was hallucinating.

"What did you say? What?" I could feel the panic returning. "There does seem to be some emergency," Mark replied, his tone distant, as if he were an airborne traffic reporter observing a pileup below. An emergency? What kind of emergency? Had someone died? Were we all going to die? "Yes . . ." Mark went on in the same disengaged monotone, "seems to be a heart attack . . . The oxygen tank is out. . . . More serious than I've seen before . . . Yes, it does seem to be a heart attack."

I was suddenly convinced that the victim was Pete—that he had died. I realized with a start that I hadn't once heard his voice in the din. I had lost him; tears flowed down my cheeks. Two women from out of nowhere, as well as Mark, tried to comfort me. I felt like a tiny child. Weirdly, I asked Mark to guess my age. He said "forty-five." I loved him for that, for knowing I was an adult. In a non sequitur of his own, he asked if I was "by trade" a mechanic, "perhaps a shoemaker—your integrity, your simplicity." That got me upset again. *Everyone,* according to Mark, had "integrity." Could the man make *any* discriminations? Was he bonkers? Where was Pete? What was the emergency? Who could be trusted?

Next thing I knew my mask had been taken off and Pete was cuddling me. We sat upright facing each other for what seemed like hours. I cried and cried, huge heaving sobs. And then I began to come down. . . .

Injections of ketalar—I think that's what the drug was called— became the new, enduring horror. Pete told me Martino's helpers only gave it to people when requested. But I saw them grab one of the men and stick the needle in his arm without any preliminaries. (Pete later insisted that before the start of the trip, the man had asked to be given it.) Otherwise, I saw ketalar offered to various people, but not forced on them. Those who accepted the offer—some took the drug twice— went through what to an outsider looked like absolute hell. One man especially: He screamed and moaned for an hour—"I'm dying! I'm dying!"

They all vomited, dry heaves. All except Sam, the man who had comforted me earlier. Sam went into instant nirvana, "saw God," did gorgeous, undulating arabesques in the air, repeated over and over "*Gracias,* Dr. Martino, *gracias,*" made love to his wife (not present), told us "to work with our hands in the earth," entered and saw the "Universe."

And then from nowhere—just as I had been fearing—three of the assistants came toward me. One, who I had earlier thought looked like a storm trooper, had a hypodermic needle in his hand. He smiled a huge, phony grin. "We have decided to offer you ketalar, Martin. You have shown great courage, you are a brave man. But now you must go further, much further." I refused it, terrified: "No, no! I've done all I can do this time. I can't do any more." They pressed me to be "brave"—to be "a real man." *That* stiffened my spine (or did I subsequently invent that desired reaction?). Finally, reluctantly, they withdrew. For hours, as I watched others go through the ketalar horrors, I was sure they would suddenly grab and inject me. Toward morning the fear diminished. But it never left me. (Originally used as an animal tranquilizer and more recently called ketamine, the drug is in 1996 known by its hip name "Special K"—and is *the* reigning high in trendy Manhattan nightclubs.)

Finally—it must have been mid-morning—it was announced that we would be allowed to rest for two hours. I curled up next to Pete, but though utterly drained, couldn't sleep. The heat and stench were intense, and my mind continued to race. My stomach was still cramping, as it had been during most of the trip. Huge farts yearning to explode lay curled rancidly within; fearing Reprimand, I allowed myself only tiny bursts of secret release.

Suddenly there was the sound of joyful music, the assistants quickly stripped the masking tape from the windows, and the gorgeous morning sun poured in.

Dr. Martino reappeared. "Testimonies" followed. Some individuals read aloud from the autobiographies they had written the previous day; others described the night's experience. There were tears, laughter, and some melodrama. Richard, a psychiatrist participant, screamed on, in a babyish yet somehow pontifical voice, about his need for love.

Then there were some concluding rituals, mostly hippie-banal: We swayed together in a circle, flowers were strewn about, the small son of one of the men was passed around to be smilingly adored, while in the background Indian music (and some weirdly sexist voice-overs: "Woman, the weak vessel, does the best she can," and so on) softly played. Then we were finally released into the outer room, where there were plentiful supplies of food, much joyful hugging, exhilaration, exhaustion.

Just before Pete, Robin, and I left for Boston, I found myself opposite Dr. Martino, whom I'd been avoiding.

"So, Martin, how was it?" he asked.

"Most of the time I was scared to death. I was right about my delicate equilibrium."

He smiled benignly at me. "And we were right that it has to be broken so the energy beneath can emerge."

"I think I was too frightened to do much. But I did say good-bye to my father." (Perhaps I meant "hello.") "I didn't go very far, though."

Martino shook his head in contradiction. "You looked several times into the abyss."

I felt astonished at this high praise, felt heroic, sanctified, Martino hugged me. "You are a very valuable person." I nodded thanks through my tears, and left with Pete and Robin.

The next day, safely back in New York, I wrote these thoughts in my diary:

"—most of my crying was over my father. In the preliminary session, before we dropped the acid, we had been told to choose in our minds 'a person to accompany us on the journey with whom we had had deep trouble.' I chose Daddy—the sweet, decent, withdrawn man who never played an integral role in my life. During the trip, I went 'up the mountainside' with him, merged with him, faced the sun, and descended. I keep repeating that 'I have finally managed to say good-bye to my father.' [He had died suddenly of a heart attack some fifteen years before; an hour's drive out of town, I had reached the hospital too late.] Even now, whenever I think about him, the tears start to flow—

"—the experience put me in touch with my cowardice and weakness, but I could not break through to a sense of my insignificance.

"—I trust only my controls; much more than what lies within or without (the Hartman Personality Test confirmed?)

"—I touched deeply the common suffering, the terrible pain and sadness we all (all except the rare Sams) carry around.

"—I cannot be comforted (as Sam is) by "calling out to Jesus Christ," feeling the "universal oneness," "believing that love never dies"—or any of the religio/mystical balms that reconciled most of the others.

"—I saw more profoundly than ever in my life that I am a terrified little boy.

"—Most people struggle to achieve some sense of balance and worth. I seem to struggle to destroy them (sensing they're falsely grounded? despising equilibrium?). But I doubt if I'll succeed any better in unleashing chaos than most people do in containing it. Too fearful it will permanently take over."

A MONTH LATER, I heard some follow-up news from Pete that made me shudder. The very next time Martino conducted one of his LSD experiments—in Vermont, and only a few weeks after ours—the local police raided the premises and arrested him and his associates. I got a fund-raising appeal from Warren Mark in the mail, but never responded to it and never heard whether there was an actual trial and if so, what resulted from it.

Some six months after that, Pete told me a more horrifying story still, about the "storm trooper" assistant who had offered me ketalar. It seems he was a New Age minister and himself an LSD therapist. A patient he had been treating attacked him one day in his church, cut out his heart with a carving knife, and laid it as a sacrificial offering on the altar. Pete did not know whether the man was under the influence of a hallucinogen.

V

ANOTHER LIFE
IN THE THEATER

WITH LSD THERAPY providing some insights but no solutions for my feelings of professional and personal staleness, I looked for sustenance to what had been my earliest love, the theater, a love that had long preceded the Ph.D. and professorial tracks. As a teenager I had toured in summer stock as "George Gibbs" in Thornton Wilder's *Our Town,* and the director had strongly urged me to think about a professional career in acting. But college—and caution—had intervened.

By the early sixties, though, I had begun to write plays, and I had found a (deceptively) early success with *In White America,* the story of being black "in white America" as told through documents, diaries, newspaper accounts, and the like. The play had opened off-Broadway in 1963, run for a year and a half, won a prestigious prize, had two national touring companies and various foreign productions.

By the time an evening of my one-act plays, *The Memory Bank,* opened in January 1970, I had become thoroughly besotted with the notion of having a second career as a playwright. Just *how* besotted, I revealed in a pre-opening night article, "The Agony and the Ecstasy," that I wrote for the *New York Times* "Arts and Leisure" section. In it, I clothed my yearning for theatrical glory in ironic humor:

> It is the afternoon of the day my play, "The Memory Bank," is due to open. I am standing in front of the bathroom mirror, shaving. In a triumph of the nontraditional, I manage not to cut myself. Perhaps I lack the strength. My brain is deep in a fog bank. Even the sky, I note, has gone from the morning's brilliant blue to what is now, at midday, a miasmic gray. Maybe the astrologers are right: tides do determine the affairs of men, telegraphing messages through nature.

I yawn. Thinking tires me. I have energy for only one activity—composing reviews in my head. Having already invented an urbanely negative notice from Clive Barnes (" 'The Memory Bank' is, contrary to popular mythology, entirely forgettable"), I catch myself about to compose a favorable review ("Not since Eugene O'Neill . . ." I begin Harold Clurman's column in *The Nation*). I am full of instant remorse and savage myself on the spot with a scathing denunciation from John Simon ("Mr. Duberman, fortunately, is a tenured member of a university faculty; we say 'fortunately' because we dislike seeing even the least talented members of the writing fraternity actually starve") . . .

I think it is time to take a pill. The idea has immediate, irresistible appeal. But I have trouble reducing it to specifics. *Which* pill? I already feel lightheaded, so a tranquilizer doesn't seem right. Or do tranquilizers bring your head *down?* That question seems to border on the metaphysical, so I quickly shelve it. I concentrate on the desirability of taking an "uppie," a Dexamil, instead. The pros and cons rack me. An intense moral struggle ensues. It is almost a full minute before I see a way to cut the Gordian knot: I will *nibble* on the Dexamil. After all, I am an American, and compromise is Our Way. . . .

My teeth are about to sink in, when an amalgam of all the Modern Voices starts whispering in my ear: "There can be no growth without pain"; "Man must face experience, not run from it." . . . I withdraw my teeth. I return the pill to the bottle. I am the master of my fate, the captain of my soul. . . .

I intone the one slogan that has never failed me: "grace under pressure." It fails me. I see with instant clarity that grace won't have a chance. The green Dexamil pill rushes back into consciousness. Then I start to get angry. "For God's sake—it's only a lousy Off-Broadway opening! There are people in hospitals with terminal diseases! There are the ghettoes! There is Vietnam! What kind of a monster are you?"

A large kind of monster, since the speech works for only a moment . . . Oh well, it'll all be over in a few hours. MOVE!!

As I walk out into the perpetual sunset of Manhattan, I have a blinding recall of the preview two nights before. It had gone splendidly: euphoric, I rush to be first out of the theater lest the delirious crowd start grabbing at my clothing. Another man is also rushing for the exit, a big grin on his face. He gets to the door just ahead of me. Pushing it open, he gives way to a burst of camaraderie and yells back into my face, "Christ, they've got a bomb, huh?!"

The Memory Bank reviews were in fact mixed to good, and though the run was brief, I felt decidedly on the verge of becoming a successful playwright.

But in retrospect, I may have lost my biggest chance when I said no to Jack Deveau. A pioneer gay male film pornographer, Deveau decided in the early seventies on a "new departure" for the medium: He would add a serious story line to the sex, creating a narrative context for the previously uninterrupted sucking and fucking. It sounded interesting to me—commercially, erotically, and (dare I say it) literarily—so I agreed to a preliminary talk with Jack about writing the script, and went up to his apartment for a screening of the then-famous films he had produced with director Peter de Rome. Peter was there, too, adding enigmatic comments about the "potential importance" of the project. Though I spent the better part of the afternoon lapping up (as it were) the films and trying to persuade myself that a radical breakthrough in form was indeed at hand, I ended up turning down the offer.

I suppose the chief reason was that in the early seventies a variety of theatrical opportunities had come my way and I was expecting an imminent breakthrough into Stardom. The 1972 Equity Library Theater revival of *In White America*—which I thought decidedly inferior to the stark original—was hailed everywhere in the press as confirmation of the play's "classic" stature (even by the *Daily News,* which had refused to review the first production because of what it called the play's "inflammatory" nature).

That same summer Edward Albee and Richard Barr produced an evening of my one-acters at the John Drew Theater in Easthampton, they were then subsequently done at the Manhattan Theater Club and two of the three were chosen for the annual *Best Short Plays* series. PBS commissioned me to write *Mother Earth,* the life of the radical anarchist Emma Goldman; Warner Brothers sounded me out about writing the book for a new Broadway musical; and CBS asked me to script the inaugural special, "The Presidency," for their thirteen-part series *The American Parade.*

To add sugar on top of the honey, I was told by a producer friend that the eminent theater critic Harold Clurman had confided to her that he was "putting his money on Duberman and Guare as this generation's best bets." Jules Irving and Alan Mandell, who were then running Lincoln Center, used nearly the same words in telling me they hoped I would let them have first crack at any new play I wrote.

Clearly, I was flying. With such laurels dangling just above my head, I should become a pornographer? Break bread with lowlifes? Yes, I probably should have. *Mother Earth* was ultimately turned down as "too radical and too ambitious"; Clurman got over his purported admiration and gave my one-acters a decidedly middling review in *The Nation;* and when I submitted a new play to Irving and Mandell for Lincoln Center's "Explorations" series, I was told it was "too good—too mature and authoritative" for that particular venue. I learned privately that they had been "dismayed" to see the homosexual subtext in my work becoming increasingly explicit; they regarded that as "the wrong choice."

Though my anointment had been unaccountably delayed, I remained sanguine. When, in 1973, I finished my new full-length play, *Elagabalus,* I told my agent to send it out to the usual (prominent) suspects—Joe Papp; Arvin Brown of the Long Wharf Theater; Wynn Handman of American Place; and of course my "fans" at Lincoln Center.

I knew perfectly well that the play would have a hard time finding a mainstream producer; it did, after all, center on "Adrian," a sexually unorthodox (and voracious) modern-day counterpart of the Roman emperor Elagabalus. But I didn't expect quite the blank, uncomprehending reception the play got. Mostly I heard nothing at all—a deafening silence. Several producers, pressed to comment, settled for variations on "Gosh, gee, I somehow couldn't get with it," or "I admire your daring, but it's really not for me." The one positive reaction ("I think it has the makings of a major play"), emphasized *makings*—I was urged to go the workshop route and "iron out the many kinks" (I don't think he meant Adrian).

Though smarting from such reactions, I decided (as if I had a choice) that a workshop might not be a bad idea; it would momentarily delay, yet could ultimately smooth the way to a full-scale production. Since I was already a member of the New Dramatists, a nonprofit organization dedicated to helping playwrights get their scripts in shape, I decided to mount the workshop of *Elagabalus* there. The New Dramatists, once a vital institution (as it would be again), was at a low point in the early seventies. It seemed—to many of us member playwrights, anyway—to have become less concerned with helping a writer take chances than in making sure no breaches occurred in the rules for how a script should "properly" proceed on its journey. Production values of any real fullness or sophistication were deplored as too redolent of the commercial theater; to avoid that disreputable association, all workshops were confined to a hundred-dollar budget, a limited rehearsal period and a maximum of five invitation-only performances, from which all critics were barred.

A number of the playwrights, myself included, were up in arms at the cocoonlike atmosphere. We argued strenuously in meeting after meeting with the New Dramatists staff and board that unless a script was presented in something like polished form, what was wrong (or right) with it could not be ascertained. And we argued, too, that confining the performances to invited guests inevitably meant audiences that were mostly a mix of relatives and begrudgingly loyal friends—not the best sources for an honest critical appraisal.

But New Dramatists turned a deaf ear to our arguments (leading a number of playwrights, within a few years, to offer angry resignations). And no exception was made for *Elagabalus,* though I did my best to argue that the "difficult" nature of the material and the play's semi-surreal structure warranted at least some extra rehearsal time. Instead, we were given the usual two weeks, denied the right actually to work on the New Dramatists stage until forty-eight hours before the first performance, and confined to the standard budget (though I did finally get permission to fill out the "set" with the couch from my own living room). Most of the unpaid cast, to survive, had to hang on to their full-time jobs, which often made them late for or absent from rehearsals. The only way I could free the director from his construction job was to lend him three hundred dollars.

Elagabalus was full of technical challenges (including—yes!—a pornographic film) that required *more* than the usual allotment of time, money, and talent. And the leading role of the androgynous Adrian—a daring, playful, willful, self-destructive, teenaged genius—required a tour-de-force performance if he was not to come off as simply a petulant, tiresome boy. Despite open calls and endless auditions, we couldn't find an actor with the needed skills—hardly a surprise, given how little we could offer in return. The actor we finally settled on proved as inept as we had feared, and after the first week of rehearsals we had to replace him with someone who, if only slightly more talented, at least *looked* the part.

No sooner was he in place than the second male lead quit for a paying job in a TV commercial. While we were trying to work in *his* replacement, the stage manager disappeared and the promised tape/sound specialist failed to materialize. The time I should have been devoting to script rewrites was eaten up by production problems, while the director was spending all *his* energy simply holding the pieces together rather than getting them to cohere. At one point it seemed all but certain that the project would abort, but we did finally manage to put together five *very* ragged performances.

Not even off-*off*-Broadway beckoned. Not even my friends were encouraging. A few managed distant, polite remarks ("Disturbing, confusing, need time to digest before commenting"). But my *closest* friends were adamantly negative, a few downright accusatory: How could I have so wantonly damaged my reputation by allowing such an unformed work to be seen in so undernourished a setting? They were right; I was bucking too hard for theatrical success, failing to await a workshop or tryout situation that might actually help me explore the script's deficiencies. Chastened, I simply put *Elagabalus* aside. I tried not to think of the play as a total loss, but I was too disheartened to invest any more time or energy in it.

It was a heavy dose of reality. What saved me from a total funk was my temperamental optimism, the distraction of a brief love affair (with a twenty-one-year-old, God help me, who one minute was mad to move in, the next mad to move on) and, magically, a timely new offer that refurbished my fantasies of theatrical apotheosis.

The offer came from the Francis Thompson Company, the firm commissioned to prepare a film to celebrate Philadelphia's 1976 bicentennial. Thompson himself called to offer me the job of scriptwriter, and our early meetings were intoxicating. The project, I was told, had been budgeted at twelve million dollars. Ten million of that would go to putting up a building (to be designed by Max Abramovitz, the architect of Avery Fisher Hall) suitable for Imax, the special process that required, among other things, a hundred-foot-wide screen. Now here were gargantuan appetites to match my own.

For the script, the Thompson people had in mind some fairly standard, benign thematic material: the signing of The Declaration of

Independence; the Constitutional Convention; and so on. I argued from the first against settling for such patriotic clichés; they would do little more than reinforce a long-standing, and misguided emphasis on the supreme importance of a few heroic personalities. Francis Thompson, a kindly, courtly man, warned me that the project did have a "commercial component"—meaning, I later learned, that the underwriters, a collection of wealthy Philadelphia businessmen, had to be satisfied. But he did suggest I come up with a specific counter-suggestion for the historical narrative. This seemed to me tantamount to a green light. As I say, I have an optimistic temperament.

I dug out all my old colonial-history books from graduate school days, and ransacked them for a resonant political theme and time frame. I finally decided to focus on the story of the Pennsylvania Quakers during the decade 1750–1760, when six Quaker members of the colony's assembly had resigned rather than comply with a call for military action against the Delaware Indians, thus ending Quaker control of the legislative body after a rule of some seventy-five years.

I went back to the Thompson people and passionately defended the centrality of what might, I realized, appear to be a peripheral story. Quaker beliefs, I argued, were in fact at the ideal heart of American ideology. It was among the radical Pennsylvania Quakers, like John Woolman and the younger William Penn—not the merchant grandees—that "liberty of conscience" had been more consistently stressed than elsewhere in the colonies, God's "Truth" declared directly, equally, available to all (with no need for priestly intervention), the profit motive held subordinate to the public interest, war and violence eschewed as instruments of social policy, the Delaware Indians asked for their "love and consent," and black slavery denounced and abandoned. This egalitarian emphasis was, I argued, the ideal spirit in which to celebrate the *ongoing* Revolution—especially since that spirit seemed notably absent from the countless other Bicentennial projects that had already been announced.

Francis Thompson raised his eyebrows and cleared his throat. "I've *got* him!" I decided, ignoring the assorted frowns on some of the other faces in the room. For the next month I put all other writing projects on hold and, working twelve-hour days, completed a fifty-page draft film treatment. I entitled it "The Independent Spirit" and euphorically mailed it off to Thompson.

The night before I was due to go back down to Philadelphia to discuss the draft at a meeting that would also be attended by several of the
wealthy businessmen being solicited as sponsors, Francis Thompson
called me at home. To my dismay, he talked vaguely of the need somehow to reintroduce the signing of the Declaration of Independence
and so on into the script. I reminded him that we had earlier agreed to
eschew such tired clichés, to which he mumbled something like "That
wasn't *my* understanding." In retrospect, I think Thompson was trying
to prepare me, in his muted but honorable way, for what I was likely to
encounter in Philly the next day.

If so, he failed. I arrived to find that my script had been completely
reworked by unknown hands, with no more than five of my original
fifty pages intact. Among other things, the rewritten draft now had the
Delaware Indians carrying out an unmotivated massacre of settlers and
Ben Franklin explaining *to* the Quaker legislators why they had to
resign from the Assembly! As I fumed about the misrepresentations,
and as several of the bigwig backers smiled contentedly, one of
Thompson's people took me aside to hint that once the sponsors had
signed on, a good portion of my original material would "probably" be
restored.

That wasn't good enough. Unless they would *guarantee* such a
restoration—and in full—I threatened to quit the project. They
refused, and I resigned. I told them I would sue if my name appeared
anywhere on the credits.

Oh, swell—another moral triumph! This accumulation of credits
in heaven was not the way to get my handprints in cement at Grau-
man's Chinese Theater. I counseled myself to stay calm: it all ended up
with a concrete slab of one sort or another anyway. Bah, humbug! Film
and theater—it was all one; the mission of the entertainment industry
was to sell tickets, and that, irreducibly, meant catering to the lowest
common denominator in public taste. Print was my medium, and I
had damned well better get back to it. At least for a while. At least until
my unaccountably delayed passport to the entertainment industry
finally got stamped.

And when I did turn back to print, I tried settling a few scores.
Asked to write a piece for the "Arts and Leisure" section of the Sunday
New York Times on the recent spate of historical re-creations on televi-
sion (NBC's *Sandburg's Lincoln*, WNET's *The Adam Chronicles*, ABC's

Eleanor and Franklin,), I took the occasion to mock the way the nation's two hundredth anniversary was being celebrated. Alluding to my Philadelphia experience, I talked about how the Bicentennial was being used to reassert all the familiar patriotic pieties in an ongoing attempt to persuade us that "success story" was a sufficient articulation and summary of the reality of the American experience.

The Bicentennial was a party, I wrote in the *Times,* to which more corporate board members than historians had been invited, apparently out of fear that historical truth might interrupt the triumphal dance. Thus far, I argued, television was proving more venturesome than the rest of the media in using the Bicentennial as the occasion for some actual introspection, offering at least occasional programming outside the acceptable parameters of national self-congratulation.

In this regard I singled out for special praise the *American Parade* series on CBS, and especially the episode entitled "Song of Myself." Based on the life of Walt Whitman, the episode had been far more daring in dealing with the full reality of the poet's life, including his homosexuality, than any dramatization I knew of—and indeed was in advance (this was 1976) of what most Whitman scholars were then willing to concede. All of which gave one reason, I wrote, to reconsider television's purported "cowardice" and the academy's purported "pursuit of truth."

As if to prove my point, Gay Wilson Allen, among the most prominent of Whitman's scholarly biographers, wrote an indignant letter to the *Times* insisting, as he had in his book, on the difference between "fantasy"—Allen admitted that Whitman had "deep homoerotic emotions"—and "physical sexuality." Were he to write his biography over, Allen triumphantly declared, he would "not handle Whitman's sex pathology differently." His "only regret," Allen added, "is that when I began publishing I could not foresee that forty years later my first name would become an acute embarrassment." I did some quick mental refiguring: Television had *far* more courage than the academy.

There was a modest rekindling of interest in my plays when E. P. Dutton published a volume of them in 1975, under the title *Male Armor*—notably, when the seminal gay theater in San Francisco, Theater Rhinoceros, selected my one-acter *Metaphors* for a double bill with Lanford Wilson's *The Madness of Lady Bright* as its inaugural production in

1977. *Male Armor* comprised five of my one-acters (including *Metaphors*) and two full-length plays, *Payments* and *Elagabalus,* both of which I had revised for publication. *Payments,* my own favorite, had originally been done as a workshop at New Dramatists in 1971, where the theme of male hustling had produced mostly horrified reactions (one friend, the actor James Coco, had whispered with mock horror in my ear during an intermission, "What did you do—swallow a brave pill?").

With a revised version in hand, I tried sending *Payments* out again to various theatrical managements. What I got back was the same familiar set of admiring negatives; The Circle Repertory's response was typical: the play, they wrote me, was "a remarkable work," yet "not quite right" for them.

And so when, early in 1976, a tiny Washington, D.C., theater called the Back Alley asked for permission to stage the revised version of *Payments,* I figured, "What the hell."

I should have remembered that my medium was print.

The Back Alley production suffered from the same limited resources I had faced earlier at New Dramatists: a minuscule budget, part-time or non-Equity actors, lack of audiences. Recognizing how poor the prospects were, and feeling that little additional work could be done on the script in such a setting, I stayed in New York for most of the rehearsal period. But a few days before the opening—which the Back Alley billed as a "world premiere," no less—I did go down to D.C. for a few media appearances.

Thus developed the only real drama connected to the production. During my interview with the theater critic for one of the D.C. dailies, the sexual attraction between us was so palpable that at the end of three hours (we had to talk about *everything*), all but eternal troth had been pledged. There was only one hitch: He hadn't yet seen the play. And when he did, and reviewed it negatively, I yelped with pain, accusing him of having savaged my work in order unconsciously (I wasn't even willing to credit him with deliberateness) to sabotage a romantic connection already too intense for his comfort.

How else to explain, I asked in a heated phone conversation, his inability to distinguish—as the *less* intelligent *Washington Post* critic had—between a dreary production and a script (here I quoted the *Post* critic to him) "full of wit," "reminiscent of the finer moments" in Fassbinder's recent film *Fox and His Friends*? What, other than his own closetry, I charged, could explain the nervous reference in his review to the play's "fiercely outspoken dialogue," or his ultimate dismissal of it as "having the feel of a nasty soap opera"?

He decried all that as "nonsense" and said that he prided himself on his ability to separate his attraction to a person from an attraction to that person's work. I said his pride was without foundation, huffily announcing that if he was that uncomfortable with my words, he could never be comfortable with my person. I broke off the incipient romance. We later patched things up and became friends. But at the time, it was as both aggrieved lover and failed playwright that I returned to New York to stanch my wounds—and to take not a little secondary comfort from feeling, as One Who Suffered, superior both to my shallow swain and to the *business* I felt he so faithfully represented.

THE BICENTENNIAL was not yet finished with me. A few months after withdrawing from the Philadelphia film project, I was asked by the Kennedy Center for the Performing Arts, in Washington, to be part of an ambitious season-long celebration in honor of the nation's 200th birthday. The Center said it planned to produce ten American plays, six of them revivals (including William Gillette's 1894 comedy, *Too Much Johnson,* and Percy MacKaye's 1909 drama, *The Scarecrow*), and four of them new plays to be chosen from a batch of six that the Kennedy Center intended to commission. The six playwrights they had decided upon were John Guare, Romulus Linney, Preston Jones (*The Texas Trilogy*), Joseph Walker (*The River Niger*), Ruth Wolff (*The Abdication*), and—me!

To say I was stunned, after my recent string of near—and far—theatrical misses is to understate the case. I was delirious. And when I was further told that I would have free choice of topic (so long as I dealt with "some phase of the American experience") and that after the engagement at the Kennedy Center, the plays would tour nationally, I thought I might quite possibly be dreaming. A front-page article in *Variety* and a long piece in *Time* on the Center's planned season of plays confirmed that I was not.

I gave euphoria free rein, even after some alarm bells went off in my head during my first face-to-face meeting (in a Manhattan restaurant) with Richmond Crinkley, who, with Roger L. Stevens, director of the Kennedy Center, was going to coproduce the Bicentennial season.

Crinkley was a Southern good old boy—charming, smooth, manipulative, unreliable—who *just happened to be* gay. Aside from an occasional dropped hairpin during that first meeting, *that* topic never became explicit between us, not even when we were joined at dinner by his demonstrably affectionate young actor boyfriend. Richmond wasn't *that* kind of gay man. Art and politics were in his view of the world separate realms; art was what the talented few did, politics was the poor substitute resorted to by the benighted many. Richmond was far too urbane ever to caution me directly against introducing gay-themed material into my pending play. But he nonetheless managed to convey the message that "free choice of topic" shouldn't be taken too literally.

In pondering what to write about, I played for some time with the notion of an evening to be called "Unofficial Heroes": the story of America as seen through the eyes of its radical outsiders—people like William Lloyd Garrison, Frederick Douglass, and Emma Goldman. I thought, too, about returning to the documentary form that had served me well with *In White America*. But when I tried my hand at it, the form felt played out for me, and I couldn't come up with an appropriate alternate format.

Then for a time I thought I might do a play on the last years of Wilhelm Reich's life, when he had been jailed by the U.S. government for subversive ideas. I immersed myself in Reich, and books about Reich, for four months; but the play wouldn't come. Then—somehow—I got on to the Beats. The "how" in these matters always seems to me more than a little mysterious: I had never been much interested in the Beats, or been much of a fan of their writings.

It was only gradually that I came to see the actual locus of my newfound interest: the relationship between Jack Kerouac and Neal Cassady. Each had been the most important person in the other's life, but neither (and especially not Kerouac) could find ways to express it apart from the acceptable buddy-buddy ones: tough-guy heroics, all-night Benzedrine sessions, screwing together in whorehouses, sharing women, treating women like shit.

That, writ large, was the destructive tragedy of growing up macho male in America (or anywhere else, for that matter). Through the Kerouac-Cassady relationship, I wanted to write a play about the horrors of "manliness"—which so many heterosexual men seemed to believe accrued in direct proportion to the *absence* of tenderness. The tragedy, as I saw it, was that Kerouac as a young man was palpably tender. Yet the sweet person inside could never get out, or stay out. With liquor in him, he could be a brute and a bully. And the older he got, the more he drank, until finally he did little but drink—and curse the radical young he had once inspired. Had Kerouac been able to connect profoundly with *anyone,* had he and Cassady been able to acknowledge the depth of their passion for each other—and I meant much more than sexual passion, and perhaps not *even* that—Kerouac might not have succumbed in his forties to alcoholism, and Cassady to a drug overdose.

Once that story grabbed hold of me I couldn't let it go. I knew it was likely to make Richmond apprehensive (to say the least), but I managed to persuade myself that the power and poignancy of the theme would somehow capture him—after all, he *was* a gay man! I knew, too, that Richmond wasn't going to be my only problem.

In those years my literary agent (and close friend) was Cindy Degener, who was married to and worked in the agency of Sterling Lord. Sterling was the literary executor of the Kerouac estate, and it was through him that I got formal contractual permission from Kerouac's widow, Stella, to incorporate a certain amount of material from his books into the play. Sterling knew, of course, that I was gay and that I had written a number of gay-themed plays. But if it crossed his mind that this might turn out to be one of them, he never mentioned the possibility or cautioned me against it. Later on, after he read the finished script, his negative reaction would have a significant impact.

I began by reading through all of Kerouac's published work—some twenty volumes of the stuff. And "stuff" is how I felt about much of it; a lot of Kerouac's "spontaneous writing" came across to me as just that, the work of someone high on bennies, unable (as Truman Capote once put it) to stop typing. I admired many sections of *On the Road, The Subterraneans,* and *The Dharma Bums,* but my real fascination was with the life, not the work.

While reading through Kerouac's books, I jotted down words and phrases that resonated for me, without necessarily understanding why. Then, when finished, I read through all those marked sections, made notes, and—mystical though it sounds—experienced some sort of transmogrification. In a way that I hardly understood myself, I tuned in to Kerouac's rhythm, felt genuinely connected to the Beat style.

The play became an amalgam of Kerouac's words and mine. As

when writing about Emma Goldman earlier, in my play *Mother Earth,* I sometimes directly incorporated lines or phrases from Kerouac's own work (with the permission Sterling Lord had arranged from the estate); more often a sentence of his would trigger a continuation of my own, spark off a page of dialogue from me or, once in a while, a scene. Some of the events in the play I wholly imagined; some of the characters became composites that I created from several real-life figures. In the end, the amalgamation became so complete that within a short time of finishing the play I could no longer identify the constituent parts, disentangle the two voices.

I finished the first draft, a whopping 250 pages, in June 1975. Actor friends did a reading of it in my apartment to help me discover what sections needed reworking, and as a result I trimmed away sixty pages. It was now ready, I thought (doesn't one always?) to be seen. I gave it the title *Visions of Kerouac*—meaning to convey that it was a subjective meditation on Kerouac's life in much the way his own book *Visions of Cody* had been a meditation on Neal Cassady's. And off the play went to Richmond Crinkley.

One week turned into two, two into four. No word. Cindy phoned Crinkley's office repeatedly, but got not a single return call. "Doubtless," she said with feigned cheerfulness, "they're awaiting the arrival of the other five commissioned scripts before offering any comments. Why not use the time to do some of the those additional revisions you've been talking about?" So I did. By August, I had completed another, still trimmer version. Off it, too, went to Richmond's office.

Now I started calling him myself. After a dozen tries, I was finally put through. He suggested a meeting, and my eager little heart soared. It shouldn't have. The meeting lasted half an hour. Richmond nervously admitted that he had not yet "finished" the new version (it was clear from his comments that he had never started it). But both he and Roger Stevens *had* read the original, and Richmond wanted me to know (his voice ominous) that "Roger thinks your play is too long."

"Was that his *only* comment?" I asked, nonplussed.

"Mmm—yes."

"That's reassuring."

Richmond giggled, but said nothing.

"The script *was* too long," I continued. "That's why I did a revision, sixty pages shorter. I urge you to read it," I added pointedly.

Richmond responded airily that of course he would, then confounded my gloom by declaring Arvin Brown's prestigious Long Wharf Theater his first choice as the tryout site for *Kerouac*. Before I could catch my breath, he was waving good-bye, off to another "urgent meeting."

I didn't know what to make of it all. *Would* Richmond ever read the new version? Or had a negative decision already been reached on the basis of the subject matter alone, with the "excessive length" being merely a convenient excuse for turning the play down? If so, why had Richmond tossed off the prospect of a tryout at Long Wharf? Was it just to get me out of his hair?

Via Crinkley's assistant, Jack Hofsiss, word soon filtered in that the main office was sharply divided. Hofsiss himself was high on the play, Crinkley unwilling to commit, and the big boss, Roger Stevens, decidedly negative. That was bad news indeed, since it was Stevens who ultimately called the shots. There had probably never been much chance that he would take to *Kerouac*. This was the man, after all, who during a recent interview with the *Washington Post* had referred to the language in the film he called " 'The Cuckoo Flew Over the Roof' with Jack Nichols [*sic*]," as "disgusting." This was the same Roger Stevens who had rejected the Tony Award–winning play *Equus* for the Kennedy Center because he had been offended "by its four-letter language and nudity." Could I really expect him to embrace a play about male love filled with raunchy Beat language and behavior? No, I could not.

Neither Stevens nor Crinkley was under any obligation to like my play simply because I wanted them to. But I did think writers—*commissioned* ones, no less—were entitled to less rude, evasive treatment. I told Cindy to withdraw the script from the Kennedy Center and to start sending it out to other managements.

She did, but the reactions were hardly what I'd hoped for. "Too long," said Circle Rep; "Too literary," said the Chelsea Theater Center. The American Conservatory Theater in San Francisco liked the play but decided the cost of mounting it would be "prohibitive." The producer Stuart Ostrow sent Cindy a note that made me laugh—grimly—out loud: "Duberman has done a wonderful job. Wish it was a musical. But of course it shouldn't be." The veteran producers Diana and Herman Shumlin took me to dinner at the Plaza Hotel to express their "enormous admiration" for the writing *and* their distaste for the contents. Sylvia Hersher, another long-established pro, told Cindy she thought the play "not good—but *great*," yet couldn't imagine who might actually be willing to stage it.

As if all this weren't disheartening enough, I learned that Sterling Lord had by now read the play and had disliked it; in his view, apparently, I had "skewed the 'sex thing' out of all proportion." (I was told this by others in the agency; Sterling never—then or subsequently— proved able, or willing, to discuss the play with me directly.) Another Big Boss putting another big boulder in the path of production.

Caught between my determination to get the script done and Sterling's reluctance, Cindy understandably became paralyzed. Several new expressions of interest, from the Arena Stage and from Cal Arts, abruptly disintegrated, and I began to feel that Sterling's fine (and powerful) hand was at work behind the scenes. Cindy herself became less available to take my calls, and our relationship, which for ten years had been a mainstay for both of us, began to suffer.

Then, two months later, and out of the blue, I got a phone call from Richmond Crinkley. "We've decided not to go ahead with your play," he announced, his voice smooth and unctuous. "Roger doesn't like it. I just called to wish you good luck."

When I found my voice, I reminded him that I had withdrawn the play months ago! I added—trying for a tone as smooth as his, and failing—that since I finally had him on the phone, I wanted him to know that of all my experiences in the theater, the one with the Kennedy Center had been the single most unpleasant. "Good-bye, Martin," he said, and hung up.

A few days later, I got formal notification in a letter cosigned by Stevens and Crinkley. It began with an infuriatingly false "After much consideration . . ." and went on to a string of pious platitudes about "wishing me every success." I wasn't about to let them off the hook so easily. My anger and hurt again to the fore, I shot back a sharp note reiterating that I was the one (did they think a historian wouldn't insist on setting the record straight?) who had decided against the Kennedy Center as an appropriate venue for my play. I wasn't surprised the news hadn't registered, I wrote, since over the past year nothing else had either. "Throughout our association . . . you've shown the lack of basic courtesy one expects even from complete strangers. . . . I could never entrust my work to people of such primitive incivility."

That *finally* got me a response from Big Boss Stevens—after a year of all but begging for some direct communication from him. He took the high road, urbanely professing "surprise" at my letter, insisting he could "not recollect" any unreturned calls, and blandly claiming that he had decided to "release" my play because "there was no time available in the coming year for a production." He suggested, in closing, that "it would have been common courtesy to have spoken to me personally" before sending off "such an unpleasant letter."

That sent me through the roof: I had tried at length and in vain to "speak to him personally"! Off went another note, this one designed to scorch: "My letter to you was not nearly as unpleasant as the treatment I've received from your office. If (as your reply claims) you know nothing of that treatment, I can only deduce that you are out of touch with what is being done in your name." I then documented in detail the neglect and evasion of the past year, including the fact that the two completely revised versions of *Kerouac* sent to his office had never even been acknowledged, let alone commented on. "After all this, frankly, I find your invocation of 'common courtesy' laughable."

In the end, the Kennedy Center produced not one of the six commissioned plays—but I didn't know that in time to stanch the worst of the bleeding. Nor did the failure to carry off the Bicentennial season prevent Richmond Crinkley from being chosen in 1979 to head the theater at Lincoln Center (disastrously, in the opinion of many). That same year, Jack Hofsiss—the good guy in my Kennedy Center melodrama—had a notable triumph directing the stage version of *The Elephant Man*.

And I ended up exactly where I started, at New Dramatists, trying to feel grateful for having at least that venue. It was quite clear to me by this point that the Sterling Lord Agency wouldn't lift a finger to get a production. Sterling's strategy, consonant with his personality, was to circumvent rather than confront. Others who worked in his office confirmed his deep dislike of the script; he apparently objected to any portrait of Kerouac that drew "undue" attention to his macho insensitivity or his possible bisexuality—regardless of how true such a portrait might be.

To some extent I could sympathize with Sterling's plight; as a friend of Kerouac's, as agent for the writer's widow, as a man uneasy (at least as I saw him) around deep feeling or unorthodox behavior, Sterling was indeed in a predicament. But I couldn't sympathize with the way he dealt with it, not even risking a phone call—though I was a client of his agency's—let alone the actual conference needed to resolve the difficult issues at stake. And I couldn't sympathize with what I was convinced was the common, bottom-line attitude toward the play: homophobia. Kerouac's reputation must not be "tarnished" with the suggestion that he had sexual feelings—or even passionately romantic ones that might suggest the sexual—for another man. *That* attitude I was determined to fight.

For a while, I tried pressing the agency to come up with additional production possibilities. But the few suggestions made seemed transparently designed to accomplish precisely the opposite; there were some vague noises about a possible Canadian production (theater or producer unspecified) "in the fall," or "maybe the Edinburgh Festival next summer" (no one at Edinburgh having requested so much as a look at the script). The most laughable moment—and the end of my patience—came when it was suggested that we (somehow) secure the interest of Paul Newman in playing Kerouac. When I said I didn't think Newman had quite the wild, rugged working-class aura the role required, I was told that I wasn't aware of Newman's "remarkable range."

That convinced me Sterling was merely waiting for my rights with Stella Kerouac to run out. According to the contract, "after 64 paid public performances" material in the play that derived from Kerouac's own books would be "forever joined" with my own words in a work thereafter owned by me. That would then allow me legally to publish the play; publication, in turn, could bring publicity and productions. If Sterling wanted to prevent my "unbalanced" version of Kerouac's life from making it into print, let alone onto the stage, he could simply sit me out, let me thrash away until the day arrived when my contractual rights to use Kerouac's prose lapsed.

But if this were the case, Sterling underestimated my tenacity. Though reeling, I wasn't about to let my play get buried. I believed in its merit (*and* its truth), and had already been through too much with the Kennedy Center to capitulate now without a fight. I decided to become my own agent and producer. I would—somehow—get the sixty-four performances needed permanently to secure my rights in the play. And along the way, I would tell Sterling as little as possible about what I was up to. Deviousness was not my style—doggedness was. Sterling didn't yet know it, but the "nice," clean-cut, eager-to-please professor had a powerful will of his own, and was a bear when cornered.

As a first step, I knew I'd have to put together a strong enough workshop at New Dramatists to drum up excited talk in the industry. That wouldn't be easy. We faced the usual uphill struggle at New Dramatists: no budget, limited rehearsals, primitive production facilities—and this time, twenty-five parts to fill. But to direct, I did get Ken Frankel, who had long been interested in the play and had recently had a hit with *When You Comin' Back, Red Ryder?*. That was a decided plus.

The next stroke of good fortune was landing Lane Smith for the role of Kerouac. He lacked the writer's magnetic good looks, and could be an erratic, volatile performer; but when he was "on" he was mesmerizing. The rest of the casting went nearly as well, and optimism filled the air. I had to caution myself not to get *too* excited about the prospects; I'd been down that road—the one with the brick wall at the end of it—too many times before.

And we did, of course, run into setbacks. Both Ken and Lane got unexpected outside offers, and we had to cut an already perilously short rehearsal period still further. Given the limited time for committing lines to memory, we were forced to let the actors carry their scripts during performances, though that meant constricting the staging and interplay. We also had to jam together six performances into three days.

They coincided with a brutal heat wave. The New Dramatists theater had no air-conditioning and only one pathetic fan. To my delight, all the performances were packed—people cramming into every nook and aisle. But that made the air still more stifling; everyone's clothing was soaked through with sweat, and during one performance, a woman, close to passing out from heat prostration, had to be helped outside.

Plus, Lane *did* vary wildly in his playing, sometimes brilliant, sometimes self-indulgent. Several of the male cast members tried to imbibe—as a shortcut to inhabiting—Beat-like frenzy by swigging tequila freely backstage and wine and beer onstage. One performance was so drunken that a bottle got hurled across the stage, just missing an actress and smashing to pieces on the floor. That particular night, the show ran twenty unscripted minutes overtime.

The audiences loved it. And in short order I got an offer from the Lion Theater Club (now defunct but which had just had a big success with *Vanities*), to re-create the production for a four-week run there. The Lion was one of a row of small, new, experimentally-minded theaters on Forty-second Street between Ninth and Tenth Avenues. Like New Dramatists, Lion could offer little more than workshop conditions. But at Lion, that included the right—playwright's choice—to invite critics.

I made the choice without hesitation. It was a gamble, but a necessary one. It seemed to me that a positive or even mixed press was my only real hope for moving the play on to the next level (and my coveted sixty-four performances).

The reviews did turn out to be mostly positive. Arthur Sainer in *The Village Voice* hailed the play as "that rare thing in today's theater—it's alive. In its gut and its head." Alan Rich in *New York* wrote that the play "succeeds in capturing honestly and powerfully, a fascinating moment in this country's literary and social history." And among the additional reviews, Gerald Rabkin in the then-influential *Soho Weekly News* called the play "trenchant, alive, and often amusing—a moving, tragic portrait."

But there was one significant dissent: the all-important *New York Times*. Mel Gussow's review was less a theatrical than a moral commentary. He accused me of presenting "a single-edged" perspective based on the premise "that if Kerouac had admitted to a preference for homosexuality, he would have been healthier, perhaps even a better writer." And, like Sterling Lord, Gussow sniffily rejected the premise.

But the play he described was not the play I had written: *Visions of Kerouac* was about a tortured, trapped man unable to connect deeply with *anyone,* male or female. Protesting Gussow's misrepresentation in a letter to the *Times,* the writer Richard Hall recalled another recent Gussow pan, of the play *Boy Meets Boy.* In now "ascribing a simplistic pro-gay message to the Duberman play," Hall wrote, "Mr. Gussow confirms his own homophobia."

In any case, thanks to the review, the tentative interest a few New York producers had expressed in *Kerouac* now evaporated. (Gussow's notice was in fact mild compared to the one Walter Goodman was to write in the *Times* when *Kerouac* was revived in 1986 at the Actors Theater, in yet another workshop. While never once using the word "gay," Goodman implied that those Beats still living might want to consider libel actions against me for the way I had portrayed their sexuality.)

At this point, my spirits low and unable to think of further options, the unexpected happened: a San Francisco producer, Lee Sankowich, entered the picture. He had happened to catch one of the performances at the Lion Theater, and had become immediately entranced with the play. Lee was best-known for having successfully revived—and toured for five and a half years—*One Flew Over the Cuckoo's Nest,* which had initially failed on Broadway. What Lee proposed was a workshop staging of *Kerouac* in San Francisco, where he had just purchased the ninety-nine-seat Zephyr Theater. If that proved successful, he would then move forward step by step to a full production, a national tour, and an opening on Broadway.

In the face of the Gussow review, this was a far more promising prospect than I would have thought possible. I had only one problem: If the initial San Francisco production failed to catch on with reviewers or audiences and Lee decided against moving forward, the play would have been killed on both coasts, making the chance of my getting the "64 paid public performances" needed to secure my contractual rights, almost nil.

Swallowing hard, I told Lee I would give him the go-ahead *if* he guaranteed that the San Francisco workshop would run for a minimum of forty performances—which in combination with the four-week run at Lion Theater, I explained, would bring the total number of performances to sixty-four and permanently lock in my rights to the material.

Fortunately, Lee really wanted the play. But he did ask me—fairly, I thought—to share the risk. He would guarantee the needed performances, but should the initial production fail, he asked me to split the cost with him of keeping the show open for the full forty performances. Though I had no extra money at the time, I immediately agreed. I figured, on the basis of my prior experiences at New Dramatists and Lion, that a workshop production entailed minimal cost and I vaguely assumed that if need be, I could get a bank loan. Anyway, I had to run the risk. There was no other way to save my play.

Over the next few months Lee and I worked out the remaining details, during which time he also made the decision to do the workshop at the Odyssey Theater in Los Angeles rather than in San Francisco as originally planned. His basic reason for the shift was the earlier experience he had had in San Francisco with *The Trial of the Catonsville Nine* and Arthur Kopit's *Indians;* though Lee had done both productions at the height of the antiwar movement, and though both had received strong reviews, neither production had proved a box office success. Lee's belief that there was "more theatrical energy in L.A. than in San Francisco" was about to be tested.

Lee generously put me up at the Beverly Hilton hotel, and when I wasn't sitting in on rehearsals—which was almost every second—I was swimming off nervous energy in the Hilton pool.

Visions of Kerouac opened at the Odyssey on September 12, 1977, and got almost uniformly good reviews, even a few raves ("a stunning portrait"; "a classic tragedy"). *Variety* hailed it as "one of the most interesting plays to come out of L.A.'s small-theater scene in a long time." In contrast, moreover, to some of the New York critics, the L.A. reviewers did not equate the play's homosexual subtext with its *entire* meaning and did not comment on the subtext in negative moralistic terms. The L.A. reviews focused instead on *Kerouac* as the portrait of a man with *encompassing* emotional hangups, arising from a working-class Catholic upbringing, that kept him at a far distance from the impassioned connectedness he theoretically championed.

The one L.A. critic who did highlight the play's homosexual subtext (Dan Sullivan of the *Los Angeles Times*) also wrote the most lukewarm review—and from my past experience, that was a correlation, not a coincidence. In almost the same words used earlier by Gussow in *The New York Times,* Sullivan insisted that in my view "Kerouac would have been happier . . . if he had quit worrying about being thought a 'faggot' and gone with the flow." (Well yes, but he would have had to stop worrying about a lot else as well.) Sullivan summarized the play as "a sensitive portrait," but he was clearly unenthusiastic about (his version of) its theme. As in New York, the least favorable review, alas, had come in the most important newspaper.

Still, Lee was delighted with the overall reception, and with the strong audience response: During the first three weeks, the 199-seat house sold out every night. He decided to extend the run into November (thus giving me more than the sixty-four performances I needed), and started to make plans for a cross-country tour that would end up in New York.

A happy ending seemed at hand. But then, to everyone's surprise, ticket sales fell off. There were a lot of theories: The Odyssey theater was in an out-of-the-way place. (So how did audiences manage to find it during the first three weeks?) The ticket prices were too high. (So Lee lowered them, and sales continued to slump.) "L.A. just isn't a serious town." (So how come the critical reception for what was irreducibly a serious play had been so good?)

Perhaps the bottom line was that *no* American city in 1977, not even the largest ones, could turn out substantial audiences for very long for a play with a strong homosexual subtext. *The Boys in the Band* had earlier managed to do so, but perhaps because it had underscored unhappy—downright miserable—gay male lives. Within a decade, Martin Sherman's *Bent,* William Hoffman's *As Is,* and Harvey Fierstein's and Jerry Herman's musical *La Cage aux Folles* would all enjoy Broadway success. But in 1977, Lee had to back off from the idea of a national tour for *Kerourac.* He decided to close the show in L.A. on November 1.

I did get my sixty-four performances, though. That was considerable consolation—even if I did have to kick in three thousand dollars as my share of the costs, and take out a bank loan to do so. With my rights secured, I was able to accept Little, Brown's offer to publish *Kerouac* as a book (publishers were always more impressed with my plays than producers)—guaranteeing the play some sort of ongoing life. And then there was the secondary pleasure of telling Sterling Lord that I no longer wished to be represented by his agency.

I CONTINUED TO PUZZLE over the repetitive mishaps I'd had in the theater, in such sharp contrast to my easy successes in academia. To what extent could I legitimately point to homophobia as a significant factor? I wasn't one who automatically ascribed failure to anyone or anything other than my own shortcomings (in fact, I had a history of overdoing the self-blame). And surely it seemed odd to think that a profession loaded with homosexuals could be homophobic. Yet not that odd, actually; just as actors, directors, scenic designers, and so on, were not expected publicly to discuss their homosexuality, neither were playwrights. The fact is, not many gay or lesbian playwrights in these years were writing gay- or lesbian-themed plays; and the few exceptions were getting performed almost solely in fledgling gay theater groups.

All I knew for sure was that my one bona fide theatrical success to date—*In White America*—was also my one play with no trace of homoeroticism. Perhaps that was coincidental. Perhaps the basic stumbling block to my success had all along been not homophobia but—horrors!—an insufficient gift for writing plays, my wish stronger than my talent. Yet that didn't quite ring true either. I reminded myself that a fair number of critics, including some of the best, had written in high praise of my work. Besides, self-deprecating though I could be, I'd always been pretty accurate in assessing my strengths and weaknesses.

All right, then, perhaps the prime culprit was something other than, more than, either homophobia or lack of talent. Perhaps—just perhaps—it was the state of the American theater itself: its long-standing, endemic distaste for work that was "too" serious (a distaste that turned to near-automatic rejection if the work had homoerotic content as well). The fact that I wanted to believe that proposition did not automatically make it false.

An opportunity came along to test it. In 1978, soon after the failure of the L.A. production of *Kerouac, Harper's* magazine invited me to do two long pieces for them on the state of the American theater. I grabbed the offer. I had earlier done theater criticism for *Partisan Review* and for Huntington Hartford's short-lived creation *Show* magazine, but that had been a decade ago. Maybe, all other avenues seemingly closed for the moment, it was *that* career in the theater that I should resuscitate! In any case, writing the articles would give me a chance to sit back and try to make some sense of the American theater scene and, not incidentally, my own experience within it.

I started the first article with Broadway, and I put my conclusion up front: "The triviality of theater on Broadway is by now nearly uncontested. Few would deny that the pursuit of laughs and the dispensing of easy comfort hold iron priority on its stages; that plays with the potential to reveal or awaken pain are avoided; that sentimentality stands substitute for emotion, surface effects for content, cartoons for people." Broadway's champions defended it for its unparalleled technical know-how, but that undeniable brilliance, I wrote, was in the service of "fatuous simplicities. . . . our theater is without ambition and ought to be allowed to seek the only level to which it aspires: a wing of the commercial entertainment industry."

Generalizations this sweeping and severe, I realized, might well have been warped by my own bitter recent experiences. And so I tried to gain perspective by looking backward. Had American theater *ever* been more than surface entertainment? Certainly the rumor of a golden age persisted, a purported period during which plays of stature regularly appeared and audiences eagerly nourished them. But during the Bicentennial celebrations, institutional theaters throughout the country had revived a variety of plays with presumably classical reputations. Some were acknowledged to be no more than "significant" period pieces: William Gillette's *The Scarecrow,* Elmer Rice's *The Adding Machine*, Percy MacKaye's *The New York Idea.*

But the works of many of our certified heavies—Maxwell Anderson, Sidney Howard, Robert Sherwood, Clifford Odets, Lillian Hellman, Thornton Wilder, S. N. Behrman, Arthur Miller, Edward Albee—were also revived. And in my not-at-all objective opinion, the vast majority came out looking perilously similar to the mainstream tradition of commercial entertainment, however superior to it in narrative complication or character delineation. In my view, George S. Kaufman fared best; in comparison with the others he seemed fresh and sturdy, perhaps because he had always been clear-sighted about the dimension of his talent and had never indulged that ruinous penchant among American playwrights (Albee being the most egregious example) for grandiloquent statements about "the meaning of life."

The Bicentennial "celebration" of our theatrical heritage had "stopped just short of turning into a mass funeral pyre," I wrote, only because Eugene O'Neill and Tennessee Williams were left standing on their feet. In the face of O'Neill's legion of genius-mongering champions, it would have seemed fatuous to deny his stature; but for me, in truth, O'Neill's wooden pontifications had always outweighed the gloomy power of even his best work.

I felt quite otherwise about Tennessee Williams. In him, I believed, we had our *one* authentic world-class playwright. He had not been well served of late—the Kennedy Center's disastrous production of *Cat on a Hot Tin Roof* had probably damaged him most—but it seemed incontestable to me that *Streetcar, The Glass Menagerie,* and perhaps *Summer and Smoke* would retain their power through time. (Though I didn't think this true of the then equally touted *Sweet Bird of Youth* and *Night of the Iguana,* both of which seemed to me badly compromised by overheated theatrics, creaky narrative structures, and swatches of forced lyricism.)

I wondered why, O'Neill and Williams aside, our significant literary

133

talents had always seemed to find fiction and poetry more congenial forms than drama. I had no theory to account for it, but I did recall that for a brief period in the sixties, it had seemed otherwise. There had then been a sudden surge of vitality in the American theater, and from several quarters.

The emergence of black playwrights like Charles Gordone (*No Place to be Somebody*) and LeRoi Jones (*Dutchman*), along with an institutional theater, the Negro Ensemble Company, eager to nurture them, had for a time looked enormously promising. But Gordone fell silent and Jones (subsequently known as Amiri Baraka) turned his energies to poetry, political activism, and polemical essays that included passages of passionate anti-Semitism.

The Negro Ensemble Company lingered on (a considerable economic feat), but at the time I was writing for *Harper's* in 1978 it was no longer generating much excitement. Its most recent discovery, the playwright Gus Edwards and his play *The Offering,* had been hailed by most critics with hyperbolic praise—an occupational hazard among people who, spending evening after evening watching inert drivel, understandably fall into rapture over a few literate lines, an offbeat characterization, the barest hint of a special vision. To me, *The Offering* seemed little more than a shaky, self-conscious mismatch of (bad) Beckett-like word poems and an overemphatic naturalism that had long been characteristic (from Lorraine Hansberry to Lonne Elder) of mainstream black theater.

And I thought the critics, with their overwrought praise, were doing Gus Edwards no service. Such unearned hosannahs almost always prove destructive in the long run. They encourage a playwright to view him or herself as a finished monument, even as they set the playwright up for instant demolition. "Faddism," as I wrote in *Harper's,* "is endemic in our culture, and tastes in theater shift with a velocity equal to that of the restaurant and disco worlds. Given to belated spasms of guilt, theater critics often compensate for their initial hyperbole by savaging a playwright's second work, though equally often it's superior to the first.

"This is one reason," I argued, "why many of our promising writers for the theater never develop. It requires unusual strength of character to survive the quick alteration in image from world-beater to has-been, and to develop the patience needed to inhabit the fertile middle ground of uncertainty." I had experienced this in my own limited career in the theater: my very first play, *In White America,* hailed as a masterpiece of the documentary form, my later efforts to shift subject and style variously denounced as weird, suspect, shocking. In my case, it was tenacity, not "character" or "patience," that had kept me angrily puffing along.

The second strong infusion of energy during the sixties had come from the innovations of the "physical" theater, as it was then known: Joe Chaikin's Open Theater, Judith Malina and Julian Beck's Living Theater, the San Francisco Mime Troupe, the Polish director Jerzy Grotowski's Theater Lab, and (to my mind, of much less interest) Richard Schechner's Performance Group. From 1968 to 1970 I was writing a fair amount of theater criticism, was therefore seeing many of the productions that emanated from these groups, and found myself in excited, if ambivalent sympathy with them.

As I wrote in one of my pieces for *Show,* "their common quest to find a place for non-verbal as well as verbal language, to search for a new relationship between audience and performers, to create a theater that might redefine and reutilize 'ritual'—as an instrument for reconstructing society and also as a working environment where actor/artists might find not only employment and 'success' but nurturance for personal exploration and growth"—was daringly innovative. Such a theater, of course, could not be created overnight, and there were a fair share of false starts and phony claims. I found the Performance Group's production of *Makbeth* disastrously silly and its version of *The Bacchae* puerile. The Living Theater, too, with its overwhelming aura of self-congratulation, often made "radical theater" seem like a synonym for self-indulgence. And Grotowski, I felt, never solved the central problem of the audience, "never (or rarely)"—as I wrote in *Show*—"achieved the deep sharing between performer and spectator which he saw as the unique mission of his group, as the essence of the theatrical enterprise properly understood."

But these groups, at their best, were electrifying. The Living Theater's "mysteries and smaller pieces," as well as segments of *Paradise Now,* contained mesmerizing juxtapositions and crossplays between physical frenzy and political exhortation. Joe Chaikin's *The Serpent,* for me the only masterwork this radical new theater movement produced, combined a witty, compressed text with nuanced physical articulations, the verbal and nonverbal embodying each other with astonishing subtlety. And if I felt Grotowski's Polish Theater Lab failed to find a way to let the audience in, and was premised on (as I wrote in *Show*) "the dubious assumption that human beings have 'fixed essences' which must be laid bare," still, the actors' efforts at psychic penetration, on "peeling off the life-mask" (in Grotowski's words) and ruthlessly assaulting their own ingrained resistance to fresh perception, produced some extraordinarily stark, brutal, intense imagery.

By 1978, only the Performance Group survived in anything like its original (and ever more tedious and mechanical) form. The Open Theater and the Theater Lab had disbanded, the S. F. Mime Troupe had declined into sloganeering, and the Living Theater, pursued by the IRS, had gone into exile in Europe.

What was left in 1978 was that ineffable, soul-destroying Broadway "know-how." The attempts made during the sixties to reexamine theater's basic elements—text, ritual, performers, audience, space—and their interrelationship, had given way to the "professional" American theater's time-honored emphasis on technical facility. Elements meant to serve the script—lights, costumes, sets—were increasingly supplanting it. And nowhere more notably than in the musical theater.

The much-touted American musical was said to be the genre that all at once best expressed our native genius and constituted our most distinctive contribution to world theater. Not to my nonmusical eye; I had always been pretty much immune to the American musical's purported charms and skeptical of its achievement. To me, what most musicals mirrored was our culture's avoidance of social reality and intense emotion; the "unique gift" to world theater seemed to me centered on technological ingenuity.

The American musical in the late seventies seemed firmly in the hands of those for whom surface effects and star turns had become ends in themselves. Lavish, lopsided attention to visual elements of limited intrinsic interest came at the expense of believable human beings or a coherent—or sometimes any—narrative line. In 1978 alone, Geoffrey Holder's costumes "starred" in the dreary *Timbuktu*, Jules Fisher's lighting came close to dominating the movement in Bob Fosse's *Dancin'*, and Robin Wagner's choo-choo train set overwhelmed the disastrously bad *On the Twentieth Century*. Gifted as those three men were, brilliant lighting or a stunning set cannot alone a bright new musical make.

Only one new musical in 1978 offered something more than equal proportions of shallowness and gimmickry: the show *Working* (based on Studs Terkel's book of the same name). It seemed to me no accident that *Working* was also one of the quickest to close. Without overpraising the play (though Lord knows that's tempting, given the sludge pile on which it sat), it was wondrously *un*faithful to the Broadway musical's mindless, callow, socially regresssive traditions. The characters in *Working* not only expressed a range of emotions, but also—and this was a still greater rarity in the musical theater—the show attempted, in however muted a form, some actual political content in its depiction of the horrors of the everyday work world. In doing so, it openly flouted the "lyric traditions" of adolescent romanticism and kneejerk patriotism—and all but guaranteed its own early demise.

The off-Broadway theater movement of the sixties had come into being in protest against the Great White Way's glitzy commercial values. But it had itself pretty rapidly succumbed to that American (or is it human?) wish for mainstream recognition. Off-Broadway's growing failure of nerve had in turn given birth to an avant-garde, off-off-Broadway theater centered in coffeehouses, storefronts, and cellars. (Joe Cino's Caffè Cino, a crucible of gay male culture, and Ellen Stewart's La Mama were the best-known.) Dozens of tiny theaters still existed in the late seventies, but their production schedules tended to be as spotty as their achievement.

I was not above citing the Kennedy Center in my *Harper's* articles as an illustration—legitimate, I felt, beyond my personal experience of the place—of how little encouragement and how few outlets for serious work in the theater still existed in the middle and late seventies. "The attitude of the Kennedy Center—that dutiful creature of the cash culture—is typical of today's institutional theater. It judges success by the length of its subscription list and the number of tickets sold, and is content to employ its resources in serving as a booking house for the banal musicals and comedies en route to or from Broadway." (Take *that,* Roger Stevens! Fuck *you,* Richmond Crinkley!)

"Playwrights—the weak, neurotic beasties—do need productions," I went on, in order to "survive and develop; need some confirmation of their worth; need the feedback that only professional collaborators and live audiences can provide." (And that plaintive note captured my lingering private resentment at the shopworn policies of the New

Dramatists.) There were still *some* theaters, of course, concerned with the feeding and care of playwrights. Many were regional, such as the Alley in Houston, the Long Wharf in New Haven, and the Arena in D.C. In New York, purported center of the American theater, such outlets as existed tended to be struggling workshop operations like the intermittently imaginative Interart Theater or the far more prosperous Circle Repertory Company.

In the seventies, Circle Rep had the most distinguished record in New York for introducing worthwhile new plays, and in particular the works of its resident guru, Lanford Wilson. Many theater people felt that Circle had a more impressive record in nurturing plays and play-wrights than did Joe Papp's Public Theater. Not that Papp wasn't him-self an outstanding exception to the shallow vision of most theatrical managers in New York; his whole enterprise was testimony to his rejection of commercial values. And Papp did care enormously about the well-being of playwrights. Once he bet on a writer, his loyalty was legendary—though some felt his loyalty was more pronounced than his judgment.

Papp wasn't the only one handing out unwarranted (to my envy-laden mind) genius awards in 1978. Sam Shepard had more produc-tions and more consistently good press than any other playwright of that generation. To me, his merits had always been inflated. His latest play, *Curse of the Starving Class,* seemed to embody his worst qualities. It was yet one more of his nightmare slices of American life, the metaphors stale ("Corporate Zombies Take Over the Farm"), the pes-simism pat and unearned, the cartoon characters impervious to nuance.

Shepard had always been involved in the music scene, and my guess was that he liked to think of his plays as theatrical counterparts of punk rock. I felt he had closer ties to Thornton Wilder: high-flown allegori-cal allusions in tandem with unacknowledged sentimentality. Ten years earlier, in *Boy on the Straight-Back Chair,* the playwright Ron Tavel had, in my opinion, worked the same theme as Shepard (the horrors of everyday life in America) with far more inventiveness, deeper sympa-thy for the afflicted, fewer cheap shots, and much less attitudinizing. By 1978 a decade had passed since Tavel had had even a minor New York production.

Perhaps my jealousy was working overtime—or perhaps my critical faculties—but I had trouble understanding the enthusiasm that surrounded several other touted playwrights in the late seventies. Maria Irene Fornes's much-discussed *Fefu and Her Friends* seemed to me a compound of languor and stilted disconnection ("If people are swept off their feet, are the feet left behind?" et cetera); but perhaps her obliqueness was simply too foreign to my own style for me to appreciate her sufficiently.

Albert Innaurato's *Gemini*—Circle Rep's smash hit of the year—revealed, I thought, a genuinely gifted comic writer, but also one incapable of resisting the cute aside and the showy set piece. And I found *Gemini*'s ending deeply offensive. Francis, the main male character in *Gemini,* is throughout portrayed as "queer"; but as the curtain falls, he decides not to abandon his girlfriend and rushes offstage hand in hand with her as his father joyously shouts, "I think they're going to make it!" Curtain. Roar of approval from the audience. So much for the psychosexual drama we had presumed to be at the heart of Francis's coming of age. So much for a playwright who seemed willing to sabotage the integrity of his own creations. So much for the limits of homoeroticism in the American theater.

Then, of course, there was the most heralded of all the new luminaries: David Mamet. He had no fewer than three plays mounted in 1978: *The Water Engine* (technically impressive, if repetitive and boring), *A Life in the Theater* (a mildly amusing departure from Mamet's usually bleak, angst-ridden angle of vision), and *American Buffalo.*

It was *American Buffalo* that produced the critical cartwheels. I found it utterly unpersuasive, a highly mannered exercise full of falsity. "If Mamet" (I wrote in *Harper's*) "believes that by flattening his tone to a deadbeat monotone he has captured authentic lowlife rhythm, he should be encouraged to spend more time on the streets." (Middle-class Marty, who used to hang out there, *knew!*) "If, as seems more likely, Mamet believes that by emptying language of content and flair he will automatically uncover deeper subtexts, he ought to reread—it is clear he has read them once—the true masters of unspoken resonance, Beckett and Pinter."

Just in case I hadn't mangled *all* the competition—not that any of them, I suspect, saw me even remotely as squaring off in the center ring—I concluded my second *Harper's* piece by writing off Irish playwright Hugh Leonard's *Da*. It had been the most-praised Serious Play of the year, hailed as a work of "searing power," as some scalding match for the Dostoevsky canon. To me, it was "a work of perky optimism and genial sentimentality—all intense emotion drowned in the familiar suds of bantering Irish blarney." *Da* won every major prize for best play of the year, except the Pulitzer (which is restricted to American authors and went to D. L. Coburn's *The Gin Game,* a play that managed to convert the loneliness and regrets of old age into a set of vaudeville routines).

Dismal and dismaying as I found the state of the American theater, the cause, I argued, lay deeper than a callow, cowardly producing fraternity. It lay squarely with anesthetized American audiences, "huddled in their swaddling clothes, demanding familiar juvenilia." Even when the reviews of the rarely produced serious play read like the myopic inflations of press agentry (as Mamet's reviews had), audiences refused to come. They resolutely turned away from any threat of being challenged rather than soothed.

And what the public wants, the public gets. The few plays with serious themes that ever reached a mainstream stage, I argued, did so "only if their subject matter has been sufficiently sensationalized (schizophrenia in *Equus*) or domesticated (terminal illness in *The Shadow Box* or in *Cold Storage*) to muffle their potential threat." And thus we had a theater, my second *Harper's* piece concluded, that justified itself chiefly in terms of musicals, and musicals notable chiefly for sophomoric quipping, circuslike razzmatazz—and an absence of content. A theater, in short, "that accurately reflects the culture's endemic puerility. Hand in hand, the two march confidently into the vinyl sunset."

Even today, when theater is no longer a site of my ambition nor playwriting a form that centrally serves me (though I do still write an occasional play), I stand by most of what I wrote in those *Harper's* articles. They may have originated in the heat of my own frustrated ambition, but heat can sometimes shed light. Some twenty years later, mainstream American theater shows no more vitality or originality than it did in 1978. The case might fairly be called terminal.

Anyway, I'd had my say, gotten a lot off my chest. It was time to get on with it.

VI

Alternate Therapies II

Aʟᴀꜱ, I ꜱᴛɪʟʟ ᴅɪᴅɴ'ᴛ ᴋɴᴏᴡ what "it" was. If what I was going through was a run-of-the-mill midlife slump, it was taking its sweet time in resolving. Not that I was lying full-time on a bed of pain, bereft of friends, pleasure, and work, reduced to watching daytime TV while munching Whitman Samplers. No, it was more a matter of feeling vaguely disgruntled and unhappy, frustrated at being unable to find the kind of large-scale, consuming project that I had always relied on to hold at bay my chronic low-grade anxiety—which, still grieving over my mother's death, was now less submerged.

Never one to *await* a new turn, to live for long in an undefined zone—it opened up too wide an abyss within, threatening to bring in train a still more immobilizing emotional downturn—I went back for a time to my first love, acting. That bit of serendipity came about when Elaine Gold, founder of the Corner Loft Workshop in the Village, invited me to bring by some of my unproduced scripts for use as classroom exercises.

I immediately liked the feel of the place, and was surprised at some of the theater "heavies" in regular attendance. José Ferrer ran a Monday night class; it was there that a one-act play of mine about transsexualism, *Reassignment,* was read. I had written it five years earlier and thought it vaguely suspect, politically. But the reading was received with rapturous laughter and acclaim.

Thrilled, I began to hang out at the Loft, sitting in on various classes and ultimately joining Frank Corsaro's. After my first improv, Corsaro declared himself "amazed"—and later told Elaine that I had the makings of "a great leading man." That was all I needed to hear! Broadway lay in my future after all! The hell with scholarship and history, with burying myself in dusty archives! So I had taken a thirty-year detour—so what? The road to Xanadu remained open.

I plunged into rehearsing a scene from James Kirkwood's *P.S. Your Cat Is Dead.* I would electrify Corsaro. All the rest—culminating in an Academy Award—would follow. But on the night another actor and I were due to present the scene in class, I arrived to find that Corsaro was ill and had been replaced for the evening by—Kim Stanley! I was awestruck. Kim Stanley! Surely my guardian angels were working overtime.

I vaguely recalled that she had been out of commission for years—what was it? alcohol? depression?—but recalling that hardly prepared me for the brilliantly bizarre performance she turned in that night. Over *my* mutilated body. The other actor and I had gotten out exactly one line, when Stanley stormed on stage to interrupt us. "Where the hell *are* you two?" she demanded, her eyes blazing.

It turned out—hours later, after most of the student audience had crept out—that she had wanted us to figure out what particular space we were inhabiting and how to convey that through our acting. But her own suffering was so palpable, so tumultuously in need of an outlet, that she careened unstoppable around the stage in a mesmerizing, terrifying assault, all at once semicoherent and piercingly insightful. "Why do you insist on playing the victim," she screamed in my face at one point, "you with such *amazing* blue eyes?" We never did get to the second line. When the tornado finally passed over, I was drenched in sweat and near tears, filled to possession with her communicated anguish and despair.

That alone would not have ended my infatuation with the Loft. I'm not sure what did, other than the gradual return of reality. I continued to attend classes for some six months, but in an increasingly desultory way, soon aware, after the initial rush of romantic fantasy had passed, that salvation was not at hand, that I was not going to be plucked from the halls of academe and placed on the staircase to stardom. I was a middle-aged academic, for God's sake, and it was in my writing, if anywhere, that I was going to have to work through the stasis that had overcome my life.

And although a consuming new book-length topic would not come, I did manage to find enough subjects for articles and reviews to keep me intermittently occupied. Increasingly they related to the emerging new field of lesbian and gay studies. Though the subject was still barred at the CUNY graduate school, my mounting missionary zeal found an outlet in teaching a course on lesbian and gay history, politics and culture to mostly straight undergraduates at CUNY's Lehman campus.

It was gratifying to feel part of a vanguard field that was beginning to generate real excitement. When, for example, *The Radical History Review* in February 1979 sponsored a panel (which I was part of) entitled "Sex in History," an overflow crowd of some five hundred people turned up to hear us. (That particular evening, unfortunately, was devoted less to the new scholarship and more to rehashing sectarian divisions that continued in force on the left even as its strength continued to decline; several members of the audience denounced the panelists for sins of omission that ranged from the failure to mention U.S. imperialism in Haiti to our refusal to ascribe all dysfunctions, historical and sexual, to capitalist ownership of the means of production.)

My sexual energy, too, belied any notion that I was a wholly lost soul, wandering disconsolately at the edge of despair. I continued to have my fair share of adventures, sexual and romantic. There was Bryan, a leftover flower child who claimed on sight that he and I were "cosmically linked." Well, for three weeks, anyway, until he announced that he couldn't go on seeing me because I was *too* open, which he had decided was "a form of sadism"—that is, calculated to make him feel insecure and inferior. I needed to learn, he sternly told me, to "come off my pedestal *slowly*." (Lord help me, I thought—there really is no way out.)

Next, I met a Romanian political refugee who claimed total devotion, and two weeks later landed in the arms of the Reverend Moon. Then there was a thirty-year-old accountant who, it soon turned out, was far more adept at smiling than listening—unless we were talking about him. I got more seriously involved with "Alfredo," a young actor/hustler who I told myself was a luckless young sparrow—and who of course turned out to be a fierce eaglet. But I chose for some time to go on believing his hard-luck tales of having been "unfairly" thrown out of Miguel Piñero's theater company and "unfairly" thrown into jail on "a bum rap for armed robbery." I even tolerated his shooting up coke in my apartment, needle dangling from his arm as he perambulated about talking nonstop of this scheme or that adventure.

But no amount of indulgence could keep Alfredo coming around once a famous clothing designer promised to put him on a Times Square billboard (he did), and spent additional rivers of money on his and Alfredo's duplicate coke habits.

It was not as if I could afford to be moralistic about drugs. During the final stages of my mother's illness, I had turned to assorted "helpers" to get through the worst of the nightmare—just as I had for years tried various potions to help me with a long-standing sleep disorder. I kept telling myself that this was necessary "self-medication," and neither worse nor better than having the occasional (socially certified) drink.

In 1977, during the Lion Theater Club run of *Visions of Kerouac,* an actor in the play had coaxed me into the dressing room one night for "a little special coke" that had come his way. I had tried the drug earlier in the seventies and had found it unappealing; touted as an aphrodisiac, it had turned me *off* sexually and had left me as well with horrendous hangovers.

But during the Lion production in 1977, my mother's melanoma had suddenly metastasized to her brain, and I was feeling desperate at my inability to do anything about it, or even to make her comfortable. She was in and out of lucidity, and terror. Visiting her in the hospital, I never knew what to expect. She would repeatedly ask me whether "everyone has had lunch" and whether her pocketbook was "safe": the condensation of two lifetime obsessions. And over and over she would whisper to me, her eyes glazed and frightened, her plans for escape. Or she would beg me piteously to get her dressed and help her sneak out. I was ready to try coke again.

The Lion Club actor was as good as his word: The stuff was terrific. Sniffing it, I felt better than I had in a long time. Either I had had lousy coke earlier, the actor laughingly said, or I had now become more receptive to its charms. He introduced me to Jacob, known in acting/cocaine circles as the Big Man—*the* best dealer of *the* best stuff. Jacob insisted on personally getting to know "the circle of intimate friends to whom I confine my trade," so down he came to my apartment to dazzle me with free lines and three hours of charismatic coke wisdom: "Never refrigerate"; "Take much water and vitamins"; "Enjoy! Enjoy!" Much as I liked the lingo—and the lift in spirits—I used cocaine only sporadically, usually when I insisted on getting a writing assignment done for which I otherwise felt no inclination or energy.

My middle-class income and squeamishness kept me this side of regular use. Plus there was the feeling deep in my gut that drug-taking was a defeat, a form of disconnection from feelings that (and perhaps especially for a writer) needed to be lived through. Some of my drug-taking friends scoffed at my "residual puritanism." "You must want to wallow in pain," they would say derisively. "It's simple foolishness, or fake martyrdom, to pass 'naturally' through grief, to willingly become dysfunctional when pharmacological help is available." "Why, it amounts," one friend said indignantly, "to eschewing the advances of modern science."

Maybe. Anyway, I could sincerely argue both sides of the debate about drugs, just as I could cyclically abstain or indulge (and always with a persuasive rationale for doing either). Not that "ups" or "downs" ever helped me much or for long. "Instead of my mood balancing out," I wrote in my diary during one period of use, "it's become irritably off-center."

My non-drug-taking friends urged a different course entirely: I had to *talk* about my pain; only that would lead to reconstructive action. But I doubted if my lingering grief over my mother's death *could* be adequately communicated. Empathy has its limits; and with busy New Yorkers especially, it seems, those limits tend to be reached rather quickly. After which point, the depressed friend is viewed as willfully prolonging unhappiness—an attitude that *increases* the sufferer's sense of isolation.

When I said as much to a friend, she told me bluntly I was talking "bullshit"—giving an "academic rationale" to justify my cowardice in facing pain directly. She said I was at a "dangerous impasse, stuck in self-pitying lethargy," and urged me to *do* something about it. "Like what?" I sardonically asked. "Find another mother? Surrender myself yet again to the tender mercies of the psychiatric profession?"

But she *had* struck a nerve. I called on my friend Pete, he of the endless faith in alternative therapies, and asked for a suggestion. What he came up with sounded utterly outlandish. He had become involved recently in one of the new "body" therapies—"bioenergetics," it was called. Pete claimed it had helped him enormously (but then he *always* said that) and recommended I give it a try. "What *is* bioenergetics?" I asked impatiently, my tone implying that I already knew it was a form of charlatanry.

Pete was patience itself, explaining that bioenergetics was an eclectic combination of body therapies "deriving from the work of Alexander Lowen," and its chief practitioner in New York was a man named John Pierrakos. "Oh, Pete," I moaned, "give it up! We're talking about a forty-seven-year-old body—and psyche—that have been pummelled and (purportedly) reshaped time and time again, only to snap right back to their original form. It's time *you* accepted the reality of imprinting. I am what I am—and probably have been since age three."

Pete nodded sagely. "Ummm . . . I hear you . . . except you do have a greater capacity for change than you like to admit, and have shown it over the years. You're not as fortified as you prefer to think. And despite your advanced years"—he smiled sweetly—"you could go right on changing." (Thank God he didn't say "growing"! That would have scotched the deal right there.) "Why not try it?" he added. "It's not like you've got anything better to do at the moment." That was true enough. And so with a shrug, I agreed on impulse to go for *a* consultation.

WHEN I ARRIVED at Pierrakos's office, it turned out he was an hour behind schedule. While waiting, I thumbed through the reading material on his end table, and found that most of it consisted of reprints of his own articles. *Just another blowhard,* I thought resentfully. *Why the hell did I let Pete talk me into this?* Picking up one of the articles, my eye lingered lovingly on every bloated abstraction—of which there were many: "We must create new concepts, new processes, and new leadership models for a New Age of Mankind"; "We must open to the benign nature of the universe, to the amplitude of life." *Oh swell,* I thought; *Dr. Pangloss tacked on to a regimen of pushups. Just what I don't need.* Yet I didn't bolt on the spot. Maybe because of the one line in the article that *did* impress me: "The more we feel the pain, the more we accept it, the less we feel it . . . when we accept the hurt we feel deeply, it gives us a sense of dignity."

When Pierrakos called me into his inner office, it was immediately apparent that this was not a traditionally antiseptic psychotherapeutic setting. On the wall were a photomural of Egyptian pictographs and a large anatomical diagram of the human torso with lines pointing to what were regarded (I later learned) as key "energy meridians." Certain objects in the room seemed startlingly anomalous: a large wooden sawhorse; several oversized plastic baseball bats; three or four huge beanbags doubling as oversized pillows. The desk and two chairs were standard issue.

Pierrakos was a trim, handsome man with graying hair and a classically chiseled face. I guessed him to be in his early fifties. He motioned me to one of the chairs and we began to talk, along the standard lines I had long since grown accustomed to in traditional psychotherapy. He asked what had brought me to his office. I explained my connection to Pete, my ambivalence about therapy of any kind, my conviction that it was "too late" for me to hope for any major personality transformation.

Until recently, I said, I had viewed my life as successful and stable. I had few overt fears, enjoyed my work, had a surfeit of acquaintances (and even a few friends), had given up on the "adolescent" notion of a "lifetime partner," was content with occasional (sometimes paid) sexual adventures with mostly younger men, and had told myself (and everyone else, including Pete) that I was no longer interested in any basic reorientation of my life, and certainly not of my sexuality. I wanted to focus my energies on becoming more of what I already was: I wanted to deepen, not spread.

I paused, thinking Pierrakos might make some comment, give some clue about his reaction thus far. But he simply sat there quietly, waiting for me to continue. The events of the past two years, I went on, had shaken my complacency. I had, despite expectations, gotten deeply, romantically involved with a man, and had been left by him. The shock of that, in combination with my mother's illness, had left me feeling disconsolate. Such hope as I could muster—and what had brought me to his office—came from Pete's conviction, more than mine, that the non-traditional therapy of bioenergetics might be a way of dynamiting my fortified defenses, even though I wasn't at all sure what bioenergetics was or whether I wanted my defenses breached.

On a deeper level, I said, I suspected that I had come to him because I was, by nature, an "impossibilist": a man who continues to seek what cannot be had; whose tenacious will refuses to capitulate to the preordained; who insists he *can* still be "happy" when all the evidence suggests he can't.

Pierrakos listened attentively. So attentively that I felt unnerved, and in a distancing gesture suddenly started complaining about his article. "This business of a 'benign universe,' " I heard myself say. "I have to tell you that it makes me uncomfortable."

"Why is that?" Pierrakos asked amiably.

"Well, how can I put it without sounding rude . . .?"

"Don't worry about that," he interjected.

"You see, I've never thought of the universe as exactly 'benign.' I don't see how anyone can, given the misery everywhere around us."

"When I speak of the 'benign nature of the universe,' I am referring to its amplitude. The rhythmic renewal of all things. Nature's continuing ebb and flow."

That's just what I was afraid you meant, I thought uneasily, putting him down as an utter lightweight. I nodded in vague assent, but said nothing.

Pierrakos allowed the pause to lengthen. Then he said, "I suspect it is precisely this universality that you are out of touch with."

Then, without waiting for a reply, he went on: "It has been a difficult time for you. Not knowing what to do to feel better, you have come here. But you keep asking yourself *why*. What I suggest is that too much of your life has been 'Why, why?' With no answers coming back, eh? You are here. That is enough." He stood up and gestured towards the adjoining bathroom. "Please go into the bathroom and strip down to your underwear."

"Strip down to my underwear?" I echoed in disbelief.

When I remained rooted to the chair, he added, "To offer a full diagnosis, I must see your body."

Still in shock, I headed toward the bathroom. Watching me, Pierrakos suddenly said, "There is surprising strength in your movement. Even as you equivocate."

"I don't understand . . ." I mumbled.

"Excellent! For you, not understanding is already an advance. The value will be precisely in the foreignness. If I may quote St. Augustine, 'Believe *so that* you may understand.' "

St. Augustine, eh? That adds a little weight to the proceedings, I thought sardonically, trying to neutralize the compelling feel of what he'd said. I proceeded dutifully to strip down to my underwear. When I reappeared, I nervously asked if I could keep my socks on. "It's chilly in here."

"Socks off," Pierrakos peremptorily replied. "It is essential to see the way your foot grasps the ground."

Off came the socks. He then placed me in front of a large mirror, and walked slowly around me, stroking his chin and grunting inaudibly.

"It is very much as I thought," he finally said. "Except for the legs." He let out a small groan. "Ai—the legs. The legs are *much* worse even than I expected."

I flushed with embarrassment. I had had polio as a teenager and had long felt self-conscious about my thin legs. I resented attention being called to them.

"There's nothing wrong with my legs," I said defensively. "I happen to be in very good shape for a man my age. So I've often been told, anyway."

"Yes, no question about it," he said without enthusiasm. Then he added enigmatically, "Even as a young child you were treated as a Greek god, no?"

"I don't think I'd put it quite that way—"

"—and as an adult, much attention, much applause, still comes your way, eh? But now it does not please you so much. Now you are more the melancholy god. Perhaps no god at all, eh? Perhaps now too much the opposite, in fact."

I felt acutely uncomfortable and reached for the familiar as an anchor: "You mean what my ex-therapist used to call my God/shit syndrome."

Pierrakos seemed not to have heard. "Now there is a dry, hopeless quality," he went on. "Great sadness. A sadness you often enjoy."

" 'Enjoy'!" I snorted in protest.

"You take great pride in suffering, in the assumption you feel more pain than others. It is your badge of superiority, no?"

As I began to mouth a protest, Pierrakos sailed right on. "You are also a man of deep feeling." (Now *that* was decidedly better!) "Feelings that are now largely immobilized. Allow me to demonstrate what I mean." With that, he directed my gaze into the mirror. I reflexively flinched, never having liked staring at myself. Pierrakos immediately picked up on this.

"I expected you to flinch. You are an intellectual. Intellectuals dislike paying attention to their bodies."

"Isn't that something of a cliché?"

"You are right. Perhaps I should have said, they do not like to touch the ground. Look at your feet. Look at how your feet curl away from the floor—as if you were touching hot coals. You are *so* badly grounded!" He let out a yelp of distress.

"Walk!" he ordered. "Walk!" When I did, he barked, "See, see? Your feet barely grasp the ground. Your walk is gingerly—like a pussycat. Now: Come and see the difference." He pulled me back in front of the mirror. "Look! Look here!" he said, poking my upper torso, his voice exuberant. "Look at the difference! Look at how easily the energy flows through your chest and shoulders! The vibrations are full, steady—really quite wonderful! And sitting solidly in the center: a great head, *alive* with energy. *Pulsating* energy!"

As I proudly stole a glance at the mirror, Pierrakos shifted his gaze back to my lower torso, sighed, and scowled. "You are like two halves of two different people. The top is a giant. But connected to what? To nothing. A Greek god with no pedestal, no base."

"Is it as bad as all that?" I asked, not sure whether to laugh at the dramatics or cry at my plight.

"We will *build* a base!" Pierrakos nearly shouted. "We will bring the energy bunched on top down . . . down into those *melancholy* legs. We will ground you to the earth!" He grabbed my hand and moved me over to the wooden sawhorse in the middle of the room. "Come! I will show you more."

He positioned me on my back on top of the sawhorse, with my arms hanging loosely over the sides. Then he told me to start slowly kicking my legs into the air, gradually increasing the tempo. As I kicked away, he watched me intently, occasionally encouraging me with a "Good, good." After a while my legs began to ache, but he cheerfully told me to "keep going—keep going!" As I started to pant, and then groan, he unexpectedly said, "Your great sadness comes from your inability to find love. You have a large capacity for love. But it is thwarted."

Tears welled up in my eyes. "This is really beginning to hurt," I said, with no metaphor in mind.

"Yes. Faster now, faster."

"Faster? This is killing me!"

"The opposite, I assure you."

"It hurts like hell!"

"*What* does?" Pierrakos asked eagerly.

"My legs are *killing* me! I can't keep this up!"

"You can, you can. Your legs are shriveled. . . . Stretch them out. . . . Stretch them! Climb into the sky, Martin. Climb! Higher, higher. Reach into the sky. Reach up to your mother. . . . The more you feel the pain, the less its hold on you. . . ."

That did it. I was sobbing uncontrollably. But when I abruptly stopped kicking, Pierrakos grabbed my legs and set them back in motion.

"I can't!" I groaned. "I *can't!*"

"A little longer . . . just a little longer . . . Feel the pain, you must feel the pain. . . ."

My whole body started to shake, my legs spastically shooting into the air. "You are very brave . . . very brave," Pierrakos said encouragingly. "You are going straight into the abyss. . . ." Then—just as I thought I would pass out—he suddenly grabbed hold of my legs to stop them and wrapped me gently in his arms. "It will be all right, Martin . . . it will be all right. . . ." he whispered soothingly. "So much pain . . . so much pain . . ."

My body shook with sobs, but Pierrakos held me tight, softly rocking me back and forth. The warmth from his powerful, encompassing hands entered directly into my body. By comparison, my embrace of him felt constricted, lame. I suddenly knew that I trusted him—trusted the *feel* of him; my suspicions dissolved.

It took a good five minutes to calm down enough to begin to breathe normally. Pierrakos gently released me from his arms and suggested I get dressed.

Afterward, we sat and talked again. He repeated his conviction that my "brilliance" was "more than matched by a great capacity for feeling." But whereas I had no trouble "activating" my intelligence, I had great trouble "finding a focus" for my emotions, getting them to work *for* me. He repeated, too, that my pain was "enormous" *and* that I "took considerable pride in it."

I said I was amazed that so much had come out of me just by kicking my feet in the air.

"And you lived through it," Pierrakos replied, smiling.

We both laughed, which prompted another homily—"You see, after pain comes laughter"—that I liked less. The follow-up made me still more uncomfortable: "And your 'aura' has changed—from muddy gray to pale blue."

"Aura?"

"The color around a person's head."

"I'm afraid I don't believe in that sort of thing."

"It's a well-established scientific fact," Pierrakos said nonchalantly. "But it doesn't matter. We don't want you becoming adversarial. Combativeness is how you have always dissipated strong feelings—feelings better put to other use."

That sounded right. But I wasn't prepared to have all strong feelings reduced to a single status. I needed to know more about *what* he and I disagreed over, before deciding which part of it I could "put aside." Especially since Pete had warned me that Pierrakos "tended to be traditional in sexual matters." And so I asked him directly what he felt about my homosexuality.

"I have no bias against homosexuality. I pass no judgment on it."

Too flat, I thought; the first part sounds rehearsed, the second part a polite way of being negative. I wanted to know more.

"Would changing my sexual orientation be any part of the therapeutic agenda?"

"I have no interest in changing your orientation. If I questioned anything, it would be the way you separate love and sex—not *who* you have sex with. And I will not disguise from you my belief that anonymous sex, or sex with comparative strangers, is not in your own best interest. It works against wholeness."

That sounded less judgmental about homosexuality than anything I had heard in psychotherapy back in the sixties, but the part about "sex with strangers" was traditional enough to leave me uneasy. Contrasting "promiscuity" with "wholeness"—even should the contrast be, in some ultimate epistemological handbook, "true"—was a time-hallowed code for portraying homosexuals as sick.

What I said was, "In my view love and lust *can* coincide—at least in the early years of a relationship, when erotic zest is at its peak—but love and lust don't automatically, or maybe even frequently, come in tandem. And there is nothing dishonorable about lust when disconnected from love."

"I am talking about *acting* on disconnected lust," Pierrakos countered, but then sighed. "Look, Martin, it can't be a coincidence that immediately after an emotional experience such as you have just had, you embark on an intellectual argument. I would like to suggest that you are doing your best to dissipate the experience."

"That could well be," I admitted. "It does sound right. So let's drop it. At least for now. But it is unfinished business. I want to make it clear," I added, mustering up a final dollop of defiance, "that I have a serious problem with some of your attitudes about sex."

"It is clear. Can we now move on?"

"What do you suggest?"

"I want to return to the current situation. You are in crisis. You need a lot of help, and as soon as possible. A crisis *faced* can prove of great benefit. I believe I can help you."

I let out an almost involuntary yelp—and to my absolute astonishment, started to cry again. I could hardly believe it. And the shock was redoubled when I felt Pierrako's arms instantaneously around me.

"You know," he said, "you're a very tough man in argument. But you are not exactly encased in concrete." That made me smile. "You're all dammed up inside, but the dam is *very* leaky. That is a good sign."

"Grand Coulee—my new nickname." I had dried my tears and started to laugh.

"Why have you stored up so much, I wonder," Pierrakos said. "For what use? When?"

"I didn't know how much was in there. All I knew was that I felt stale and unhappy. If anything, I felt dried up."

"Parched would be closer."

"Right now I feel completely drained."

"I will tell you what I recommend." Pierrakos shifted from an intimate to a professional tone. "For the moment, I cannot see you myself; my schedule is entirely booked. But I would like you to work for now with André Cossen, one of my associates. He is very good. I know you will like him. Think about it. I will write down his number for you, and when you feel ready you can call him for an appointment."

"Are you sure you can't see me yourself?" My disappointment was palpable. *Same old story,* I thought bitterly. *I open myself up—and it turns out the person isn't available.*

"Hopefully, there may be an opening in my schedule later on. I assure you that you will like André very much."

There was a pause. Then Pierrakos took my hand and, his voice earnest, urged me not to use my disappointment that we could not work together as an excuse for retreating into isolation. "You need help. You need it *now*. There is no reason for you to suffer like this."

As my tears welled up again, we hugged good-bye. And I thanked him.

★   ★   ★

I DID CALL ANDRÉ. And I did like him immediately—he was sweet and warm—just as Pierrakos had predicted.

We worked together once a week for more than three months. The sessions continued to be powerful: floods of rage, tears, tenderness. And I continued to be amazed at how close to the surface and how full those feelings were. Before long, I was regularly using one of the plastic baseball bats to pound my fury into a large beanbag on the floor, yelling out all kinds of bottled-up grievances, cursing those who had "betrayed" or "abandoned" me, cursing my mother for having loved me *too* much.

Sometimes I thought the "new" therapy was no different from working out regularly with a punching bag. But I didn't much care. It was enough to know that the physical techniques of bioenergetics were capable of unlocking an astonishing swell of feelings—whatever I might then be able to do with them—and was surely unlocking more than the "talking cure" had ever been able to. Wielding the baseball bat, I cursed the talking cure too—cursed the traditional therapy I'd gone through years before, cursed (mere) words, cursed my skill at manipulating them into formulaic accounts of what I was feeling, cursed the fact that despite all the talk, the feelings remained undiminished, and the behavior remained the same.

I was *so* impatient with verbal "explanations" that whenever André even hinted at a discussion of the "analytic assumptions" that underlay bioenergetics, I would abort it. I feared my own ability to pick apart the assumptions as simplistic. I didn't need another intellectual exercise. I needed the chance to vent emotionally—and *that,* the physical work was indisputably providing. Where all the venting might lead, I nervously postponed thinking about. But within weeks of beginning bioenergetics, I felt lighter and more optimistic.

It's not as if André and I never talked. But we did so mostly *after* the excercises had unlocked me. Words did have *a* place in the therapy, but optimally they came anchored in emotion rather than as substitutes for it.

I talked a fair amount about sex, partly as a test of André's attitudes; I was ready to pounce, and possibly run, should he react with even a scintilla of disgust or derision. I dredged up some of my raunchiest recollections, and was careful to embed them in a defense of sexual "adventuring" which (in certain moods) would have provoked disagreement even from me. I told him about how I used to frequent male hustler bars, and sometimes still did. I reported with salacious gusto on Haymarket, the roughest of them, as well as its somewhat tonier, recent replacement, The Cowboy.

To test André's outer range, I mustered as much graphic detail as I could, reaching back several years to tell him about my pickup one night in the Haymarket of Freddy R., a blond, square, beachboy type from Long Island, vice president of his community college, athlete, hot-rod builder. About Freddy, who had appeared so neat, trim, and polite, and who within minutes of getting back to my place had his tongue up my ass and was groaning, "Please—piss on me—*please!*"

"Did you?" André asked evenly.

"It wasn't easy, on demand. Besides, we weren't in the shower."

"So did you?"

"I managed to squeeze out a few drops on his chest. He groaned in ecstasy, begged for more. But I was not about to risk uric acid on the Persian rug."

We both burst out laughing, which ruined that test.

But I did later get André to rise to the bait when I questioned the importance of "having *one* other person to share things with." Would the need be as great, I wondered aloud, if we learned from childhood to share more intimacies more readily with a wider variety of people, instead of withholding ourselves for that mystical, magical, Completing Other? I quoted, in order to mock, Bruno Bettelheim's insistence in *Children of the Dream* that kibbutz kids, saturated with peer group familiarity, grew up "incapable of intimacy." The disinterest in "intimacy" might be accurate, I declared, but it was wrongly ascribed: Children raised on a kibbutz grew up lacking not the "capacity" but rather the intense need characteristic of *our* culture to find the Completing Other—a need we then choose to equate with "emotional depth."

Waxing ideological, and only partly believing my own words, I insisted (as I had in some of my articles in the seventies) that the going formula for human happiness—the monogamous pair-bonded lifetime couple—was no more than a Puritan hangover, an outmoded cultural formula for regulating sexuality, for putting unnatural restraints on the human need for variability and adventure. And it was a formula that regularly produced disaster, I insisted; after erotic zest faded—

often in a matter of just a few years—the two partners discovered that they had cared less about each other than about getting their credentials as bona fide adults (that is, as "persons capable of coupling"). I even argued that a variety of sexual partners and experiences was what kept one on that exploratory edge essential to *real* growth.

André would grimace, giving no response or an oblique one. But during one session he did finally say, "I don't expect you to give up what you call your 'adventuring' overnight. But it will never fill the void you complain of, the loneliness. Only a committed, ongoing relationship can do that." *Aha!* I thought. *He* is *a dutiful disciple. He does share Pierrakos's traditional views on sex and relationships.* So, big surprise. So, the truth was, part of me did, too—and at the moment, the painfully unhappy larger part of me.

I had recently gone back and forth over whether, and to what extent, I really needed a lover, a steady companion. In one mood, happily engaged in work, juggling a full writing and social life, I would tell myself that as a scholar and writer I in fact cherished, above all else, isolation, privacy, and freedom from the responsibility of having to account for my time to anyone else. I didn't need someone to "fill" the apartment, sit opposite me at breakfast, share my bed at night. The daily mechanics I could (usually) manage nicely alone. And as for the exceptional moments, I could share those with a few close friends. Sex I preferred in the context of adventure; familiarity and fantasy cohabited poorly, I told myself. They *could* be combined, but on some middling ground of excitement that lacked the high amplitude I prized.

But in other, less fortified moods, when I felt less need to cover over my sadness at not having had a partner since my twenties who had lasted more than a few years, I could acknowledge to myself that the trouble with sequential relationships was that one was always having the first conversation, and that my need for intimacy was something only dailiness could finally provide. In that mood I would feel, perhaps exaggeratedly, that deep down, beneath the bravado, my lack of a long-term lover was evidence of some sort of character disability; that in truth I fled the mutuality I claimed to want, that I was stiff-pricked only in pursuit of invulnerability, that although I often lamented the discontinuity of my sexual and emotional lives, I ran from the peaceable companionship that could combine them.

And before long I was confessing all that to André, confessing that the sense *had* been growing in me that I needed to be with some *one* other person over a long period of time. That it was in the space some-where between work addiction and frenzied pleasure that real satisfac-tion, and depth, lay. That dailiness was the key that unlocked the best, and scariest, places.

I talked a lot, too, about my mother. I talked about what I wished I had been able to say to her, yet never had: That I did understand the frus-trations and disappointments of her life—and the bravery with which she had met them. That her strength was my strength—and I wanted to thank her for it. That her capacity to love, however contaminated with demand and control, was at base large—and that, thanks to her, I had the same capacity, similarly misdirected and misused.

During one session, bathed in tears, I spoke to her directly: "Ma, I've spent so many years, so much energy, resenting you, denouncing your complaints and manipulations, that I never had anything left over for appreciation and praise, never let myself credit and enjoy the deep connection between us. Thanks, Ma . . . thanks . . ."

As I cried, André hugged me tight, told me how glad he was to know me. Touched by his words, grateful for his comfort, I simultaneously felt cynical about their source. *He's picked up his cue,* I thought, *respond-ing not to me but to the training manual's instruction to be supportive after the patient has arrived at a painful juncture. It's different from traditional therapy only in that the support is physical as well as verbal.*

But I also realized that if André *hadn't* put his arms around me, I would have had a whole different set of complaints: "He's just another uncaring, distant, sadistic male—*straight* male—just like all my previ-ous therapists." But André cut through the cynicism before it could solidify: "You know, Martin, when you blot out your desolation, you cut yourself off from positive feelings as well. It's all part of one stream, and every boulder in the path affects the flow."

TWO MONTHS INTO BIOENERGETICS, André told me I was "moving at a great clip" and in his opinion was ready to undertake a ten-day "inten-sive." I had no idea what that meant, and he explained that it was sim-ply a way of accelerating the therapeutic process. The Pierrakos group had a commune in the mountains at Phoenicia, New York, called the Center for the Living Force (the name alone made rational me a little queasy) and that was where "intensives" took place. They involved concentrated "self-exploration." With the "guidance and support" of a five-person team, an "intensive" consisted of a variety of practices, from physical exercises to meditation to periods of isolation—all in the context of "the community's healing and love energy."

I gulped uneasily. Pete had mentioned to me early on that Pierrakos was considered "far out" even in bioenergetic circles. Unlike others doing "body work," Pierrakos had introduced "a spiritual dimension." Indeed, his wife was considered a medium, a "channel" through whom messages were delivered from the non-corporeal world. At the time Pete told me all that, I had quickly buried it, realizing that I was in danger of letting what I loosely thought of as "an ideological difference" become an excuse for discontinuing a physical therapy that was having a demonstrable impact on me. When André suggested the intensive, I swallowed my doubts yet again, and said yes.

ON ARRIVING AT THE CENTER for the Living Force—an attractive collection of unpretentious cottages and community buildings set on three hundred acres in a wooded valley surrounded by hills and crossed by streams—I was introduced to my five-person "team," all of whom seemed pleasant and one of whom (Alex) I felt an instant, urgent attraction to.

The first session—many were to follow in the next ten days—began promptly at seven-thirty the following morning. Early on in that first session, following a sequence I can no longer recall, the image of a vicious rat gnawing away at my innards got established as a powerful symbol of the unconsolable, unappeasable hunger I was carrying within. It was my job, the team told me, to give the rat my attention; the rat was really "little Martin," the angry child still inside me who desperately needed to be accepted and embraced. Alex, role-playing the rat, cowered in ferocious terror in front of me, then slowly allowed me to touch and comfort him.

Over the next few sessions, I developed raging resentment towards Alex's wife, Liz. Pounding out my fury on the beanbag, I accused her of "ingratitude" at having Alex in her life, of holding him to her through coldness and reserve. Startled at my vehemence, the team held firm, neither contradicting me nor comforting me. Before I knew it, my anger had turned to tears, and I was bemoaning the absence in my own life of someone to love. Next I knew, Alex had been transmogrified into "Daddy," and I was asking for permission to sit on his lap, where I sobbingly asked him "Why won't Mommy let us be together more?" *Jesus,* I thought between the tears, *what the fuck is going on? Am I having a complete breakdown, a total regression—or both?*

Neither. But I was certainly behaving in uncharacteristic ways, letting fantasies and feelings rip, completely forgetting, wondrously, that I was an esteemed forty-seven-year-old professor of history.

Between sessions, I wandered the grounds, actually taking pleasure—previously unthinkable for my city-bound psyche—in mini-walks in the woods (mini was still all I could manage). Gradually, in an unpressured way—at meals, at a stream, in the rustic building where I had been assigned a room—I met various members of the community. Some of them were East Coast bioenergetic therapists who spent weekends at the Center; others were occasional visitors like myself. There was also a small number of year-round residents—the Center was only five years old—from whose ranks came most of the staff, including part-time farmers, dieticians, bookkeepers.

It soon became apparent to me that, as Pete had warned, the community *was* traditional in its views on sexuality and relationships. At dinner one night, a woman stared disapprovingly at me when, in answer to her question about my marital status, I said "I'm not married. I'm in fact gay." She quickly disclaimed any disapproval—too quickly, I thought, as if eager to avert possible discussion.

Later on, I did meet one man in the community—and only one—who openly described himself as gay. But he was skittish around me from the beginning. And when, one day, I brought up politics, asking if he might be interested, back in the city, in attending one of our "Gays for Bella Abzug" meetings, he stammered, "Maybe—doubt it though," and thereafter was always hurrying off on some urgent business whenever I ran into him.

Another night at dinner, Larry, one of the year-round residents, made an offhand comment about not liking the ice cream parlor in town because it was "so gay." I didn't say anything at the time, but the remark rankled, and I told him so when I saw him the next day. He used the word "gay," he said, to mean "superrefined" rather than, specifically, homosexual, and claimed "not to be in touch with any negative feelings within myself toward homosexuals."

But then—more believably, and with impressive frankness—Larry told me that he felt "a strong feminine component" in his nature, and that it frightened him. He, too, was a writer, and had been going through a period of "blocked creativity" that he ascribed to his inability to accept "the feminine within." He confessed to having deliberately avoided me since my arrival in the community, and thanked me for approaching him so openly; it had helped him acknowledge more directly the inner struggle he was going through. Since I'd expected bland denial or a belligerent "What's it to you?"—the usual responses when a homophobic remark is challenged—Larry's attempt at *self*-scrutiny threw me happily off guard.

Larry was himself at the top of the evening's agenda at the very first community meeting I attended. It seemed that on the previous evening Larry—though married to Margaret—had gotten drunk and picked up another woman at a nearby commune, Rainbow Farm. Only his inability to get an erection had prevented consummation.

The community discussion—again to my pleasant surprise—was not one-dimensional. Though people clearly disapproved of Larry's behavior and reaffirmed the community's commitment to a traditional model of monogamous pair-bonding, what was said to him was mostly loving and supportive. He was reminded that non-monogamous urges came from his "lower self," that destructive part of every personality where "distorted concepts, negative feelings, and blocked energy got hoarded." He was encouraged to "do more work" on confronting and exposing those "negativities" in order to transform them into "higher" feelings of "love, joy, and physical vitality"—and to avoid any orgy of self-blame.

No more complicated argument surfaced—the kind any gay Manhattanite might have offered—about the "need for sexual variety" or the impossibility of any one person satisfying all erotic moods and appetites. But I warned myself to stay focused on the impressive amount of warmth and support that had been expressed, and to steer clear of the ever-ready skepticism that might prematurely derail me.

Besides, I told myself, the community wasn't *that* conventional. Though it adhered to a traditional model of coupledom, it deviated significantly from a traditional view of sex roles. Men were encouraged to develop their warm, gentle, nurturing side, and women spoke out decisively at community meetings, seemed to share equally in decision-making and, on spiritual matters especially, usually took the lead. (That, to be sure, could be viewed as the *most* traditionally hallowed female role: Woman as the repository of piety— Whoops! I was at it again. . . .)

Pierrakos's wife, Eva, was the dominant spiritual force. In my ten days at the Center, I never laid eyes on her, let alone met her. There were veiled allusions to a recuperation from cancer, but I suspected a more encompassing determination to remain mysteriously aloof. It was through Eva, when she was in a trance state, that the Guide (never further defined, other than as "the spirit force") transmitted "lectures." The words were lovingly taken down by other hands, and then subsequently discussed and interpreted in ongoing study groups.

The lectures, according to the center's official brochure, explained "man's inner realities—the various levels of human consciousness and how these influence our lives—and the cosmic laws and metaphysical conditions in which we exist." Taken together, their embodied insights purportedly marked the way to fully realized awareness: the Path. This was the ideological cement, the Ur-Text, that held the Center for the Living Force together. (And, since many in the community were prosperous therapists, the Center had a secure economic base as well— something rarely characteristic of communal enterprises, past or present. Daily operations ran smoothly and efficiently; meals were on time and delicious; chores of every kind seemed to have been parceled out to minimum complaint and carried out with maximum grace.)

I heard it often said during my stay at the Center that "there were many paths to The Path." But I distrusted the seeming openness of that slogan; the basic ideology, I suspected, was *not* subject to challenge. Indeed, I never heard a scintilla of skepticism expressed about either the supernatural sources of Eva's trances or the Guide's inspirational omnipotence (only once anyway, when a member of my team did let slip that he went "back and forth" on "the spiritual issue"—and then refused to elaborate further). But, I kept reminding myself, the workings and mysteries of the Path were not my concern. I was at the Center to "do the body work," in which I did believe, and strenuously to ignore the kneejerk cynicism that might interfere with it.

That meant trying to ignore, as well, the community's apparent unconcern with events in the outside world. During my entire stay at the Center, I only once saw a newspaper, local or otherwise. By putting my mind to it, I managed to come up with a sympathetic explanation: A New

Age and New Person could be most rapidly brought into being by minimizing contamination with the soulless world that elsewhere predominated. Besides, I told myself, many at the Center did maintain contact through their therapy practices in Manhattan and elsewhere—contact with other people, if not with their "misshapen" worldly concerns.

On my fourth day at the Center, I went to my first "Core Energetics" session, which most of the community attended. Barbara (a member of my team) and I were paired. Following a series of exercises that focused on "grabbing upwards after one's desired goal," accompanied by occasional moans and shrieks, a woman named Lisa suggested that those of us who felt the urge should come, one by one, into the center of the room, express what we were grateful for in our lives, and then listen to what others had to say to us in response.

As various people took turns, I was able to join in the chorus of comments, shouting my encouragement and praise at whoever occupied the center of the room. The more feelings I got out, the more they mounted in intensity. Seeing how animated I was, Barbara urged me to claim the center for myself. The next thing I knew, I was in the middle of the room, terrified, feeling dizzy and nauseated, my fingers suddenly spastic, locked into a vise. (I, who as a teacher and lecturer had grown comfortable over the years with public speaking—who, indeed, thoroughly enjoyed it.)

Lisa and several others rushed to my aid. Two of them held my feet while Lisa told me to hold my breath. I was hyperventilating, she said; it was nothing to worry about. Another of the women hugged me tightly and told me about her own terror the first time she had tried to "speak out." As they continued to pat and comfort me, I slowly quieted down, and then began to speak. I said something about how much I had to be grateful for, and how much I wanted to lay claim to that. I talked about the bursts of joy I had felt while walking in the woods, the strength I sensed all around me, the climate of *forgiveness*—here I started to cry—that I had found at the center and which I felt was beginning to heal me.

Shouts of encouragement came toward me from various parts of the room. I was "a natural leader." I was "full of strength and courage." I was "like one of the mountains." I was—this from beloved, sexy Alex—"more ready than anyone I have ever seen to step into the abyss and *hold* there, determined on finding your truth." It was a tidal wave of affection and appreciation. As I wrote in my diary that night, "I was as amazed at the fullness of my emotional connection as at the fullness of their loving response. An astounding experience."

And so it went for most of the next few days: the sophisticated, skeptical, world-weary New Yorker blissfully awash in the simplicities of nature and human affection. I barely thought about the city, though normally I could never leave it without feeling vaguely in jeopardy. And this despite two days of steady downpour, a stuffy little bedroom, and an injunction from my team not to let myself read *anything*. Reading, they suggested, had long been my main mechanism for (among other things) keeping anxiety at bay; I had to give it up temporarily, if I wanted my feelings to come unstuck.

I agreed to the experiment and, in my mounting euphoria, decided that bioenergetics was allowing me to *experience* my deepest feelings, rather than simply to talk about them (psychotherapy), or to learn how to distance myself from them (yoga and transcendental meditation)— all of which I had earlier tried, and all of which had left my hungers unappeased. On my own, I decided—the incipient fanatic emerging— that masturbation (that other lifelong release from anxiety) might also defile "the process," and I forswore it for the duration.

Bursting with vigor, I sampled all the community's offerings, determined to do everything possible (to quote from the Center brochure) "to bring to consciousness, energize and dissolve the barriers we have created against the spontaneous flow of life." To steam open my pores, I sat in a Native American–style hut filled with glowing coals—and then plunged into the ice-cold stream nearby. I had my aura read, my body massaged, my biorhythm chart diagnosed, my numerological prospects analyzed.

The biorhythm expert warned me to take "extra care" on the eleventh day of the month; it seems I would then be subject to a double—possibly even a triple—"planetary crossover," putting me in great danger of some sort of accident. But that warning was small potatoes compared to the alarming numerological reading I got. It was based, I was told, on a highly complex Galaxial Science that derived from "Tibetan celestial mathematics unintelligible to most Westerners." (My informant, though Western, had studied in Tibet for ten years.) And what the Science revealed, I was portentously told, was a set of starkly challenging Learning Lessons.

It seemed I had "come into this incarnation with a heavy karmic burden from my 'background life.' " In 1885 I had been the only son of a wealthy, aristocratic New York family: "Coat and tie at dinner. Sterling silver and crystal. That sort of thing." I had hated that life and had deeply resented my father's tyrannical control; but I had lacked the courage to rebel, other than furtively. As a result, I now had a "heavy residue problem," an accumulation of anger that made me "ready to tangle with authority of every kind, to 'muscle-up' at the slightest provocation."

"You've been active all your life in political causes, haven't you?"

"Not *all* my life."

"So much wasted energy tilting at windmills! Such a negative energy flow: always mobilizing *against* something!"

Not so fast, thought I. *Impressed with bioenergetic therapy, I am. A bliss ninny, I'm not.* "Some things out there," I said (the tone a trifle more pompous than I might have liked), "*have* to be fought against. The world is full of injustice. I don't regret for a minute any of the time I invested in the antiwar, gay, or civil rights movements."

"You are simply playing out your background life, rebelling against your father."

"That's what my shrink used to say."

"Psychotherapy could do nothing for you. You're already overinvested in words and in 'figuring things out.' "

"That sounds familiar, too."

"You need to turn your energy inward, use it for yourself. And you have a lot of energy going for you."

That launched a lecture on my Third Ruler. ("Rulers," it seemed, were lines on the circadian chart, the length of the line indicating the depth of the personality trait.) My Third Ruler, it turned out, was so long it nearly went off the side of the chart; this was proof positive of my "obsession with logic." Fortunately for me, my Second Ruler, which controlled personal relationships, was longer still. I was "a very loving person, with a strong need for a stable home."

Just as I was puffing up with pride, my earlier animosity over that remark about "wasting energy in politics" dissolving, the bad news came. My Sixth Ruler was so positioned as to be "an antipical retardant" to the Second Ruler. It demanded variety; it would not let me settle down. It made me "too multifaceted ever to be satisfied with one person, one activity, one mode of life." (*Well,* I thought, *that's not* all *bad news.*)

"If you had consulted me at age eighteen and said, 'I'm in love, what should I do?' my answer would have been, 'Don't ever marry. Don't bother. No one female could ever satisfy your needs. You have too many contradictory impulses.' You need a warm, comfortable home, but you could only achieve that with a woman who isn't threatened by your need for a variety of relationships—or who has a chart much like yours and herself requires more than one person for fulfillment."

"Does it matter that I'm gay?" I asked "innocently," fully intending the question to throw a monkey wrench into the proceedings.

To my disappointment, the answer was "That makes no difference at all."

"Gender is irrelevant?"

"You *will* have more difficulty finding a multifaceted male than a female. Besides, in my experience"—that was the first tentative phrase I'd heard—"on the gay level, the male has a higher degree of possessiveness. And that would work against your need for multiple outlets."

Uh-huh. When the reader suggested that we go on to a discussion of "the dangerous number ten in my interior karma," I called it a day. Before leaving, he gave me a final summary: "We're all climbing a mountain. Everybody has a ten-pound knapsack, but you have a thirty-pound one and yet insist on keeping up. Sooner or later, that could destroy you." I did not schedule a second reading.

Still, I thought later, trying to keep my enthusiasm alive, the conclusions weren't so different from what I had heard or learned about myself elsewhere. And as for the arcane vocabulary, it was no less transparent and made no less sense than a lot of the psychoanalytic mumbo-jumbo I had subjected myself to for years—all that stuff about my "unresolved libidinal feelings for my mother" and my "doomed, repetitive search for the lost father." Well, maybe numerology made a *little* less sense. But I was determined to hold on to my high.

An unpredictably wild community meeting rekindled it. The evening began with two of the community's "witches" going at each other, spitting out venomous incantations and threats. The energy ran like a current through all of us. People started to snarl and square off. A low growl began in my belly, then grew in intensity—until suddenly I found myself thrashing around on the floor, cursing, yelling, physically tangling with half a dozen different people. Some of the fighting was—or sounded—fierce, but a sixth sense (or Sixth Ruler?) seemed to prevent anyone from actually getting hurt. The mauling, raging storm went on for some two hours. When it finally died down, we got back into our chairs, exhausted, "cleansed," smiling tenderly at one another, congratulating ourselves on having released a stored-up mélange of antipathies, on having created "a clean slate."

And then came the contraction: For a whole day, I felt barely able to move. My team told me that was to be expected; up to now, I had gone at "such a rapid clip, that a pause was inevitable." They urged me to sink—for once—into apathy, to experience fully my need for inactivity and rest. I lay around, nearly catatonic, feeling I should force myself back into engagement. "That's what you've always done," Alex said (insightfully, I thought), "forced yourself to maintain a constant level of intensity, even if that means an unnatural exertion of will, or a reliance on pills. Part of you doesn't believe in your own creativity; so you constantly, artificially, keep the flame up full blast. You lack faith in the natural ebb and flow of life. You must learn to accept an alternation of rhythms, of intense activity being followed by deep rest."

To help me better experience my body's need for quiescence—and the natural springing back to life that would follow—the team prescribed a deep massage, all five of them working on my body simultaneously. They dimmed the lights, put on a background tape of Indian music, and began to massage me with some kind of oil—ten hands at once working every part of my body. (But avoiding my penis, I groggily noted; I wondered if that was standard policy or a precaution adopted when working on gay men, a class notoriously prone to arousal).

A sense of deep peacefulness alternated with tears and joyful laughter. After twenty minutes or so, I turned on my back. It was then that I abruptly flipped over into another reality, tripped out, entered an earlier time frame—the team's later words for it; I didn't have any.

I was back at Camp Idylwold, where, as a preteen, I had spent every summer for some six to eight years. I was with my bunkmate and best friend, Billy Katz, with whom I often crawled into bed at night. I saw myself in my gray woollen sweater with "C.I." sewn on the front. I saw the bumpy dirt road leading into camp. I saw—Morty Offit! And now the tears really flowed. Beloved Morty, whom I had adored, the senior (age sixteen? seventeen?) who had taken me (age ten? eleven?) under his wing. I saw—I was back in the middle of—our last, painful good-bye. Morty was leaving camp midway through the summer to join the army. (Was it 1941?) As the taxi pulled up to take him to the railroad station, I hid behind a bush, too overcome to face him. But just as he was getting into the car, he spotted me, got back out, came over, and put his arm around me. "It's going to be all right, Marty. It's going to be all right . . ." Then he was gone in a blur, the last time I ever saw him. . . . I was blinded by tears. . . .

As I groggily came to, one of the team members gently suggested that I could "redo" that "crushing departure," transform it into a posi-tive memory. I had been loved and blessed; Morty had cared deeply for me. *That* was what I should try to remember—not the obliterating sense of loss. It wasn't a matter of reinventing my history, the team explained, but rather relocating its essence so that I could experience it differently. I was entitled to my grief over Morty's departure, but the grief could be recalled within the original context of his love for me; to remember the caring was to soften the pain.

I felt hugely comforted, cried some more, and then started to sink back into other memories—family memories. As if on cue, I refigured them as they appeared.

I was in Russia with my father, then twenty years old, as he fled from the army, walked his way to a port town, desperately sought pas-sage to America. I could *feel* the bitter cold, his aloneness, his fear and bravery. I traveled with him to the United States, to his shabby apart-ment, the overhead El reverberating outside his window—friendless, uneducated, poor. I was overcome with compassion for him. And with pride: No "nebbish"—as I had long characterized him—could have done his deeds.

I was in our house in Mount Vernon, New York, sitting in my room, staring out the window at the cherry tree whose branches, top-heavy with gorgeous pink blossoms, reached up to the pane. I was sitting with my parents and sister at the table on our patio, enjoying a meal. I was in front of the house the day we nailed up the sign, THE DUBER-MANS, right next to the big magnolia tree. We *were* the Dubermans, despite everything. There *were* positive memories. My family life need not be seen as an unvarying monochromatic gray. . . . I sobbed and sobbed. . . .

*   *   *

ON MY LAST NIGHT at the Center, I had dinner by candlelight with my team, joined by a few other members of the community with whom I had gotten friendly, and by André, who had come up from New York for the occasion.

The next morning we met at seven for our final session. We went into the woods and sat on the rocks next to a mountain stream, at a spot where the water fell with special fullness. We held hands, meditated together, spoke from our hearts. I realized, and said, that for the past few days I had felt the occasional urge to walk farther upstream, to get closer to the source. Something had held me back. I now realized what it was: I wanted to go there with these people. It was through them that I had gotten in touch with deeper resources of strength within myself than I had ever known. . . . As we said good-bye, I was swept by waves of sadness.

THE NEXT DAY, back in New York, I was desolate: punchy, frightened, unable to stop crying. Then, toward nightfall, I started to get angry. Had I been conned? Had I, yet again, allowed others to pass judgment on my life, accepted those judgments as valid, put myself through needless spasms of self-doubt? Wasn't bioenergetics a greater instrument of self-torture than any of the more obvious ones I had begun the therapy to alleviate? The anger astounded me—and the swiftness with which it replaced my sadness. Wasn't that itself a clue?

During my session with André the following day, I continued to rail against the "smug," formulaic words I had heard at the Center. I mimicked the community's likely analysis of my anger: "Your 'lower self' is resurgent." I dismissed their "Aimee Semple McPherson certitudes," their authoritative charts and credos, as "stone engravings on air." I raged at the assumption that one could—at any age—radically alter one's perspective or personality. Haven't they heard about imprinting? Couldn't they see that the path of wisdom was to *accept* the basic parameters of one's personality after a certain point in life and to stop pursuing the chimera of "fixing" it, making it different or better or perfect?

At the end of the session, my fury vented, I heard myself say that "at bottom" what might well be going on with me was simply desolation; after ten days of closeness, I was again alone.

To deal with the crisis, André and I met the following day as well. Right after the session, I recorded it in my diary:

"Stupefied. Trouble moving my body around. Hopeless, stuck. But haven't hit the depth of my hopelessness—that it's all a repeat, another game in the void.

"Banged my head into the pillow like a battering ram. Screamed at André, at all the fools on the Path who don't have the guts to face meaninglessness, who have to fall into the arms of mystical mumbo-jumbo. 'Not me,' I yelled, '*no way!*'

" 'Is your life working?'

" 'Don't give me that shit. It works like all lives—in some areas, some times.'

" 'It can work better.'

" 'It can't. It's too late.'

". . . Then tears . . . then vomiting . . .

"Then: 'I don't understand anything.'

"André says I have to give up in order to gain, that I cannot have everything, cannot have sexual adventures and drug-induced highs *and* continuity—which is the only long-range solution for loneliness. He says I have undergone 'a brutal expansion' during the intensive, made 'enormous strides.' I now have to allow myself the contraction. Meaning what? I feel more zombie than human. Can't connect to anyone or anything.

" 'Let yourself feel the full depth of your despair.'

"At which point, I gather, I either kill myself or find Jesus. My therapy is ruined. It turns out to be a cosmology."

Then I added this to the diary entry: "It's my isolation, my loneliness, that's driving me nuts. Ten days in a warm cradle has rocked me right off the cliff. . . . Is it as simple as missing being with people?"

When I saw André the following week, he warned me that my "resistance" could prevent further progress. (*Now that sounds familiar,* I thought. *Shades of psychotherapy: Shape up or ship out*). Andre suggested a joint session the following morning with Pierrakos to try and break the deadlock.

In preparation for it, I reread the diary entries I had made during the intensive. I cried at the descriptions of the farewell candlelight dinner and the final session at the mountain stream. *Maybe the anger is breaking up*, I thought, *maybe the contraction is ending. No*, I decided, *that's* their ter-

minology. I felt trapped, forced to choose between autonomy and alone-ness. Or was that *my* terminology, *my* dichotomy?

At the session the next morning, Pierrakos contended that it was, that *I* had created an either-or dilemma that no one else was insisting upon. He said I had seized on that strategy as a way of once more iso-lating myself; it was a "reflex function of my childish impatience and perfectionism."

"Forget the Path!" he demanded. "No one has asked you to join it, no one cares if you join it! Concentrate on *your* process."

"Which is tantamount to saying 'Put aside your intelligence.' "

"Not at all," Pierrakos shot back, exasperation in his voice. "What you need to put aside are the categorical judgments your intelligence creates in order to distance yourself from available love and support."

That sounded devastatingly plausible. And the stalemate might have been broken then and there. But in response to my further accusation that he and the Path were homophobic, Pierrakos insisted that he was not, and then added—fatally—that he did regard male homosexuality as "a flight from woman," did find it "regrettable" that I had chosen to "block out half the human race."

To which I replied, fury mounting, "I don't—other than genitally." Why, I asked, didn't he also lament the way *heterosexuals* 'block out half the human race'?

"I do regret," he answered in a measured voice, "that men, men much more than women, do not relate to each other on a deeper emo-tional level. But I do not regret their failure to relate sexually."

"You're applying different standards for gays and straights," I said angrily. "I have always had strong emotional connections, though not sexual ones, with women. Why do you equate the absence of sexual desire with 'flight'? Or if you do, why don't you say the same thing about men who refuse to acknowledge feelings of desire for other men? I'm capable of emotional intimacy with men *and* women, and most straight men are capable of *neither.* Yet somehow in your view I and other homosexuals don't qualify for full admission to the human race. What *does* qualify one, if not the capacity for intimacy? Merely the ability to have sex with a member of the opposite gender?"

Pierrakos sighed deeply and then, a note of finality in his voice, qui-etly said that I was "inventing" disagreement between us in order to create needless distance. He added—to my astonishment—that he thought "overall" I was "in a very good place," and he hoped that henceforth I would concentrate on the physical work and continue to move ahead.

The stalemate had not been broken. Yet I didn't immediately stop the therapy. Both André and Pierrakos had said enough that was cogent, and positive memories of the intensive were still so strong, that I kept going back for another few weeks.

The final break came when, still sick with grief and despair, still feeling encased in cement, I took André's advice to make a return overnight trip to the Center: "Take yourself to a place where there's caring and warmth—and fuck their theories!"

But this time the Center turned out not to be caring and warm. I arrived in the middle of a week-long workshop for non-Path therapists. With everyone locked into airtight schedules, I had to catch hugs on the run. All the "see you laters" intensified my loneliness; I seemed the only one unattached—to a person or purpose. I finally grabbed André and told him I felt desperate, as frightened and aimless as I had ever been. He had twenty minutes between workshops. I pounded the baseball bat into the beanbag, cursing and weeping. "Hang in there," André said.

The next morning Pierrakos also found twenty minutes for me. He concluded that I needed a deep massage and a session with the one member of my team available that day. I had both, and both brought out racking sobs. But the emotional checkmate held. By then I was feeling physically ill, feverish. I decided that I had to get *that* under control before I could cope with anything else—which meant I had to get back to the comfort of my own apartment. Would that really be taking care of myself? Or was I using the unavailability of people at the center as an excuse for closing down my feelings again? I didn't know, but on shaky balance decided to leave.

When my bus pulled in to the Port Authority, I discovered that New York City was in the midst of a gigantic blackout. A cosmic counterpart, I thought humorlessly, to my own shutting down. All I could make out in the dark were looming caverns between the outlines of buildings, thousands of tiny, darting shadows. I was scared to death. Somehow I found my way home, lit a candle, turned on the portable radio, and listened with grimly mounting cheer to the repetitive accounts of waterless buildings, lootings, fires. I felt comforted by the news of a city gone more amok than any broilings of my own inner world. I took a sleeping pill and was soon cozily detached, comfortably apart from the maelstrom within and without. I prayed for the power *not* to come back on.

I was sick for a week with a heavy cold. And I never went back to André's office. To this day, I don't fully understand why. Part of me thinks I "came to my senses," saw to the ersatz heart of the whole ridiculous cosmology. Part of me thinks that I fled out of fear, that I had opened up too quickly to too much pain—to say nothing of hope—and needed to clamp the lid back on. Probably both explanations contain some truth—and which the greater part, I still could not say with assurance.

VII

INTENSIVE CARE

I'VE ALWAYS HAD TROUBLE with my body image. Though I recognized, abstractly, that I was considered good-looking, the news had never really taken hold.

I had worked out the reasons several times over in therapy; they had something to do with global feelings of not being intact, not "right." Such feelings were commonplace among gay people in pre-Stonewall America. Few of us liked ourselves. How could we, growing up in a society that insistently linked homosexuality with pathology?

Karl, my therapist in the mid-sixties, had never once suggested that negative cultural definitions of homosexuality might be *somewhat* responsible for my feelings of distress and discomfort. Rather, he indicted homosexuality itself, implying further that social disapproval was a perfectly understandable response to behavior that was intrinsically disturbed.

Karl had explained—at length and insistently—that I had early in life focused my (appropriate) feelings of inadequacy at not being heterosexual on my body, and had then, as a compensatory mechanism, embarked on the relentless pursuit of intellectual distinction. Being deeply competitive and willful, I had, according to Karl, become a warrior of the mind, straining in the bargain to be—or to be perceived as—a "nice person."

But neither this, nor any other psychoanalytic insight, had ever done a thing actually to improve my body image. And so in 1978, at age forty-eight and by then nearly a decade removed from Karl's ministrations, I had finally decided on direct action: I joined the burgeoning gym craze and signed up for a membership at the New York Health and Racquet Club. My "individualized" program centered on thrice-weekly workouts on the Nautilus machines, which were touted as building "strong but lithe" bodies. "You'll be noticing a difference almost immediately," the strong and lithe instructor cheerfully predicted.

And I did. Within weeks, my body had taken on a firmness it hadn't had in years. Within months, I was the possessor of undeniable muscles—discreet ones, natural to sight and touch. Even *I* could see them! The makeover made me so euphoric (Down with psychological insight! Up with behavioral modification!), that I added half-hour jogging sessions on the club's indoor treadmill to my routine.

Gary, a man nearly twenty years younger than myself whom I'd been seeing for some six months, didn't seem to notice. But then, he hadn't been noticing much of late. From the beginning, ours had been a tumultuous affair, always out of synch, one of us always in pursuit, the other always in retreat, a settled, mutual commitment never more than momentarily achieved. Among our chief difficulties was that Gary was a devout Catholic and was still considering a vocation in the priesthood. (As recently as that year, he had been turned down for admission to Maryknoll Seminary.) But Gary insisted that he was in love with me and that "nothing could match in holiness a solemn lifetime commitment between us."

That line alone, I suppose, should have sent me running. But like all disappointed cynics, I was, beneath my skeptical surface, a hopeless romantic. Once the geyser of bottled-up longing for a partner had been released, it proved difficult to cap. I was soon telling myself that Gary was as deeply committed as he kept claiming and, moreover, was not a kid; at twenty-eight he had a master's degree and a job teaching ten-year-olds in a Catholic school, and was insistent on leading (as he put it) "a principled life." In short, he was far removed from the wild, bereft young men who in the past had so often magnetized me and then disappeared. He could unnerve me with talk of "wanting little of the world, and nothing for myself," but since *he* had pursued *me,* I thought it safe to assume that St. Simeon Stylites was not his true role model (or asceticism his calling).

Not even our mismatched sexual fantasies induced much caution, though as usual, sex did become the metaphor for our interaction. Gary from the beginning assigned me a particular image: the well-established, sure-footed, ruggedly dominant top. I was supposed to fuck him a lot and maul him a little, like any self-respecting husband.

All of which I went along with at first, thinking we were engaged in initial explorations; besides, our deplorable sex-role bipolarity did wonders for our short-term functioning. But these "explorations" turned out to be rigidly final parameters. No deviations permitted. No expression allowed of my own actual range of need or fantasy—no five-year-old pleas to be held and cuddled, no "womanly" bid for submission or passivity would be acknowledged, let alone met. For his own psychic convenience, he had taken my forceful veneer to be the whole of me.

Gary considered sexual urgency of any kind vaguely dishonorable. In the great Catholic tradition, love had no necessary expressive connection to sexual pleasure—indeed, I sometimes felt he gauged the extent and validity of our love by its *dis*connection from sex. Occasionally I got glimmers of St. Jerome: the wonders of marital chastity, the mortal sin of orgasm unrelated to procreation. When, one passionate night following orgasm, Gary asked me if I believed in the Devil, my "no" met with incredulous silence, and a slightly smug furrowing of the brow.

As part of the package, Gary insisted on monogamy. I did agree with the view that—at least in the initial stages of a relationship— monogamy *was* important; it encouraged the partners to work out fears that might arise (of intimacy, of abandonment, of whatever) within the relationship, instead of dumping and dissipating them on some anonymous other. Yet my allegiance to that view was unsteady. I shifted between the traditional model that linked sexual fidelity with emotional depth, and the newer one that separated the two, treating sex as a branch of sports. Once, in the ten months or so that Gary and I were together, I did go into a gay bar, where I drank a lot, went home alone—and the next day dutifully reported the episode. Gary raged at me for hours, until I tearfully pledged never to repeat so flagrant a "breach of trust."

By that point I was in love with him, ready to pledge almost anything, my iron vows never again to get deeply involved turned into tissue paper. His very foreignness, his haunting difference, held me in thrall, my certitude concerning spiritual nothingness drawn powerfully to his conviction that there was More—something unknowably beyond, yet knowably benevolent—even as I felt, in tandem, the frightening conviction that our values could never be bridged.

Once Gary realized he had won me, his interest—as I had feared from the first—waned. He became unpredictable, one minute loving, the next abruptly disconnected. And it now became clear that I was not masculine *enough* to meet the outer limits of a fantasy life that he revealed only after he felt I was securely in tow. What he really wanted, it turned out, was a stereotypical brute, a Tom of Finland Neanderthal—but with a brain.

He initially tried for a mental adjustment: Since I didn't look like a brute, I would have to work extra hard at *acting* like one in bed. That meant a decided tilt toward S/M. He insisted I pinch his nipples hard; then harder; then *much* harder. Next, he told me to use a belt on his ass; then to raise welts on his ass; then to take the belt to his whole body. I did—once. And was afterward repulsed. I didn't care whether my reaction sprang from some old-fashioned notion of what sex between lovers "should" be, or from a healthy conviction that you don't—you can't, you shouldn't—beat up somebody you love (no matter what fantasies are being fed). What I knew for certain was that the scene made me feel awful, about myself *and* about "us." I told Gary I would never again take a belt to him. *Never.* And when, a few weeks later, very drunk, he begged me to repeat the scene, I refused unequivocally.

We never recovered, though we continued to see each other for some time thereafter. Gary needed his fantasy brute much more than he needed commitment or closeness. And now that he began to move away from me, I reversed roles and became the pursuer—which, as Gary scornfully implied, no true brute ever would.

After I started working out and my body took on some somatic facsimile of "brutishness," Gary disdainfully announced that "bodybuilders don't turn me on. They're phony, asexual, disgusting." Only the *naturally* strong physique—as if the artificial weren't, for me, challenge enough!—appealed to him. The Health and Racquet Club, alas, had no "individualized program" for turning out real-life Maine lumberjacks. Interestingly, Gary himself had precisely the kind of body he craved in others, which made his tastes puzzling—that is, if one believed the theory that we're erotically attracted to people with whom we can "exchange" qualities we feel lacking in ourselves (rather than duplicating those we already possess). But Gary *was* a puzzle, an unpredictable mix of surface sureness and secret guile.

Having contemptuously denounced the Nautilus machine–made

body, Gary decamped for a summer language school, notifying me three weeks later that (1) he did not want me to visit him, as earlier planned, and (2) he was again actively considering the seminary.

Still later, it emerged that his renewed sense of a vocation was part and parcel of having fallen for a seminarian who had "allowed" sex to happen—*once*—and had then enlisted Gary in a joint vow of celibacy. That struck Jewish me as a possibly new definition of "brutishness." But to Catholic Gary, it proved the thrilling essence of his anchorite quest, the completion of his search for morally uplifting punition.

I took his loss hard. When I wasn't mournfully trying to figure out what *I* had done wrong (had I been too moralistic—or cowardly— about pursuing the S/M dynamic?), I was angrily berating Gary for having drawn me in and having then so abruptly vanished, and berating myself for having once again gotten ensnared by the "wrong" person. I firmly resolved, yet again, to count my manifold blessings and retire from an unseemly (at forty-eight) romantic search that hadn't been worth the candle in the first place. What I really wanted, I told myself, I already had: good friends, congenial work, and occasional, varied sexual partners.

As the pain, over many months, began gradually to subside, I mechanically kept up my gym routine, having gotten rather fond of my new shape even if it had failed to meet Gary's standards. Some six months after Gary headed off for the seminary's certified version of homosocial heaven, I was doing my standard twenty-minute jog on the treadmill one day when I felt a mild, dull pain in the center of my chest. I walked around the exercise room for a few minutes, the pain eased, and I got back on the treadmill. After another few seconds of jogging, my pace much slower than usual, the pain returned. I decided it must be due to something I had eaten, or maybe to a wayward bug I had picked up. Though I didn't feel sick. Well, no point pushing myself. I called it a day.

So it went for the next two weeks. My general health remained fine; I felt alert, had plenty of energy, and developed no additional symptoms. In fact, the only time I felt the dull chest pain was in the gym, whenever I tried to jog. It was annoying. Holding to my gym routine felt like a necessary stay against the lingering emotional pain of losing Gary. But I decided to be sensible and drop jogging from my workout until the mysterious bug had had a chance to subside.

Straphanging on the subway one afternoon, I glanced up at the billboard advertisements. A public service ad caught my eye; stark and clean in design, it stood out from the surrounding clutter. The ad was divided into four boxes, each containing the same drawing of an upper male torso. The print on top read, "THE FOUR MOST COMMON SYMPTOMS OF A HEART ATTACK." I glanced idly at the first box. A red circle was drawn around the torso's chest cavity. Below were the words, "The single most common symptom of the onset of a heart attack is a dull pain in the center of the chest. It can continue for many weeks without additional symptoms developing."

I never read the second box. I went straight home and called Gerald, my doctor of a dozen years. Dialing his number, I felt a little foolish. He had given me my annual physical only a few weeks before and had pronounced me, "fine, better than fine for someone your age—you're remarkably fit." He had joshingly added, "You gays keep yourselves in such good shape"—we had gotten beyond the "gay thing" years before—"you're going to inherit the earth." "And without procreating," I had joshed back.

I felt foolish, too, because I could already predict Gerald's response: "For God's sake, Martin, you're as healthy as a horse. We just did an electrocardiogram on you. It was perfectly normal." Over the years I had periodically raced up to Gerald's office with one or another dire symptom: a mole that had changed color; an earache; a cough that would not abate. In every case I had expected the delivery of a death sentence and had gotten instead the warm reassurance of continuing good health. It was a form of confession: direst sin and fear absolved at the very door to Purgatory.

Gerald reacted to my alarmed call predictably, but I was not to be put off: "I'd feel better if you had a look." He gave his ritual sigh, itself a reassurance, and said I should come up to his office at four thirty that afternoon.

I was a little disquieted when Gerald began by suggesting we do a "stress EKG" rather than the traditional "at rest EKG" of our yearly physicals. He had me climb up and down a wooden block with three steps. After five full minutes I was barely winded. "You have now," Gerald announced, "gone beyond the point recommended for people in your age group. And with hardly any effort. As I've said before, you're in remarkable condition. Keep going."

Up and down I went, Gerald ticking off at intervals the mounting evidence of my (in Gerald's words) "almost obscene good health . . . You've just passed the time ordinarily recommended for a man aged forty . . . thirty-five . . . thirty . . ."

"You're jealous," I said. Already feeling embarrassed at the familiar denouement that loomed, I thought a little banter might help.

"I certainly am."

"I'll send you a brochure for my gym."

"Eternal youth holds no appeal for me."

I was now in exuberant good spirits. "You prefer premature senility? When are you going to give up smoking, at least?"

"Okay—stop!"

For a second I thought Gerald meant, "Stop the banter."

"Stop the steps. Jump onto the table so I can hook you up."

Gerald wheeled the EKG machine to the table and attached the "electrodes" (as I had always called them, fantasizing an imminent execution).

"I hope you realize," Gerald said sardonically, fastening the last of the electrodes to my ankle, "that I stopped you after you had gone *beyond* the time recommended for twenty-five-year-olds!"

"With a new washboard stomach to match. Which you've cruelly failed to comment on." I was in giddy high spirits.

"Lie still." Gerald turned on the machine. "You can breathe normally, but don't move until I say so."

The machine purred away. Gerald bent over to study the marked graph paper as it emerged from the machine's side—tracings of my abused heart, I merrily mused, able to think comically about Gary for the first time. After a minute or so, the purring stopped. Gerald ripped off the graph paper, quickly rolled it up, and walked into his adjoining consultation room. "You can get dressed," he tossed back over his shoulder.

An ominous rumble struck my midsection; Gerald usually pronounced an instantaneous verdict. "Does it look okay?" I called after him, gathering up my clothes in record time and following him, still in my underwear, into his office. Gerald sat behind his desk, quizzically silent as he watched me fumble into pants and shirt. "Did something show up on the EKG?"

"Yes." Gerald paused—melodramatically, I thought, the panic rising.

"Yes, it showed up a perfect tracing. No abnormality of any kind."

"My God, Gerald!" I yelled, "Why didn't you say so?"

"Do you believe me?"

That caught me off-guard. "Well, of course I believe you," I said, with just a touch of suspicion in my voice. After retrieving my shoes and socks from the examining room, I added, "I tell all my friends that you're not only a marvelous diagnostician but that rarest of things, a nice man."

Gerald smiled uneasily, apparently liking the compliment. "Try to have a pleasant weekend."

We were now at the door. "You *do* have a penchant for drama, Martin. Sorry, not today; you're in perfect health."

"That does *not* disappoint me." I was halfway out the door.

"Or completely convince you—right?"

"Well, ninety-eight percent. We've all heard the classic tale: Patient gets clean bill of health and drops dead on the sidewalk outside doctor's office."

"That has happened. But won't to you."

"Famous last words. Don't take your phone off the hook!"

We both laughed. "Call me in a few weeks," Gerald said, "and let me know whether the pressure is entirely gone."

"Did you have to add that?"

"If I didn't, you'd accuse me of being lax."

I capitulated with a groan.

Well, I thought as I reached the sidewalk, *yet another new lease on life . . . Try not to let it depress you.*

I ran a few errands and then—what better day to get back on the horse?—went to the health club. I did my usual limbering-up exercises: stretching, some push-ups and sit-ups, ten minutes on the stationary bike. Then I leaped with bravado onto the treadmill—though I was careful to start at a slow pace, more a fast walk than a jog. After a full five minutes I still hadn't felt so much as a twinge in my chest; euphoria mounting, I gradually raised the speedometer. The hotshot hunk running full-out on the treadmill next to mine, sweat flying off his body, looked over disdainfully at the dreary older man who after ten full minutes was still at a crawl.

I tried to hold my competitive genes in check and to raise the speedometer *slowly*. Before long I was actually jogging, though still not at full clip. Give or take a little humiliation—the hunk smirked again in my direction—I was still not feeling any pain, and again increased the speed. But only a little; I didn't want to press my luck.

But I had. A dull pressure, barely perceptible, started up in the center of my chest. Within a minute, the pressure had notably increased. I quickly turned down the speedometer. Previously, the pressure had disappeared immediately after I stopped jogging. This time it didn't.

I turned the machine off and walked slowly back to the locker room, all the while trying to down the rising anxiety with furious little speeches to myself about having *just* gotten a clean bill of health. I showered and dressed quickly.

THAT EVENING I MET an old friend for dinner at Duff's in the Village. Leo had long since moved to California and we now saw each other only on his periodic trips to New York. Ever since graduate school days, ours had been a close friendship, but in recent years the lack of regular contact had taken the usual toll. Typically, we would try to cover too many bases in too short a time, catching each other up on surface events or reducing recent trials of the heart and triumphs of the will to bland recitation. Our evenings often ended with my feeling unspoken sadness that our once-vital friendship had dimmed.

But now and then we would surprise ourselves and feel the sort of animated excitement in each other's company that we had once taken for granted. We had just such a dinner that evening in late September 1979; fueled by three, then four Stolichnayas on the rocks, we grappled more directly than in years with the peculiar constellation our friendship had settled into. We talked for hours, unleashing buried grievances and tenderness, and when we parted on the street, hugged fiercely, very near tears. Having unexpectedly recaptured our closeness, separating felt bitterly unfair. I hadn't had exactly a surfeit of communication of late, and all else seemed suddenly unimportant. We made extravagant promises to write more often and more intimately.

The bittersweet mood stayed with me as I headed back from the restaurant to my apartment a few blocks away. Despite the vodka, I felt lucid, and mused, as I walked, on how strange it was that a middle-aged man of considerable experience and some insight could still be made to feel so unexpectedly vulnerable. The hunger to connect never really disappears; there was some comfort and pleasure in acknowledging that.

But it was short-lived.

Suddenly—literally between one step and another—the entire width of my chest felt caught in a vise. The pain was so excrutiating, I nearly fell to the pavement. Legs buckling, I managed to lurch a few feet to the side of a building, then leaned against it to maintain a precarious balance. I was in agony; no physical pain I'd ever known had been remotely comparable. It felt as if my chest would burst from the explosive pain that now began to radiate over my body. I started to sweat; a wave of nausea came over me.

I was on Seventh Avenue near Tenth Street, the heart of the Village, midnight of a weekend. People must have passed me, yet I can't recall a single face, nor trying to call out to anyone. The pain was obliterating. I know I didn't pass out, and I know no one came to my aid. Some portion of my brain—or will, or instinct; who can name or locate the saving remnant of consciousness?—pushed through the information that I was near St. Vincent's Hospital and *had* to get there.

Somehow I did. I have only a blurred memory of staggering through the hospital's main entrance and—I had visited friends in St. Vincent's several times—heading straight for the booth a few steps to the left of the entrance. A young man was sitting inside the booth doing paperwork. He glanced up at me, annoyed, said something curt like "Be with you in a minute," and went back to his paperwork.

My instinct for survival took over: "I need help *now!*" I almost shouted.

Barely glancing up, the young man pushed a form at me. "Fill this out," he said, handing me a pen.

"You don't understand. I have to see a doctor *now!*"

"You can't go to the emergency room"—I could see it right behind the swinging doors a few feet away—"until you fill out these forms. Or have somebody fill them out for you."

"No one's with me. Look—I feel *awful* . . . I'm going to pass out. . . . *Please*—I need a doctor! I'll do your damned forms later!"

Given how weak I felt, I was amazed the words came out, let alone with such force. Maybe I seemed *so* pulled together that the clerk had been thrown off. (*A lifetime problem,* I thought self-pityingly: *No one ever believes I'm in trouble.*)

The clerk's eyes narrowed as he sized me up: Was this another nut job? *This can't be happening,* I thought, *it's too crazy. Is he actually going to make me fill out a form? . . . a form? I could die because of this kid. . . . Fuck him—I'm going into that emergency room now!*

At which moment, the clerk finished his assessment, jerked his head toward the revolving doors and in a bored, surly voice said, "You can go in. But make damned sure you fill out these forms before you leave!" I not only assured him that I would, but *thanked* him, thanked him twice. Maybe I was in shock. I like to think so.

Anyone who has ever been in the emergency room of a city hospital knows that bedlam reigns. I had a blurred awareness of frantic activity on all sides. That reassured me: Instant, expert attention was at hand. Within seconds, I was flat on my back being given an EKG, a young doctor standing above me, reading the printout with furrowed brow. When he finished, brow unfurrowed, he told me I could go home. Given my classic symptoms, he added, he had expected to diagnose a heart attack. But the EKG was fine.

"But I feel terrible. I don't think I can get home."

"You've got indigestion, that's all. How far away do you live?"

"Charles Street. A few blocks."

"You'll be fine. If you're not better in the morning, call your own doctor." And with that he was gone.

"I've just seen my own doctor," I called into the void.

A nurse appeared and bustled around me impatiently, as if to say a *real* patient needed the space. Somehow I got myself up and dressed. In fact I was feeling better; a pat on the head had at least served to reduce panic.

And somehow, too, I got back home to Charles Street, climbed the three flights of stairs, and got into bed. By now it was nearly two A.M. but the acute pain in my chest had returned. At five A.M. I was still frantically awake, and feeling desperate. What should I do? Where could I turn? Twice over, at Gerald's office and at St. Vincent's, I'd been given a clean bill of health. Yet I felt certain this was no simple case of indigestion.

I phoned my sister, Lucile, who lived five minutes away. As soon as she heard my voice—which she later said was faint and frightened—she got alarmed. I explained what had happened and told her the pain was awful.

"I don't know what to do. Everybody tells me I'm fine."

"I know what to do. Sit tight. I'll be there in a few minutes."

She arrived with an ambulance, which she'd called immediately on hanging up. I was taken back to St. Vincent's and back to the emergency room. Once again, the EKG was declared normal and, once again, I was told to go home. Lucile insisted I be admitted for overnight observation and my sister, when worked up, is not easily denied. I was reluctantly given a bed.

And many hours later I was still in that bed, still unattended. It was a Sunday; on Sundays, it seems, hospital staff is skeletal, and doctors do not appreciate being paged at home. By now I was incontinent. Lucile decided to throw a calculated tantrum. She went to the nurses' station and, acting even more distraught than she felt, demanded that a specialist be called to examine her brother. If the doctor wasn't there within the next half-hour, she screamed, she would sue the hospital.

That apparently did it. By now I was in and out of consciousness, so I have no recollection of what followed. As Lucile tells it, a cardiologist arrived soon after and quickly decided I was in serious trouble. He had me immediately transferred into intensive care. Two days later, blood enzyme levels confirmed that I had had a heart attack—a major one.

PLACED ON A STRETCHER, I was wheeled into a room with three beds, the middle one unoccupied. A sallow, sixtyish Italian-American man dressed in a robe (I later learned his name was Sal), was sitting in a chair beside the bed near the door, reading *The Daily News*. He nodded pleasantly in the direction of the stretcher, but said nothing. Sitting up in the bed near the window, browsing through magazines, was a husky, healthy-looking man in his early forties. As soon as he caught sight of me being wheeled into the room, he jumped off his bed and came up to the stretcher.

"Hi, howya doin'? I'm Bill. Bill Grabinski, your new roommate. Welcome to the terminal unit."

"Awright, Grabinski," said one of the nurses, elbowing him off to the side, "We've got a very sick man here. Cut the shenanigans."

As she and the other nurse unhooked the bed rails and started to roll me slowly from the stretcher onto the bed, Grabinski hovered nearby, bantering with the nurses in what had clearly become a routine.

"Watch his IV," one nurse called to the other, "it's tangled under his arm. Careful it doesn't pull out."

"You betta hope," said Grabinski, looking straight at me. "Or next thing you know, in comes the seventeen-year-old intern to puncture holes in your arm. He usually hits by the fourth or fifth try."

One of the nurses chuckled despite herself, and in a mock-stern voice told Grabinski to get back into his bed and "behave yourself."

"Sure thing, Nurse Lisa," Grabinski said, sounding vaguely like Butterfly McQueen, "Ah sure wouldn't want to be sent to bed again without mah supper."

"*Liza,* Grabinski, not Lisa. *Liza.*"

"You know how us Polacks is, Miss Leeza. Can't hardly talk, let alone spell."

Liza made a nasty face and called out to the orderly standing at the door. "Gil, you need to clean him up after we get him in bed. Go get a basin and a new gown."

Grabinski held his nose high in the air. "Shit in his pants, huh?"

The nurses ignored him as they completed the effort to roll me from the stretcher onto the bed.

Grabinski was not one to be ignored. "Why *do* people shit during a heart attack, huh? Is it a physical thing? Or just fear of dying?"

"Because I told him he was going to be put in a room with you," Liza snapped.

That was the first time I had heard the actual words spoken: "a heart attack." The doctor had said only that I was "a very sick man," adding in a mechanical voice, "But you're going to be fine, just fine."

The IV had stayed in place and Liza now injected into the socket an anesthetic that I later learned was called lidocaine. Then she leaned down close to my ear and asked me if the pain had eased. When I said, "Maybe a little," she turned to the other nurse, Joanne, and asked her if I'd had morphine yet. When Joanne said I hadn't, Liza consulted my chart, shook her head angrily, left the room for several minutes, and then returned with a hypodermic and a small bottle.

"This *will* reduce the pain," she said emphatically, injecting the morphine. "How's that? *Much* better, isn't it?"

"Better than what?" Grabinski piped in, "being in a cobra pit?"

Liza scolded Grabinski affectionately, telling him I needed to get some rest now and to try to keep it down "to a dull roar."

Within minutes I started to drift off. I vaguely remember hearing Grabinski exclaim over my tan ("A *tan!* In late September! The guy must be rich!"), and Liza sardonically saying that St. Vincent's didn't discriminate, that to saints like her and Joanne, everyone was entitled to equal treatment. The very last words I heard were from Grabinski, humor drained from his voice: "Yeah, sure . . . so long as the poor are paid up on their Blue Cross premiums," and swearing that they weren't moving *him* to some "fucking V.A. hospital."

WHEN I GROGGILY CAME TO, a siren was going off in my head. Then shouts, the sound of running feet, a swift crescendo of noise—and suddenly six or eight nurses and doctors were pouring into the room. Within an instant they had surrounded Sal, groaning in the bed next to me; a Laocoön jumble of gyrating arms and legs pushed and pulled him as disembodied voices shouted instructions.

Catching sight of my gaping astonishment, a nurse rushed over and pulled the curtain around my bed. Just before she closed me off from the chaos, I caught a glimpse of Grabinski, hunkering down in terror on his own bed.

One voice louder than the rest suddenly cried "Stand back!" There was an urgent shuffling of feet, then a strange sizzling sound, as if a juicy beef patty had just been thrown on the grill. Some muffled voices conferred; then the sizzling sound repeated. Then a pause. More conferring, another sizzle.

Then the voices and movements quieted to a whisper, like sails gone abruptly slack when the wind shifts course. I heard the scraping of machinery being moved into the corridor, then some renewed activity as they rolled Sal, who had stopped groaning, from his bed onto a stretcher and out of the room. A hand reached in and pulled back the curtain around my bed, opening up the room again. Everybody was gone, as if it had been a mirage. Just me and Grabinski.

"What was all *that?*" I asked.

"That was Sal."

"What were they doing to him?"

"They were trying to save him. They didn't."

"You mean—?"

"You got it. There's no more Sal. Too bad you didn't get to know him. A good guy, a sweet guy. Always offering me some of the food his wife brought in. She's a great cook. Sure beats the slop in this dump. Wait'll you see the pear salads they call lunch. This is going to be hard on her."

186

The bellowing giant who had roared his welcome at me the day before lay motionless on his bed, his voice a flat monotone. I was feeling shell-shocked myself. Sal was *dead*? Had I actually seen him before they gave me that needle yesterday? I couldn't remember a single detail about him, just a sallow blur. How did they get rid of bodies in a hospital? I started to feel groggy again. I wanted to sleep.

"Is the monitor bothering you?" I heard Grabinski say just as I was dozing off.

"The what?"

"The monitor, the monitor," he repeated impatiently, pointing to my waist.

I looked down and saw what looked like a big corset over my stomach, wires coming out on all sides. I was dumbfounded: How had they gotten it on? What was it for?

As if reading my mind, Grabinski, some color back in his voice, pointed to his own belly and told me everybody in intensive care had a monitor—"so don't get to thinking you're something special." He explained that we were all hooked up to a TV screen, with somebody staring at it twenty-four hours a day. "If anything goes wrong, they pick it up on the screen before you even feel it. Then they call the code. That's what happened to Sal. Heart failure."

Gil, the orderly—hadn't he washed me the day before?—came into the room. He and Grabinski exchanged a few grunts of condolence about Sal (the straight male version of emotion, I silently scoffed). Then they started the buddy-buddy teasing (the *other* note, I contemptuously thought, in the macho male emotional range). Grabinski, who clearly liked his food, wanted to know "why the fuck dinner was late," though why he "gave a shit about boiled fish and rhubarb with cherry Kool-Aid for a chaser" he "sure the fuck" didn't know. "I'm a man," he yelled, "not a rabbit!"

Gil, predictably, picked up on "cherry" and did a little riff about yes indeed, cherry—that was just exactly what his man Grabinski *did* need, he sure agreed with him there. *Ho, ho, ho,* I thought sardonically, wondering "how the fuck" I was getting the energy, one day into a heart attack, to *be* sardonic, to care about straight men and their little-boy routines. The two had another good laugh when Grabinski allowed as how Nurse "Lisa" had tried to give him a back rub the night before, but when he asked her who was paying for the lotion, him or the hospital, she had told him to give *himself* a back rub. They guffawed no end over that, Gil baiting Grabinski as "a no-good mother," and Grabinski predicting that next time they'd probably send in Sister Eloise—eighty years old, with a cleft palate—to do the back rub.

Then Gil surprised me by turning shyly serious, asking Grabinski if he had had a chance to copy over Gil's lyrics yet. Grabinski surprised me more, telling Gil, without any hint of a wisecrack, that he had "real talent." But, he added, reaching over to his night table for a batch of paper, he had had trouble with a few of the words. Together they decoded some of Gil's more enigmatic spellings, the final puzzler—"testimony"—yielding only after Gil, in his own version of charades, sang a few bars in demonstration of "giving testimony to the Lord."

Grabinski promised to complete the "copying" (which, it had become clear, meant translation into standard English—Gil's native language being Spanish) in the next day or two, thanked Gil for having given him "something to do," and said he would expect free tickets to his first big concert in Central Park. Gil swore he would not forget his friends after he became famous, and, grinning, bowed out of the room with a sweep of his arms magnanimous enough to include me.

So much for my too-quick stereotyping, I thought remorsefully, and in recompense said something admiring to Grabinski for helping Gil out. He pooh-poohed that, saying I "sounded like a professor."

"All I did was say my first full sentence since arriving here." I laughed, trying to make light of my follow-up confession that in fact, yes, I was a professor. Grabinski looked blank, as if he hadn't heard me, and started talking about how familiar I looked to him. He had the feeling he knew me from somewhere else.

"Do I look familiar to you?" he asked. When I said no, he wanted to know if I lived "down here in the Village?"

"Yes, just a couple blocks away, on Charles Street."

"I knew it!"

"You live down here, too?"

Grabinski laughed uproariously, as if I'd made a huge joke. "I'm a Polack. From Staten Island. I live with my sister." Still grinning slyly, he asked me what bars I went to in the Village. A ten-watt bulb went on in my head: Could this possibly be leading where it dimly seemed to be?

Grabinski pressed on: "Ever been to the Eagle? Now, *there's* a hot bar. I go mostly to One Potato. The guys aren't as hot, but I like the nice, neighborhood feel to the place."

My mouth must have been hanging open. "Whatsa matter?" he asked with genuine concern. "You got angina?"

In fact, I was—along with astonishment—feeling some congestion in my chest.

"Oh, that's nuthin'," Grabinski reassured me. "You get that after a heart attack. If it's not like a jackhammer, it's nuthin'."

"You had a heart attack, too?"

"Just short of it. The pain knocked me to the sidewalk. Oh Christ, what pain! I don't even know how I got in here. They said they 'caught it' just in time, I coulda popped off right there. Still might." He laughed. "They're doin' some tests. Might need an operation."

"Sorry to hear that."

"So what bars do you go to? You ever go to One Potato? I know I've seen you *somewhere*."

Clearly angina was of mere passing interest compared with the main event of spilling the beans. I couldn't match Grabinski's gusto (what *was* that sensation in my chest?), but the good fortune of finding myself in a room with another gay man (even if he wasn't like any other I'd ever known, give or take some erotic fantasies) had to be seized.

So we got down to it. I explained that I didn't go to bars much anymore. He said he loved them and couldn't get in from Staten Island as often as he'd like. I asked how he had known I was gay—"Was it the gold lamé bed jacket?" He laughed and said he could "always spot a sister." As proof, he described one of the (more adorable) interns as "definitely in the club; he keeps checking me for hernias, you know what I mean?" An understandable obsession, Bill modestly allowed—"I mean seein' as how big I am."

From that, he segued into the saga of another admirer: the eighteen-year-old son of his neighbors and best friends on Staten Island.

"The kid is nuts about me, but scared to death his folks will find out. His father's an ironworker, like me."

"Not likely to be sympathetic," I lamely offered, aware that the "congestion" in my chest was getting just a mite sharper.

"Yeah, they'd have a shit fit. It's not that we do that much, you know. I like people my own age. *He* came after *me*."

Then Bill wanted to know if *I* had a "special friend." "Quite a few," I said flippantly, wanting the conversation, and the chest pain, to stop. Bill's eyes lit up; he wanted to hear *all* the details. But when I said I really wasn't feeling so good, he immediately shifted gears and told me to press the button for the nurse. "You *are* a little gray around the gills." The button? He pointed to the device pinned to the left side of my sheet.

"When you press it, the light goes on at the nurses' station. Joanne or Lisa—Liza—will come racing in, sometimes even within the hour. I'll press my buzzer, too. Where the fuck are they? You know none of the nurses here are nuns, so it's not like a real Catholic hospital. Thank God! I can say that 'cause I'm a Catholic. You're a Jew, right? Though you look like a WASP."

"Right again," I mumbled, just as Liza came bounding into the room, hands on hips, voice at full tilt.

"Why are you *both* ringing? You want matching bedpans, maybe?"

Grabinski grinned, relishing the prospect of another skirmish. "Just make sure the enamel's not chipped, sweetheart. I got a lot to protect here." (He made a vague feint toward his crotch.) "Who's running this dump, anyway?"

"The Holy Father," Liza shot back. "He runs everything, remember?"

"I thought maybe it was the Mafia, given all the tough gun molls around."

Liza tried not to smile. "Listen, Grabinski, there are two of us covering fourteen rooms. You need something or not? I'm too tired to play games."

"You do look tired," Bill said, furrowing his brow in mock concern. "Take my advice and get an EKG. While there's still time."

Seeing Liza momentarily stuck for a topper, Grabinski plowed on: "Hey! Why shouldn't patients be sadists too? Why should you people have all the fun?"

"This is the last time I ask, wise guy. Why did you ring the buzzer?"

When I explained that I had some chest discomfort, Liza got instantly serious and went for the blood pressure gauge in the corner of the room. She shot Bill a furious look, as if to say, "You ought to be ashamed of yourself, trading one-liners with this man feeling sick." I said I didn't have pain exactly, more like a feeling of phlegm that I couldn't cough up. Liza put a stethoscope to my chest, took my pressure, and then asked a string of questions—"Any nausea? Dizziness? Pain down the left arm?"—to all of which I said no. "Good!" she pronounced, clearly relieved. "This is nothing to worry about. Go to sleep." She started toward the door.

"Why do I have that congested feeling?"

"It could be anything."

"For instance?"

"Tension . . . the damp weather . . ."

"I'm always tense. And it isn't damp in here. In fact, the air-conditioning's a little chilly."

"Right—it could be from the air-conditioning. You've probably caught a little cold."

Grabinski butted back in. "Bullshit! Ask a direct question around here and they look at you like you just farted in public!"

Turning to me, he formally pronounced on my condition: "The congestion is inflammation in the damaged part of your heart!"

I could feel the chill start up my back. Damaged? My heart was damaged? Panic rising, the resumed banter between Grabinski and Liza sifted through as a distant echo only ("Thank you, *Doctor* Grabinski"; "Don't think you can insult me by calling me a doctor!"). I swallowed hard and asked Liza if Grabinski was right. Grabinski answered for her: "A heart attack always leaves some damage. Sometimes more, sometimes—"

Liza interrupted him. "It's much too early to worry about that. You're doing just fine, Mr. Duberman."

"That's what they tell everybody," Grabinski said. "Standard bullshit. They make it up as they go along."

"Grabinski hates it when other patients get good news," Liza said acidly. Then turning back to me, she resumed her comforting tone: "The doctors will be doing some tests on you in the next few days, and then we'll know a lot more. In the meantime, I suggest you stop listening to your friend over here."

"Ignorance is bliss," Grabinski piped in again. I felt a wave of resentment toward him. "The doctors are ignorant, the nurses are blissed—they're all on pharmaceutical coke, ya know. And the patients are supposed to be deaf, dumb, and blind."

"You qualify on all counts," Liza shot back. She gently puffed up the pillows on my bed, patted me on the hand, repeated that everything was going to be "just fine," and suggested I try to get some sleep.

"Aren't you going to sing him a lullaby?" Bill sneered. My anger at him went up another few notches. Turning to Liza, I asked for another injection, but she said not enough time had passed since the last one.

"This is a *Catholic* hospital, Marty m'boy!" Bill joked. "We believe in the power of positive suffering!"

I wanted to yell "Shut up!" I'd had enough jokes. I was scared. But, I thought guiltily, *He's your ally, you'll need him.* So instead I said something about how tired I felt, how I needed to sleep. Bill looked at me as if I'd just defected to the enemy. Ostentatiously picking up a magazine from his night table, he announced that *he* had to complete his crossword puzzle—and before long was wondering aloud, "What continent is New Zealand on?"

Liza told me that Dr. Hawley—the cardiologist who the day before had finally converted a diagnosis of "indigestion" to one of "heart attack"—would soon be in to see me. She reassured me that Hawley was "one of the finest cardiologists in the hospital."

"And a good skier, too," Bill muttered. "Takes *long* weekends. And a *sharp* dresser. You mean he's back from Chile?"

Liza ignored him, gave me another pat on the hand, and left.

"Just kidding," Bill said after she'd gone. "Hawley *is* good. I wish he was *my* doctor."

"Why isn't he? Can't you ask him to be?"

Bill snorted. "There's a lot you don't understand. I'll explain some other time."

He went back to his crossword puzzle, and I turned over on my left side to sleep. I found myself staring straight at the empty, already remade bed Sal had been in a few hours before.

"You know," Bill said, "you got real cute buns."

I pulled my hospital gown around my back and grunted thanks.

"Sleep tight," Bill said, "and don't be dreaming about *my* intern."

A MAN STANDING AT THE SIDE of my bed shook me awake and briskly introduced himself as Dr. James Wescott Hawley, the doctor who had admitted me to the intensive care unit two days earlier. I mumbled something about not remembering that day too well, to which he impassively replied, "That's to be expected, Mr. Duberman, given the condition you were in. Now then, let's have a look at you. Lift your hospital gown, please."

Hawley put his stethoscope on and bent down to examine me. That meant turning his back on Grabinski, who promptly put his finger right next to the crease in Hawley's butt and rolled his tongue lasciviously around his lips. When I started involuntarily to laugh, Hawley took the stethoscope out of his ears and said peremptorily, "Please do not talk while I am examining you." I dutifully apologized, turned my head to be out of range of Grabinski's gyrations, and fixed my gaze on Hawley. It was just as Grabinski had earlier said: He *was* wearing a finely cut Italian suit. (Bought on that ski trip to Chile?). "I'll bet he wears sunglasses indoors," I thought distractedly to myself.

With my gown off, I got a full look for the first time at the girdle of wires and bindings that encircled my stomach and chest. It looked like a homemade bomb about to detonate; I prayed that Special Agent Hawley could deactivate the damned thing before I blew sky-high.

Grabinski, not five feet away, was now dangling his legs off the side of the bed and intently watching Hawley's every move, like some rapt sports fan trying to second-guess the next play. Sensing Grabinski's gaze, Hawley pulled the curtain between the two beds and went back to examining me. He moved the stethoscope around my chest, alternately telling me to breathe deeply, then naturally. He repeated this several times, then put the stethoscope down and sighed. (*Jesus,* I thought, *what's wrong?*)

"The first thing I need to know," Hawley said, "is whether or not you want me to be your cardiologist."

"I thought you already were," I said, surprised.

"You came in through the emergency room," Hawley explained, adding, with a slight sniff: "From off the street. And a good thing, too, since time is critical in these matters."

"Well, they did try to send me home—twice, in fact."

"Yes, I know," he said, waving a manila folder, "I've read your chart. You were wise to persist. Patients often know their bodies better than any physician can."

He opened the folder again. "This history that the resident took down. Did you tell him everything?"

"I answered all his questions."

MARTIN DUBERMAN

"It says here," Hawley said coolly, studying my chart, "that you sometimes use cocaine. Can you be more precise about 'sometimes'?"

I heard a low whistle from Grabinski's bed.

I knew it would be stupid to lie about or even minimize my occasional use of cocaine, but I myself wasn't sure—denial probably playing a role—how to describe my use with precision. I wanted Hawley to know the full truth, but did *I* know it? "I was not a regular user," I finally said. "At a friend's suggestion, I first used cocaine to break a writer's block—I'm a writer, as well as a professor." (This was the moment, I sensed, to get in my credentials.) "The coke did break the block. Then I heard it was great with sex, and so I tried that. That worked, too."

"Contrary to common belief," Hawley said emphatically, "Cocaine is not an aphrodisiac."

"Not in terms of erections maybe, but it sure as hell inflamed my sexual imagination." Grabinski, behind his curtain, let out a loud guffaw.

"Let us not waste time debating fine points," Hawley said, his voice tinged with anger. "How frequently do you use cocaine?"

"Infrequently. My body can't tolerate it more than once in a while. And I hate the hangovers."

"Once a day? A week? A month?"

"Maybe a couple of times a month. But some months not at all. It's hard to give you an accurate picture. I'm more of a binger—an occasional blast." I was trying to give him as honest a picture as I could. "Why? Does this have some relevance to my heart attack?"

"Cocaine is basically a benign drug," Hawley said—to my surprise, and relief. "Only in large doses does its use become problematic. You apparently use it infrequently, in which case I would say cocaine is not a factor in your heart attack. On the other hand, I would hardly recommend its use for someone who's a heart patient."

"Should I *never* use it again?"

"Certainly not for some time. Later, perhaps, much later . . . but only in very moderate amounts."

Astounding as that exchange may sound today, when Len Bias horror stories have long since become commonplace, in the late seventies Hawley's attitude toward cocaine did not brand him as some mad maverick. Over the next few days, I checked out his view with several residents, and all of them confirmed the then-standard attitude that

194

cocaine, used in moderate amounts, was an essentially "benign" drug, posing no significant threat to a healthy person.

Since cocaine was apparently not the villain, I asked Hawley what *did* account for the attack. I was especially curious about why my EKGs had been normal.

"The EKG is a gross diagnostic instrument," Hawley answered.

"Then why use it?"

"You ask a lot of questions, Mr. Duberman."

"I'm an intellectual, what can I tell you?"

Hawley was not easily ruffled. "I suggest we talk more tomorrow. After I get back your blood enzyme results. They will provide the conclusive evidence that an EKG cannot. That is, *if* you decide you want me to take your case."

"Well . . . *yes!* Of course!" (I mean, like what were the options? I already disliked the man, but if I said no, would the hospital send in six other cardiologists to audition?)

Hawley smiled for the first time. "Very well, then, I'll see you in the morning. And every morning thereafter." He turned as if to leave.

"Wait!" I called out, my anxiety suddenly uncorked. I didn't know what I wanted to say, but I knew I needed something more. What came out was a plaintive generality: "Am I going to be . . . okay?"

Hawley stood quite still, letting a beat go by. Then, his voice deliberate, even grave, he said, "I see no signs of complications." Then he paused again. "Frankly, Mr. Duberman, you are something of a medical anomaly."

"I don't much care for the sound of that."

"You're relatively young. You're in excellent shape, have no history of high blood pressure, don't smoke, and don't drink to excess. In short, you should not have had a heart attack."

"Then why did I?"

Hawley managed a thin smile. "That's what we have to find out, isn't it? Despite what you may have heard, Mr. Duberman, cardiology is not an exact science."

"You *are* certain I've had a heart attack?"

"Quite certain. It *did* show up on your third EKG. Showed up quite plainly. I'd say you are very lucky to be alive."

"So everyone's been saying."

"Everyone's right."

He went on to tell me that a heart attack requires prompt treatment, that I had not gotten it, that the mortality rate from first heart attacks— even when promptly treated—was forty percent, and that I had survived only because I was in excellent physical condition. Repeating yet again how "lucky" I was, he then delivered the punch line: "You should know, Mr. Duberman, that your heart muscle has sustained considerable damage."

I involuntarily groaned. "When you say 'damage,' does that mean I'll never be able to—to do much?"

"Not at all," Hawley responded cheerfully. "No such thing. Your prognosis remains excellent. You can come out of this as good as new. This heart attack may prove the best thing that could have happened to you."

"Better than a trip to Europe?" Grabinski called over through the curtain.

Ignoring him, Hawley said that if I heeded the warning given me, I could live out a normal life span—perhaps longer than normal, since I would now be taking better care of myself than most people ever do.

Hugely relieved, I still had to know more. "But you said I'm an anomaly; I had no risk factors. So how can I take better care of myself? I can't give up smoking if I don't smoke. I can't lose weight if I'm not fat, I—"

Hawley interrupted me. "I omitted two risk factors: stress and genetics. Your father, I believe, had his first heart attack while still in his forties?"

"Yes."

"So clearly a genetic predisposition *is* at work."

"Is 'genetics' really a diagnosis—or an excuse for not having one?" I was surprised at my boldness, since I already felt utterly dependent on this man.

Hawley smiled patronizingly. "It is certainly true that we have not yet captured in the microscope the 'gene' for arterial disease. Someday, perhaps."

"Fair enough," I said.

"In any case," Hawley continued, "stress is unquestionably the single most important factor. And it can be inherited." I must have looked puzzled because he went on to explain that while stress "isn't a gene, it, too, can be inherited—as part of a family's lifestyle. You don't yourself seem like a particularly stress-filled person," he added. "At least, not to the casual eye."

I assured him that my friends would readily attest to my qualifications as a classic Type A, a driven, product-oriented perfectionist.

"Fine," Hawley said, "now we have not only the cause of your heart attack, but also its cure. Genes can't be reprogrammed, but a stressful life can." Viewed properly, he said yet again, my heart attack could be seen as a great opportunity. "We will have to discuss this at some length."

With that, he turned again to go. "Could I ask you one other thing?" I said, stopping him halfway out of the door. He turned reluctantly back into the room.

"Yes?"

"The nurse said that if I want a sleeping pill at night, you have to write the order for it. I barely slept last night."

Hawley frowned disapprovingly. "It would be better to do without. We don't like to get patients into bad habits."

"I already have that habit. I've had a sleeping disorder since my college days. My mother did, too."

"I can assure you that sleeping-pill addiction is not passed in the genes from mother to son."

"I never thought it was. But it *can* be part of a family culture. Type A—remember?"

I was getting testy. I had already been through all this with Nurse Liza, had already explained that without a chemical assist I would be unable to sleep—especially given the added terror of being hooked up to a wired corset, expecting the dreaded "code" to be called on me at any moment. I had even balefully predicted a second heart attack induced by withdrawal symptoms. At which point Grabinski had demanded that he be moved to a room "without any addicts in it." I had dutifully laughed, but had secretly thought of having him killed.

"I don't understand," Hawley said haughtily, "why you should feel the need of a sleeping pill every night."

"What is there to understand?" I said, trying to keep my anger under wraps. "I'm your everyday hyper, intense New Yorker."

"You think too much, that's your problem," Grabinski butted in from the next bed. "You intellectuals worry about everything. Everything unimportant."

"You mean unimportant things like heart attacks?" I snarled back. I *was* going to have him killed.

"What is that you take at night?" Hawley asked, cutting back to the issue at hand.

"Doriden," I said.

"That is not a drug I can in good conscience recommend." My guess was that the recreational use of Doriden's kissing cousin, Quaalude, had reached his ears. "I will write you an order for a low dose of Nembutal."

I disliked barbiturates, but wasn't about to argue.

"Thank you," I said, with maximum humility. Hawley, the sharp aroma of moral disapproval at his back, departed.

Grabinski pulled back the curtain separating our beds. "Liza will stand over you while you take it. You know that, don'tcha?"

"Huh?"

"Yeah, that's the rule. You have to swallow the sleeping pill while they watch. They're afraid you'll store them up and commit suicide." For some reason that seemed hugely funny and we both roared.

"Anyway," Grabinski said after we'd quieted down, "now you have the answer: " 'Avoid emotional stress.' Nice work if you can get it, huh? . . . What's *he* got to worry about, with his silk suits," he added grumpily.

I was puzzled over what had made him turn suddenly ill-humored. But I didn't want to ask. I felt drained from the shuttlecock exchange with Hawley.

The silence hung there between us. And silence was a red flag to Grabinski.

"Hello!" he called over after a minute or two, as if rousing the dead. "Hello over there! Remember me—your ICU buddy?"

"Sorry. I'm worn out. Amazing how fast the energy goes. I guess that's called having a heart attack."

Grabinski seemed hurt. "A lot of people around here do that," he said, in what sounded to me like a non-sequitur.

"Do what?"

"Forget I'm alive." There was real pain in his voice. This was not another routine.

"What are you talking about? You're the nurses' pet, anyone can see that."

"Yeah, I know. A laugh a minute. That's Grabinski. But you don't see any of the doctors giving me two minutes of their time, do you?"

"Didn't you tell me that intern couldn't keep his hands off of you?"

"He's an intern. Not a doctor. You know how long Hawley talked to you? Eleven fucking minutes. And he *talked* to you." His anger was palpable—and the reason for it now luminously clear.

"Don't you have a doctor?" I asked tentatively.

"I've got interns. Lots of interns. They troop in and out of here. Twenty-five-year-old brats. One tells me I'm healthy as a bull, gonna be 'just fine.' The next one looks all gloomy at me and says I'm 'a time bomb, ready to go off again at any moment.' "

"He said *that?*"

"But no doctors. Doctors only talk to people with money. Especially a star like Hawley, who can fart and walk at the same time." Grabinski was fuming.

When I tentatively asked about his medical insurance, he let out a derisive snort. He told me that he'd been laid off—"Ironworkers aren't exactly in demand, in case you haven't heard"—and his policy had been dropped.

"How come?"

"When you find out, let me know," Grabinski said bitterly.

"Doesn't the union carry you?"

"The union takes care of its own—those who are working."

"That's awful," I mumbled.

"Yeah, sure is awful," Grabinski snapped. "Why don't you get up at the next Pride rally—he spat the words out—and give a little speech about all those gay men who can't afford their discos and their cocaine; who can't even afford to get sick. Tell 'em I sure am glad some faggots get decent care; we wouldn't want the race to die out, right?"

"I know what you mean," I said feebly. "I understand. . . ."

"Why the fuck would you understand? You've got money."

"Not a lot, no."

Now *I* was feeling hurt. I didn't want to be labeled his class enemy. I was a socialist, for God's sake! A supporter of SDS! An antiwar activist! Fortunately I said none of that. Grabinski may have been gay, but it was already clear that he and I were miles apart politically. My presumed wealth *and* my radical politics would have put me totally beyond the pale.

But I was feeling pretty angry myself. Why was he yelling at *me?* I didn't set up this miserable system. I wasn't responsible for its inequities. Or was I? The mix of feelings came out as the idiotic suggestion that if he asked, maybe Hawley would take him on as a patient.

"Will you pay for it?" Grabinski snarled.

"Don't you have *any* money?"

"Look: I got no money. I got no job. I got no insurance. The picture clear? I live with my seventy-five-year-old sister in a house on Staten Island that our parents left us."

"Jesus!" I said, trying to interrupt the angry flow.

"Right—thanks for reminding me: I got Jesus." He crossed himself, looked toward the wooden crucifix nailed to the wall of our room (and of every room in St. Vincent's), then quieted down a little, enough for me to say something about how I thought it was a law that city hospitals like St. Vincent's had to take in anybody who appeared at its doors.

"Right, they have to take you in—but not keep you. Since the day I arrived in this dump, St. Vincent's has been trying to persuade me to go into a V.A. hospital on Staten Island. You ever been in a V.A. hospital?" I allowed as how I hadn't.

"It figures," he said, the anger back in his voice. "The medical care sucks. V.A. hospitals rank high on *one* statistic: their mortality rate. I'm not leaving here!" He was almost shouting again. "That's it! Period! Let them drag me out if they want!"

I wanted to say something comforting, but drew a blank; what, realistically, *could* be comforting? Only, I suppose, getting across that I did sympathize and wished there was something I could do. But I got tripped up on the fear that sympathy might come across as patronizing, so what came out was some vague reassurance that they could *never* make him leave against his will. Grabinski, of course, knew better. But he let my words go unchallenged.

For a minute or so neither of us spoke. Then Grabinski, his voice much calmer and warmer, said, "Well, at least they put me in a room with another faggot. My luck's not all bad." That was so unexpectedly graceful that I could feel tears well up. Somehow Grabinski had found the magnanimity, despite his misery, to get us out of the logjam. "We oughta be able to help each other in this hellhole," he added.

He must have sensed that I was about to say something weepy and admiring, because he fended it off with a quick return to sarcasm: "Just don't start giving me any of that brotherhood bullshit, okay? I heard all that crap at some Gay Pride rally I made the mistake of going to three years ago. What a load! Because we both suck cock doesn't make us 'brothers'!"

Of course, he had just proven that it wasn't all bullshit. But I settled for an offhanded "It's a promise."

He slipped immediately into high gear. "Now, about that little cocaine heart-to-heart you had with Hawley—man, aren't you the deceptive one," he chortled. "Mr. Brooks Brothers with a needle in his arm!"

I laughed. "Nothing like that. I never shot anything in my life."

"Sure, sure—tell it to the marines! As if I give a shit!"

"Haven't you ever tried it?"

"Twice. Both times it ruined the sex. The first time, all I wanted to do was lick the guy's armpit for twelve hours. The other time, I wanted to put on a black velvet evening gown and play dominatrix with the cop who lives next door."

"Quite a range. True of everybody, I guess, on cocaine. That's what I liked about it."

"Who needs it? Me, I stick to suckin' and fuckin'. That's all I ask outta life. Of course, I do the fucking. The one time I tried it the other way, it felt worse than root canal. But you! I dunno; it's beginnin' to sound to me like you're some sort of sex maniac."

"If only."

"Don't fool me. I can tell. Yup—I can see you at ninety: won't eat your tapioca pudding till you get your blow job. I wanna hear *all* about your sick sex life. Spare me no details. We've got lots of time! . . ."

As Dr. Hawley was leaving my bedside one morning after examining me, he casually threw back over his shoulder, "We'll be starting some heart tests on you, probably tomorrow."

"What tests?" I asked, instantly alarmed at the possibility that some unexpected complication had arisen.

"Oh, pretty routine stuff. Nothing to worry about."

"I'm a worrier. What kind of tests?"

Hawley sighed with annoyance, turned back toward the bed, and begrudgingly said, "We'll be doing an angiogram on you. Now—do you know any more than you did?"

"What's an angiogram?"

Hawley sighed again. "It's a diagnostic tool. It allows us to take pictures of your heart."

"You mean like an X ray?"

"No, this is an internal procedure. We thread a device through an interior artery."

That set all my alarm buttons going. "Why do I need to have that? I thought you said my recovery has been completely normal."

"Angiography gives us a far more complete view of your heart than we can get from any other diagnostic procedure. Once scar tissue begins to form, it obscures the true picture, the extent of blockage." He turned toward the door. He had said all he was going to.

"Will it hurt? I'm a devout coward."

Hawley managed a thin smile. "You'll feel very little. Now stop worrying. Just leave things to us."

Uneasy, I put in a phone call to a friend, Naomi Weisstein, a scientist who was well-connected to a network of physicians. She said she would check with them about the advisability of an angiogram so soon after a heart attack, and get back to me. Though diplomatic in what she said, Naomi sounded apprehensive, which made me still more uneasy. I also ran the idea by a few other close friends. They understandably hesitated to give any firm opinion; the worry lines in their faces gave it for them.

When Naomi got back to me later in the day, she reported that her sources had expressed uniform surprise and some alarm. None of them had heard of an angiogram being done within the first week of a heart attack. None was willing to say outright that I should refuse to go through with it, but all had expressed various degrees of misgiving over what they suspected might be an experimental procedure, and therefore one fraught with potential danger.

The decision was left to me. And, still shaky and weak, I was in no condition to make it. I felt caught in the headlights of an onrushing train, and without the energy to move my body off the track.

Then I remembered Bonnie, an intern who had come to see me soon after I'd been admitted. Bonnie had recognized my name—I had interviewed her parents for one of my books—and had wanted me to know that if I needed anything I could call on her. As luck would have it, she happened to be on rounds that very day, and I asked her if she could spare me a few minutes whenever she had the time.

She came by that same afternoon and I filled her in on what was going on—Hawley's announcement of the angiogram, my friends' uncertain advice about whether I should comply. Bonnie, looking stricken, sat on the edge of my bed and took my hand.

"If you repeat to anyone what I'm about to say," she said gravely, "I will never be allowed to become a doctor. Do you understand?"

I assured her that I did, and that I was deeply grateful to her for taking such a serious risk in my behalf.

"Okay, then. It's like this: St. Vincent's is testing a theory that the best way to get an accurate picture of what's going on, is to do an angiogram as soon after a heart attack as possible. Every patient who arrives at St. Vincent's with a heart attack is getting angiography within the first week. So far there have been no fatalities—"

"*What?*" I interrupted with a gasp.

"Well, you know, don't you, that angiography always carries *some* risk, even when done many months after an attack?"

"I certainly did not know."

Bonnie's brow furrowed in silent disapproval. "Well, you *should* know. You can't make a reasonable decision without all the facts."

"I can't make a decision, *period*. I don't know what to do. Do you think this theory is true?"

"It might well be. No one has an answer yet. . . ."

Her voice trailed off. Neither of us spoke for a while; then I asked her—unfairly, I knew, but I felt desperate—whether, if she were in my position, she would go ahead with the angiogram.

She hesitated, visibly torn about what to do. Then, very quietly, she said, "If I were you, I would refuse to go ahead with the test."

I thanked her, gave her a hug, and told her our conversation had never taken place.

And when Dr. Hawley next appeared in my room, I told *him* that I would not do the angiogram.

He looked stunned, then angry. But—ever the total professional—he quickly regained composure. "That choice is, of course, yours," he said, his lips drawn tight with disapproval. "But as your physician, I must tell you that I feel you have made a very unwise decision."

I then silently made a second decision: As soon as I was safely out of St. Vincent's, I would look for a new cardiologist.

Grabinski was hugely taken with my "bodacity" and as a reward for "bucking the authorities" offered to share his hidden stash of gay porn with me. As we were ogling one of the mags the next day, Liza suddenly walked in and Grabinski tried to push it out of sight. But in case she had already caught a glance, he explained (*much* too breathlessly) that "some gay guy on my block who's been trying to get into my pants" had sent him "this weirdo physique magazine. It's got this article on intestinal parasites," Grabinski rushed on, "which he's trying to convince me is the reason I get these stomach problems. He wants to believe I have this secret gay life that I won't admit to him."

Liza raised her eyebrows suspiciously, but avoided saying anything more than, "You are a weird one, Grabinski."

That episode, in combination with my refusal to have an angiogram, produced a distinct change in the staff's attitude. Liza, the nurse who knew Grabinski and me best, remained friendly, if a little less willing to trade mock insults. But there were several incidents that suggested word of my "rebelliousness" (and/or "queerness") had quickly gotten around. I would henceforth be known as a "difficult" patient, meaning one who did not automatically do as he was told and who thereby jeopardized hospital routine and lines of authority.

I'll never be sure, but it seemed no coincidence that the technician who'd previously drawn blood no longer drew mine. Instead an intern was sent in, an intern who confessed—after jabbing my veins five times with no result—that I was his very first assignment, someone to "practice" on. Grabinski, understandably, found my loss of privileged status highly gratifying, and with the class lines between us less distinct, we drew closer.

The most telling indicator of my reduced status revolved around what Grab (as he now told me to call him) and I later referred to as the Drama of the Impacted Stool. Four or five days into the heart attack, I still hadn't had a bowel movement. So when it finally felt as if I was about to, I rang the nurse's bell for the portable potty. In came Alicia, a sour-faced nurse I had seen only once or twice before. She scowled with displeasure, took thirty minutes to return with the potty, told me to "mount it"—and was gone.

As Grabinski made noisy genuflections toward the "throne," I waited—and waited—for release. Every five minutes or so, I'd get a wave of contractions and feel sure success was at hand. But the wave would pass—and no stool. Finally, I gave up and rang for Alicia. The news that I had *not* produced a stool led to a hands-on-hip scowl, as if I had deliberately turned in a false alarm to annoy her. When I told her I was in considerable discomfort and suggested she send for a floor doctor, she stormed away at me: "You think you're the *only* patient on this floor?" she bellowed. "You're not a privileged character, you know." (Well, *now* I knew.) "You'll be seen when it's your turn to be seen."

After yet another half-hour, an intern did arrive; he decided I had an impacted stool, announced grimly, "I hate this procedure!" and extracted the stool manually. He was fairly gentle, though I could have done without his periodically saying, "I'm trying to go slow so we don't unduly strain your heart." I wanted to say, "It couldn't be more of a strain than sitting on the potty for an hour trying to *push* out a stool." Thereafter Alicia was known to Grab and me as "Hitler's Bride."

The drama over, Grab and I turned to our nightly argument over what to watch on TV. Of late we'd been resolving our differing tastes with a minimum of friction, but that night—I accused him of being grumpy about all that anal play I'd had with the intern—he was intractable. A *long* boxing special was scheduled for the entire evening—Sugar Ray Leonard versus Andy Price! Duran versus Gonzalez! Holmes versus Spinks!—which Grabinski insisted he had to watch in its entirety, and with the set at maximum volume. I fumed and argued, but to no avail.

When, in my annoyance as the *third* hour of televised boxing unfolded, I dared refer to the so-called sport as "brutal," Grabinski scorned me as a "bleeding heart." When I asked him to turn the volume down a *little,* so I could read, he said, "Too much reading has turned you into a pussy." When I told him I *had* to watch the ten o'clock news, he advised me it would be the same as last night's. When I accused him of unfairly hogging the set, he accused me of being menopausal.

"Now that's a thought," I said. "Maybe I am."

"Now what are you talking about?" Grabinski said, clearly displeased at the de-escalation.

"Men *do* go through menopause, you know."

"Speak for yourself."

"I am. Maybe that's what this is all about." Grabinski groaned at the prolonged interruption.

"What *what* is about?" he said irritably.

"The staleness I've been feeling these past few years."

"Oh poor you," Grabinski shot back. "I'll bet your professor's salary is a mere thirty thousand bucks a year." Chastened, I didn't dare admit that it was in fact forty thousand. "Now will you please *shut up*," he said, "so I can watch this." And with that he turned resolutely back to the screen.

The class lines might have softened, but they were still intact.

OVER THE NEXT FEW DAYS, Dr. Hawley continued to show up for my daily examination. His manner seemed little changed—which is to say, he was as contained and uncommunicative as ever. And he continued to assure me that my recovery was proceeding in an "uneventful" way—"though, of course, only an angiogram could have given us a true picture of what is going on with you."

What *was* changed was his willingness to answer my persistent (and admittedly repetitive) questions with even the minimal responses he had previously mustered. "I've already answered that," he would say, when I asked whether it was really true that I could "come out of this as good as new." And to my apprehensive, "How could that be, when you've also said the damage to my heart has been extensive?" I would get a steely, "Because it can."

I had other anxieties that I knew better than to express to Hawley (or to Grabinski). Even if I did make a full recovery over time, who would take care of me in the short run? I lived alone; would I be able to shop or cook meals? Would I be able to navigate the flights of stairs up to my apartment? How long would I have to stay in the hospital? When could I go back to teaching? Would CUNY give me a paid leave, and if not, how could I afford to live?

During that first week, some of those worries got resolved. Friends and colleagues flooded the room with greeting cards and flowers (one wag reported that the history department had voted five to one, with one absention, in favor of my recovery); the chair of the department assured me that I would get at least a term's leave, and probably more if I needed it, at full pay. My sister, who also lived alone, offered to take me in for a few weeks after I left the hospital. Though I didn't think that was a good idea, given the periodic tensions in our relationship and the importance (in my mind) of becoming independent again as soon as possible, I thanked her for her generosity and promised to think about it.

Few people had been allowed in to see me during the first week. The intensive care unit had strict rules: Only relatives could visit, only one at a time, and only from two-thirty to three o'clock each after-noon. My biological family was a small one; both my parents were dead and I felt strongly connected only to my mother's two sisters, Theresa and Flo, and to Flo's son, Ron (who was then living with his own family in Belgium). So I was able to pawn off two close friends, Barbara Hart and Seymour Kleinberg, as relatives, and they, along with my sister, dropped in nearly every day.

To Grabinski's mind, this constituted a crowd. He had not had a single visitor of his own that first week, and it was painful to watch him try, as a forlorn substitute, to chat up anyone who came to see me— even as he visibly fought off resentment at the attention and support I was getting. It was the same story with the mail. Grabinski never seemed to get any, and after a few days I took to concealing mine, or pretending that the get-well cards were "bills that had been for-warded."

At the end of the first week, I was allowed some non- family visitors, and they brought a decided brightening in Grabinski's mood. With some he was able to argue; others he could ogle. With Pete—he who had engineered the LSD trip with Dr. Martino—he did both. Pete was convinced that I had had a heart attack because I was "blocked up" with unresolved grief over the death of my mother and the breakup with Gary, which had left me, as he put it, "unattended, unloved."

As remedy, Pete was quick to urge one or another of his ongoing discoveries from the world of "alternative healing." Initially he pushed acupuncture as the quickest way to "unblock and shift my energy." He knew an acupuncturist, he said, who made hospital calls, and was *sure* that St. Vincent's would agree to a consultation; or, that failing, he offered to "sneak" the acupuncturist into my room. "Rubbish," said Grabinski. "I'd rather take my chances with cobra extract."

The two of them went at it for the remainder of the visit. To Gra-binski's remarks about "planetary platitudes," Pete (rightly reading Grabinski as Catholic), countered with, "Just like the notion of a Virgin birth." Grab reddened with anger. "I suppose," he sputtered at Pete, "you also believe in Hare Krishna, Scientology, and all the rest of that moronic bullshit, like est." I myself regarded Scientology as wiring and tin cans, and as for est, I was convinced that nobody with Werner

Erhard's smug composure and shallow sloganeering could possibly know anything important about the human condition. But I knew Pete had dabbled in both—and was about to rise to Grabinski's bait. So I jumped back to the comparatively benign subject of heart attacks.

It didn't work. Pete soon left, with a curt nod to Grabinski and a final warning to me that I was in dire danger from both an insufficient will to live and the "pseudo-rational" hospital rituals.

GRABINSKI'S REACTION TO PETE was benign compared to the fury he worked up at my colleague, Ann. She taught American literature, was single, was given to a steady patter of arch complaints about the fact, and arrived bearing a stuffed chicken she had cooked herself ("as proof *I* can care, not that you are cared about.") Those amenities over, Ann wanted to know *exactly* how I was feeling.

"Better," I said noncommittally.

"On some days, he can make it rain," Grab put in from left field. He had obviously disliked Ann on sight.

She ignored him, sensing trouble. "No, no, no," she said impatiently to me. "I mean, what have you learned from your brush with death? How has it changed you?"

"It's made him very nervous," Grabinski said before I could answer.

I said, "It hasn't taught me anything, at least not yet."

Doubly stymied, Ann clucked in disapproval and shifted to telling me about the "wonderfully received" lecture she had recently given at Swarthmore on "the cult of domesticity in the nineteenth-century novel." I smiled feebly; Grabinski picked up a magazine.

From there, she segued into her own unhappy domestic plight and how tough it was for a single woman in her forties to get laid. "Especially," she added, "in academia, where all the energy goes to the head and everything else atrophies."

"It's not that easy for gay men over forty, either," I offered tentatively.

Ann got all huffy. "Poor baby! No place to go but Turkish baths and backroom bars! And if you get desperate, you can tootle off to your hustler bar of choice. I couldn't find anyone to pay for it if I wanted to. *I* have to settle for the Metropolitan Museum on Sunday afternoons!"

"Want me to fix you up?" I offered. "Almost every hustler I've ever known swears he's bisexual."

"Meaning he likes blond men *and* Latin men."

Grabinski was now back on the alert. "Nobody's bisexual. That's just a bullshit cop-out."

"No," I contradicted, "some people *are*."

Ann cut through the budding argument with a heartfelt "God, I wish *I* was gay! Women are so much *nicer* than men! But I, alas, am stuck with heterosexuality. And that's why I made the decision I did today."

Which was when it came out: Ann had decided on an "ass-lift" to compensate for her diminishing allure.

"A *what?*" Grab bellowed. "What the fuck is an ass lift?"

Ignoring him, Ann zeroed in on me. "Now, don't try to talk me out of it," she insisted, before I'd said a word. Ten days after a heart attack I didn't have the interest or energy to argue her out of *anything*. It still exhausted me just to wash myself—*in* bed.

"My mind's made up," she went on. "It's a very common procedure."

"I've never heard of it before," I said blandly.

"I thought gay men were interested in asses."

"Not in sagging asses," Grabinski offered sourly.

"Well, of course not!" Ann responded, with a little screech. "That's my point."

"Why not just exercise more?" I asked.

"Surgery is more reliable. I might just splurge and go to Dr. Porteno—you know, the surgeon in Brazil who does all the jet-setters."

"Doesn't sound like something you oughta cut corners on," Grabinski offered deadpan, glowering. He looked as if he might hit her.

She got the message, and was out of the door within minutes, pleading the need to prepare for the next day's classes. I sighed with relief and thought of asking Nurse Liza to re-instate the "family-only" visitors policy.

I tried to assure Grabinski that the "ass-lift" had been an elaborate put-on, that Ann was a genuinely nice person given to occasional fits of bitterness. Grab would have none of it. He mumbled off and on for days about "privileged bitches worried about sagging asses when half the world goes to bed hungry at night." At one point, he made me laugh out loud: "If age flattens your ass, it at least oughta firm up your character."

I agreed—this was wisdom—and only hoped that when and if my friend Robert returned from his vacation in Italy, he wouldn't spend his *entire* hospital visit describing how beautiful and inexpensive the Italian boys were.

Not that I was counting on a visit. A close friend of twenty-five years' standing, Robert, on learning of my heart attack, had sent a huge box of calla lilies—flowers I had always lugubriously associated with death—and had promptly decamped for Italy. From there, I received exactly two postcards, one professing boredom and the other astonishment at the ready availability, for cash, of Italian teenagers.

His withdrawal hurt me deeply and when, many months later, I told him so, his explanation was that when someone he cared about was in serious trouble for which he could find no solution, he had to distance himself; it was a trait he didn't much like in himself but felt he had no control over. I tried that on for size and decided it just wasn't good enough; when a friend was in crisis one *had* to be there, whether or not it was psychologically difficult (or, as I suspected in Robert's case, personally inconvenient). Our friendship never recovered.

I was often surprised at who did or did not appear at the hospital. Robert's absence was as much of a surprise as Jan's presence. He and I had had a brief affair four or five years earlier that had long since dissolved into an infrequent dinner. Within a minute of meeting Jan, Grabinski took to calling him "Chopin," in honor of his gentle, melancholy good looks. After Jan left, Grabinski, frantic with envy, demanded to know why we weren't still lovers. When I guiltily mumbled something about Jan having been too unrelentingly passive and adoring, Grabinski went through the roof.

"You are fucking *nuts,* do you know that? Anybody who wants to worship at *my* feet can stay for the rest of his life!" He never tired thereafter of telling me how hot Jan was and what a jackass *I* was for not keeping him chained to the bed. "*Your* trouble," he said, "is that you're so wrapped in intellectual bullshit and that gay lib crap that you can't appreciate a good piece of ass when it's dumped in your lap. You keep thinking of gay men as your 'brothers' and you'll never get a hard-on again. Unless you're into incest." He grinned happily.

"I stopped being active in gay politics a while ago."

"Maybe that's what broke your heart. Maybe you should rejoin." Grabinski snapped on the television set; he'd had his say.

That was an unexpected zinger, I thought: "Maybe that's what broke your heart." I couldn't get it out of my head.

★   ★   ★

WITHIN TEN DAYS OF THE HEART ATTACK, I was considered improved enough to be given bathroom privileges; soon after that, I was allowed to paddle *slowly* down the corridor twice a day. Then, some two and a half weeks after the attack, I was awarded "film privileges." That meant not a riotous night out with the Marx Brothers, but the right to sit in the corridor lounge and watch the film *My Heart Attack,* as narrated by the ancient projectionist, Sister Bernadette (she of the miracles).

The film actually proved informative. I learned that a myocardial infarction (the official name for a heart attack) was brought on by an accumulation of plaque in a coronary artery. As for what caused the accumulation, there were a variety of theories (science apparently being very similar to history), including some recent studies that suggested plaque accumulation was less significant in causing heart attacks than were "severe life stresses." The specific items mentioned—from carrying a large mortgage to marital troubles to job insecurity—seemed largely irrelevant to my own circumstances; but there was no denying that, as I had told Dr. Hawley, I was boilerplate Type A. The film offered much technical information about how, under extreme stress, the cerebral cortex could—by a process "not yet fully understood" (meaning, of course, not understood at all)—send the muscles of the heart into dangerous spasms known as fibrillations.

The film's ultimate message, though, was upbeat: Lots of "exciting" new treatments had become available. There were beta blockers and bypass surgery, ultrasound imaging and balloon angioplasty, electrophysiology and implantable defibrillators. I found the words scary, to say nothing of the gruesome procedures the film insisted on detailing; it was more than I wanted to know—or could thereafter forget.

The film concluded with a recovery program "designed especially for you" (and doubtless for the four quite different patients watching with me, as well). Within six to eight weeks of the attack, I was to be allowed modest walks. ("Thirty years ago, the average American walked four and a half miles daily; today, to our detriment, we walk only one and a half miles.") The film also recommended that I develop the habit of standing while talking on the phone, that I avoid large meals at night, and that I buy a pedometer in a sporting goods store. In a few months, I would progress to a stationary bike—but only when

211

supervised at a special cardiac treatment center. It seemed one could suddenly pop off from "unauthorized acceleration."

From now on, the film warned, I had to be very careful about my diet and my weight, avoiding all animal fat and fried foods, and loading up on fish, fruits, and vegetables. That was precisely the diet I had long been on, give or take the occasional ice-cream-and-cookie orgy. But then I had already heard from Dr. Hawley that I lacked all the usual risk factors, except for stress and genetics.

The film was downright hectoring on the subject of stress, expounding relentlessly on the relentlessness of the Type A personality. We *must,* Sister Bernadette intoned, recognize our limitations, stop fancying ourselves as "searchers" or "artists" pushing ever onward into the unknown. We were to count the blessings we had rather than hankering after those we had not. Wanting to believe those basic transformations possible, I silently vowed to take up yoga and meditation again.

Above all, the film counseled, we were to "avoid emotional stress; nothing should become important enough to raise your blood pressure." Like injustice? Like sex? As if reading my mind, Sister Bernadette promptly said: "And after a few months, you will be able to return to sex, at least in modified form." What was "modified" sex? Did that mean sex without love, or sex only with love? I made a note to ask Dr. Hawley for a definition when I next saw him; that ought to drive him crazy, I thought.

It did not. At least initially, he treated my questions about sex as if they were among the most familiar (and tedious) in the heart attack patient's repertoire, and he settled for a stern summary remark: "You cannot expect to jump back into life immediately. Any questions you might have about sex are premature."

"Is that like the orgasm?" Grab—who was already eavesdropping—put in. (He had earlier predicted, "If you want to see paranoia big-time, wait until you ask them about sex.")

Unrattled, Hawley replied coldly, "I have to remind myself constantly, Mr. Grabinski, that there are no stupid questions—other than unasked ones."

Grab, familiar with WASP patronization, immediately flared. "The only questions you guys seem to like around here are the ones relating to insurance policies and wills."

212

At that moment, the floor nurse arrived to cart Grabinski off for "tests." "Tests" were always unspecified and always required a minimum wait of two hours, the patients lined up in wheelchairs in the corridors while the X-ray technicians cracked jokes with each other or traded ball scores as they ambled lazily through their routines.

Furious that he was being removed from a conversation about to center on sex—that is, if *he* had anything to say about it—Grabinski tried his best to postpone departure. First he claimed he was "under the weather" and needed to rest. When the nurse irritably told him to *get into the wheelchair,* he wanted to know whether they were actually ready for him—or, as he put it, whether "the runway was clear for takeoff." To which the nurse snidely replied that she hadn't known he was on such a tight schedule.

"So," I said, turning nervously to Hawley, "I would like to have at least some preliminary answers about sex."

Hawley avoided my eyes. "You are doing *very* well, Mr. Duberman. So far there are no complications of any kind. But a heart attack *is* a heart attack. In my experience, it's much more difficult for a young man, a relatively young man, to deal with a heart attack than for an older man already less active in his life."

What was that uncharacteristically long speech about? I wondered anxiously. *Is he telling me I can't ever again risk having sex?* But what I said was, "Hell, I was playing squash three times a week!" I was surprised at the vehemence in my voice. "I was beating twenty-five-year-olds. Regularly!"

"Squash is not a sport we recommend for middle-aged men," Hawley said evenly.

"Yeah, I know," I said, hurt to the quick at the demotion. "From now on I'll be riding a stationary exerbike three times a week, to the accompaniment of Mantovani."

Hawley was not deterred. "As the film has already told you, Mr. Duberman, soon after you leave the hospital in another few days, it *will* be perfectly safe for you to have modified sex. I mean, you're not planning to have sex while still *in* the hospital, are you?" From Hawley, that was a major humanizing note.

I laughed, brushing away the vision of me and Grab getting it on under an oxygen tent, then joining in an assault on the intern with the blond personality. I said something more or less mature about being the kind of person who likes to plan ahead, who needs to have something to look forward to.

"If all goes well—and I see no reason why it should not—you will be able to have modified sex in six weeks' time. Now you have something to look forward to. Like any physical activity, of course, sexual intercourse places demands on the heart, increases its need for blood. If the blood flow is not sufficient, the result can be angina. Or worse."

I must have looked alarmed, because Hawley immediately went on to add that patients tended to overestimate the amount of energy expended in sexual intercourse. "The strain on the heart is about the equivalent of climbing two flights of stairs."

"Oh, I have to climb more than that to my apartment," I said with a bright, happy face.

But Hawley was ready with the downer: "Death during intercourse is a rare event, even when undertaken a few weeks after a heart attack. Just to be sure, take a nitroglycerin pill before and after. And stick to modified sex."

"Intercourse"? "Intercourse"? He had used the word three times. It had begun to grate; it was not a word gay people used about gay sex. And as for "modified sex"—that had to be at least the fifth repetition.

"What *is* modified sex?" I finally burst out. "Does that mean sex with yourself? Sex with your clothes on? Sex with someone you do—or don't—love?"

Hawley actually chuckled. "I would have thought it was perfectly obvious what 'modified sex' means."

"Well, it isn't. Not to me. People have sex in quite different ways." I realized I had opened the path to a discussion I wasn't sure I wanted to have. But I needn't have worried: Hawley didn't get it. The hospital scuttlebutt about the two queers apparently hadn't penetrated his Olympian fortress, or he wasn't going to admit it had.

"Modified sex," he recited in a singsong voice, "means the man lies on his back, the woman straddles him, places his penis into her vagina, and moves up and down until she brings him to orgasm."

Dumbfounded, I resorted to political correctness as a delaying strategy. "Brings *him* to orgasm? What about *her*?"

"We leave it to each couple to work out the details," Hawley said haughtily. I could tell he was about to bolt. "As you know," I said tentatively, "I'm not married. I'm not part of a couple."

Again picking up the wrong cue, perhaps deliberately, Hawley became stern again. "Impersonal sex—sex with strangers—should be avoided. It entails too much anxiety. Studies suggest that the risk of heart attack *is* greater during extramarital sex."

I tried another delaying tactic. "My pattern's the reverse. I feel more anxiety having sex with someone I care about—because of the need to please and impress." Even *I* thought that sounded a bit bizarre, but I postponed self-recrimination for later.

"I see," Hawley said noncommittally.

I wanted to scream, *"You don't see! What I'm really into is smelling piss-stained jockstraps!"* But since I wasn't, and did want an answer, I said instead, with some exaggeration, "I have been seeing one person fairly regularly."

"Fine," said Hawley. "For now confine your sexual activities to her."

That was it—he'd pushed me over the edge. "It's not a her. It's a him," I blurted out.

"I see," said Hawley, falling back on his signature phrase. He recovered so rapidly, I barely caught the momentary twitch. "The same advice holds," he said tersely. Then he turned to leave.

"No, it doesn't," I said with some force. Suddenly, all the throttles were open. "And he isn't much into getting fucked. He can't do it at all in the 'modified sex' position. Besides, he doesn't believe in one person doing all the work. Nor do I." Whew!

"My training is in cardiology," Hawley said icily.

That further incited me. "My questions involve cardiology."

"Not in any way that I can see."

"Let me spell a few out then. Is there an advisable length of time for having sex?"

"I believe ten minutes proves adequate for most men."

"Not for most gay men."

"Yes, I've heard you homosexuals are—how shall I say?—obsessional about sex." He was dripping acid.

"And is sex three or four times a week excessive?"

"I believe the more apt word might be insatiable."

"Gay people *like* sex," I said, smiling the smile that aims to kill.

"You'll have to excuse me now, Mr. Duberman. I have other patients to see."

"Then let me get to the bottom line." I was so flushed with anger, I was afraid to vent it directly—afraid I could bring on another heart attack, afraid that Hawley might abandon me before I could fire him.

"I have scant knowledge of variant positions," Hawley said. He might just as well have said "of variant lifestyles." "Anyone with a history of heart disease," he added coldly, "would be ill advised to allow their pulse rate to go above 120 during sex. You'll have to work out the details for yourself. I will see you tomorrow morning." With that, there was no holding him further. He turned and walked out.

WHEN GRABINSKI GOT BACK from X ray in the record time of an hour and a half, I was still simmering. I gave him a brief replay, highlighting my daring and Hawley's iniquity, and he chuckled merrily throughout. This disconcerted me. I had expected him to be as indignant as I was.

"Well what didja expect, Professor?" he said, laughing. "This is *their* place. The hospital. The planet. They own it all. They own the fuckin' world. I thought a political type like you would have learned *that* much! *They don't give a shit about us!* Hell, if they really wanted us to get well, they'd provide us with a daily supply of huggers! That's what we *really* need!"

"With *what?*" I had come to expect these lightning-quick Grabinski shifts, but still couldn't always distinguish comic effect from comic intent.

"Forget your IVs, your EKGs—patients need hugging! Every hospital oughta hire professional huggers."

"Well, you softy, you!"

Seeing I was touched, Grabinski shifted straightaway onto the safer ground of camp.

"I'm not saying, mind you, that hugging would help as much as some nice hot cum trickling down my throat. That's the real mother's milk."

"Did you know cum *eats* cholesterol?" I said, trying to top him, needing a little delirium. "It's true! A gay doctor friend told me."

"I'm gonna ring for Nurse Liza," Grab said deadpan. "They might as well do a bypass on you right now. Brain bypass."

We were now in synch, racing together toward complete silliness.

Grab suddenly stuck his hand up, as if halting traffic, and in a hushed, melodramatic voice asked me if I'd been "abusing" myself again. He advised me to "tell the truth—as your priest, I can take it."

None of this was very funny, but we were shaking with laughter.

Suddenly, Nurse Liza appeared in the doorway, hands on hips, the pretense of a scowl contradicted by the merriment in her eyes.

"Are you boys crazy?" she asked with mock severity. "We can hear you down the end of the hall! Are you looking to make yourselves sick, or what?"

"We *are* sick, nursie dear," Grabinski managed to say between stiffled laughs, "you don't know the half of it!" Suddenly we were howling again, as if Grabinski had just made the funniest joke in the world.

Liza now looked a little alarmed. "Awright," she said, "that's enough. Now cut it out. You're gonna do yourselves some real harm if you keep this up."

She came over to the side of my bed and practically pinned my shoulders against the pillows. Gradually, I subsided. That is, until Grabinski, keeping an absolutely straight face, turned a furrowed brow to Liza. "Isn't this pathetic?" he asked, pointing to me. "Don't you think you better send in an intern to have a look at Duberman? In fact, maybe two interns. It must be those anal warts that have been bothering him."

Liza squinted suspiciously. She knew Grabinski was putting her on, but couldn't quite pinpoint the degree.

Then he suddenly overreached. "I've been meaning to ask you something, Nurse Liza," he began blandly.

"Yes?"

"Your boyfriend works for United Parcel, doesn't he?"

"How did you know that?" she answered sharply.

"Oh, you know—hospital scuttlebutt. The same way you know about the two of us, right?" Grabinski didn't even pause for the beat. "Anyway, what I want to know is, is the rumor true that lots of those high school athlete types United Parcel hires wear black pantyhose under their uniforms? Mind you, I'm a big fan of high school athletics. Watch every Staten Island High home game."

Liza literally gasped, marched straight out of the room, scrowling angrily and mumbling something about our minds being sicker than our bodies.

It even brought *me* back to earth.

"Grabinski, you really are something," I said in genuine awe. "We have to take your show on the road."

"Shut up, you fool, and pass me the poppers."

★ ★ ★

THE VERY NEXT DAY, all the life-sustaining laughter dissolved in tears. Liza came into our room to inform Grabinski that he was being transferred to the Manhattan V.A. hospital. "Your blood enzymes are negative, and you're no longer in any danger of a heart attack. They'll do some further tests on you at the V.A." Liza said it all with her eyes averted, as if confessing that she was fabricating. Grabinski flushed with anger and started yelling that it was "all a goddamned lie—all lies! You're trying to get rid of me 'cause I don't have any insurance—like my fancy friend Duberman! Right? *Right?* It's a fucking *caste system,* that's what it is!"

To my astonishment, Grab suddenly began to cry. Huge tears streamed down his cheeks. His chest heaved with sobs. Then the anger surged back: "I'm not leaving here, you hear me? I'm *not leaving here!*" He was off his bed now, shouting. Liza fled the room, returning seconds later accompanied by two orderlies and a floor doctor.

One of the orderlies asked Grabinski where his locker was. When he refused to say, Liza pointed to it and the orderly started to pack up Grab's things. They were transfering him *now*—then and there!

I finally found my own voice. "Hey, wait a minute. You can't do this. You haven't even given him any time to prepare. . . ."

Liza looked embarrassed. The orderlies acted as if they were deaf. One continued to pack; the other went out into the corridor, returned with a wheelchair, and told Grabinski to get into it.

"You'll have to fucking *drag* me out," he said, tears still in his eyes. "I'm a fucking taxpayer, you hear? You can't *make* me leave!"

"You'll get good care at the V.A.," Liza said weakly, looking as if she was about to cry herself. "Really, Grabinski, the Manhattan V.A. is a *good* hospital. I promise you."

Grabinski gestured angrily toward the young floor doctor, who'd been standing there, flustered and passive. "I recognize you!" Grabinski yelled at him. "Don't think I don't remember you! *You're* the guy who told me that first night that I had a 'serious heart problem.' So suddenly it's not serious anymore, huh? 'Cause now you found out I don't have any goddamned insurance to line your pockets! You'll get yours, buddy—don't worry, you'll get yours. I'll see to it!"

To my surprise, the doctor's response was gentle and honest. "I'm sorry, Mr. Grabinski, really I am. We wish we could keep you here, but the rules are the rules. . . . It's not exactly a fair situation. I know that. . . ."

The acknowledgment quieted Grabinski down. For a few seconds everyone was frozen in place. Then one of the orderlies stepped toward Grabinski. "Awright, awright," Grab said in a dispirited voice, "I'm coming." He knew damned well they *would* drag him out, and he decided to go on his own terms. He came over to me and gave me a big, prolonged bear hug. I was crying now, too.

"*You,* I'll see!" he said, as he disengaged and bravely tried to flash a smile. "How about Ty's, Saturday night at six?"

"You're on," I said. "I'll have them wheel me over."

"And don't forget to bring my mags," he added as he settled down into the wheelchair. "You can have them this week, no longer."

As they wheeled him out, I called after him, "Hey, Grab! Grab! I'm listed in the phone book!"

"Yeah, yeah, I'll call you." The words echoed distantly as they pushed him down the hall.

And that was it—gone, just like that. Gone for good, as it turned out. We did talk once on the phone, when he called me several months later. We even said something about getting together for a reunion after we "got our sea legs back."

But we never did. We had drawn together for sustenance, two odd ducks trying to quack loud enough in unison to ward off the terrors of being caught in a "total institution" utterly under *their* control. We had made each other laugh, manufactured just enough courage to dilute our shared sense of helplessness, provided our own version of intensive care. But back out in the "real" world, we fell prey to habit, reestablished more familiar alliances, let go of St. Vincents's painful, poignant memories as quickly as we could.

I WAS MYSELF DISCHARGED a few days later. Discharged the decorous way: No orderlies threatening to drag me out; no worries overwhelming me about the quality of my future health care. Loving friends bundled me safely off to my own apartment, and the staff huddled round to wish me bon voyage. (Well, Liza did, anyway; most of the others waved a perfunctory good-bye from a distance.)

And Dr. Hawley, ever correct, came by for a final summarizing chat; a pervert I might be, but I was his patient and doing the "professional" thing was central to his self-image.

"Your heart attack," he told me, looking out over my forehead, "represents an opportunity, properly viewed, to change your life. If you are wise, you will seize it. I would urge you to consider psychotherapy."

When I explained that I had already spent many years in psychotherapy, Hawley said, "Perhaps you were in the wrong hands." (I had spent many years hearing that, too.) When I alluded to my several forays into "alternative therapies," Hawley tersely dismissed "that sort of thing" as "unscientific," not something he could recommend.

"Whether or not you decide to give psychotherapy another try is entirely your decision," Hawley said, indifference etched in his voice. "But I can tell you this much without qualification: If you do not make real changes in your lifestyle, you are an excellent candidate for a second attack. And a third—should you survive the second. You must find some way to reduce stress in your life. Genetics may have predisposed you to a heart attack, but by itself didn't cause it. Stress did."

"But don't all New Yorkers live with too much stress?" I asked, already knowing the answer, and looking more for another argument than for enlightenment.

"*Some* stress is necessary, can even be creative when properly managed. You lead a life *centered* on stress."

Undoubtedly true—and difficult to hear when encased in such obvious disdain. Hawley never used the words, but he might just as well have said outright that as a responsible physician he had gone through the motions, but really didn't give much of a damn *what* I—a degenerate—did after I was out of his sight. Even if I had not earlier decided to find a new doctor, I had the strong sense that he would have told me his practice was already full.

FOR SOME SIX MONTHS after being discharged from the hospital, I had limited mobility and steady anxiety about physical symptoms (chest pain, fatigue, depression) that periodically convinced me another attack was imminent. My new doctor, less judgmental but far more directive than Hawley, gave me strict instructions to get back into life as quickly as possible—but not *too* quickly. Go calculate *that* formula on a daily basis! The sum of what it seemed to mean for the first six weeks was that I should not climb the flight of stairs in my apartment more than once a day, and should remain utterly cheerful (like Hawley, the new doctor kept repeating how "lucky" I was to "still be here").

I remained "cheerful" mostly by staring almost nonstop into the television tube. I hadn't even owned a set previously, but friends loaned me one, and I became gratefully devoted to it, to being able to space out, content irrelevant, at my fourth movie of the day, my fifteenth newscast. Beyond that, I did little except go for checkups, ride the exerbike at the Cardiac Fitness Center, prepare "sensible" meals, and try to "redo my attitudes toward life" (another of the new doctor's directives). "If you intend to survive," he said, "it is essential to develop habits of modest expectation," to aim at "emotional equilibrium," and to forgo forever the "high-intensity drive"—romance! Broadway!— "that has previously ruled your life."

Oh, is that *all I have to do to survive? And you say I have* weeks *to accomplish the transformation?* After a lifetime's training in pushing for more and better, for placing difficult demands on myself and others, I was now to adopt (or was it *pretend* to adopt?) a posture of placidity utterly foreign to my nature. I was to become the man who wanted little and was happy (*oh* so happy!) with what he had. It was like telling a linebacker to drop his cleats and play contentedly at the minuet of croquet.

It was hard going on all counts. I gritted my teeth, kept my eyes glued to the tube, and tried to ignore the refusal of my gut to stop churning, my moods to stop careening, my flounder dinners to stop leaving me screaming for a hot fudge sundae. I tried to take on faith the guiding assumption behind my new regimen: that if I *acted* serene long enough, I would end up *feeling* serene. New behavior repeated often enough purportedly becomes habit; and habit, in time, reprograms internal desire, even temperament. I could, after all, become a daffodil.

It was the better part of a year before my energy and confidence came back with any consistency. The real milestone in my recovery came after a thallium stress test revealed some obstruction of arterial blood flow on the right side of the heart, but none on the more critical left side. Horowitz, my new doctor, called that a good result. He took me off Inderal, and said for the first time that he saw no reason, at least for now, to contemplate either an angiogram or bypass surgery.

Thrilled and relieved, I finally began to emerge from depression and from the feeling that (as I had written a friend the previous year) "I've lost ambition and buoyancy." Now, in 1980, I felt otherwise, felt some kind of rewarding life might still lie ahead. It seemed a good time to take stock, to begin to sort out what (and who) did or did not matter to me, to try to think about what had caused the two-year stalemate, personal and professional, that had preceded the heart attack—and to try and avoid a recurrence.

Those two years had seen many losses—primarily my mother, but also Gary, and also the sense of lively engagement, political and professional. The country's turn to the right and the gay movement's (to my mind) one-dimensional absorption in a reformist civil rights agenda had left me feeling politically unanchored and disillusioned. But in distancing myself from the gay movement, I now realized, I had put myself at a distance, too, from absorbing activity that had filled my days, puffed up my self-esteem, and given me some cherished friendships.

Similarly, I had experienced a vacuum in my life as a scholar. I had begun to reinvent myself as a historian of sexuality, but the large-scale history of sexual behavior that I had embarked on back in 1974 had ultimately run into so many research obstacles and such yawning gaps in the available evidence that by 1978, I had abandoned the project as prematurely ambitious. And no new large-scale project had replaced it. As for my alternative life as a writer, I no longer felt on—or even near—"the verge" as a playwright.

My personal life had underscored rather than compensated for the professional staleness. It had continued to be marked by some decent friendships, some short-term affairs, and a variety of sexual adventures. I hadn't in any sustained way managed to combine sex and love in one package, and the cultural bill of goods I'd been sold (or was it a set of universal truths?) continued to insist that life was best when one *did* combine the two. Whether or not that was true, I had to face up to the fact that I hadn't even managed the two separate halves very well. I often tended to choose as friends people as self-absorbed and career-oriented as myself—and then dared to feel hurt and surprised when they proved unavailable or difficult. And I had never been very good at simply enjoying sex for what it was—pleasure, not romance, not emotional nurture; always lurking was the hidden hope that casual sex would evolve into something it wasn't: matehood. None of which was helped along by my penchant for the Garys of the world, who had little to give, and my indifference to the courting of more available men like Jan.

My discontent had at times felt encompassing, had induced a surge of self-recrimination too reminiscent for comfort of how I had been taught to think about myself during my years in psychotherapy the previous decade. One diary entry from 1976 had encapsulated the periodic sense I had had of personal and professional failure:

"Inwardness, a sense of limits, memory. I feel deficient in all three—like most Americans, perhaps. Much of my life *seems* to embody those qualities, but may only parody and counterfeit them. I do spend long hours in isolation, reading and writing—but rarely in contemplation. Trained in habits of rationality, I do impose a superficial order on my experience—but that conceals, and perhaps even fosters, a deeper rebelliousness against all constraints. A professional historian, I'm an official recorder of memory, but that has *heightened* my awareness of memory's limited truth—or usefulness: We *cannot* recover past experience, personal or collective, in a form sufficiently detailed, accurate, and intimate to illuminate or lighten our present griefs and appetites.

"Yet these counterfeit qualities feed real inhibitions: my inability to submerge in past *or* present; my ambivalence as to what it is, in myself *or* the world, I should accept—or try to change.

"So the shuttlecock sails back and forth, a scoreless game."

As balm for such feelings of desolation, I had sought help in experimental LSD therapy, bioenergetics, even Tibetan numerology, and they had left me feeling that my temperament was unalterable, my fate isolation (quite different from solitude—the difference between feeling unable to connect and not wishing to). Much had happened, but little had changed. I had tried telling myself that I was, after all, in my late forties and that by that age most people had long since settled, however unhappily, for who they were and what they had.

I had tried telling myself that my restlessness and discontent had a positive side: an enviably youthful ability not to "settle," not to equate—as the Old Culture encouraged us to—adulthood with stability, unvarying moods, and sober-minded moderation. I had tried to count my many privileges and blessings, and had vowed many times over to stop troubling deaf heaven with repetitive, whiny cries. But I didn't seem to have the knack for consistent affirmation. I could mouth the words, but inside I continued to feel trapped and deprived. I might not have been an obvious candidate for a heart attack, yet in a real sense my arrival at the St. Vincent's intensive care unit had been overdetermined.

How to make it come out differently from this point on? Yes, my life had too much stress in it. Yes, I would go back to yoga and meditation. Yes, I would faithfully do relaxation exercises. Yes, I would go regularly to the Cardiac Fitness Center to ride the exerbike.

But how did one start having "realistic" expectations? How did one aim—and hope for—half a result? ("I am *so* pleased to have gotten that workshop of my play; and no, *of course* I have no wish for a commercial production, nor for fame, riches, a wide audience, or critical praise.") And how did one stop wanting—or develop a new strategy for getting—sustained closeness with another man? Especially since I now thought I understood at last that my drivenness originated not (à la Freud) in an excess of repressed anger, but (à la Harry Stack Sullivan) in an excess of unrequited tenderness (which, to be sure, made me angry).

Should I surrender any lingering hope for a mate, dismiss (or try to dismiss) it from my mind as foolish romanticism, and somehow learn to concentrate on cultivating more nurturing friendships? But could one find those in frenzied, career-mad New York, where twice-monthly lunches were conflated with closeness, and an exchange of gossip with intimacy? Should I leave New York? Could I hope to survive away from a city whose rhythms and intensity had been deeply carved in my boyhood bones? And was it really any different in Iowa?

Well, I told myself, a stutterer doesn't develop a golden tongue simply by coming to the realization that he has a speech problem. Introspection could carry me only so far. I needed to start to *move*, to rejoin the world. I needed to consolidate the insight I'd had that there's a difference between acknowledging periodic despair—it's there, in me and in the world—and assuming that despair is a permanent condition. Things could be bad *and* getting better. If I put one foot in front of the other, maybe I could manage the goal of "moderation" at least behaviorally—in how I lived, if not in how I dreamt.

As the preoccupations and fears of the past year began to recede, I slowly reactivated myself in various directions, particularly in resuming research on gay history and in reinvolving myself in the gay movement. I had still been in the intensive care unit when the first ever national March on Washington for lesbian and gay rights had taken place on October 14, 1979. The organizers estimated some one hundred thousand people had attended—an unprecedented number (even if six months later, a fundamentalist Christian group, "Washington for Jesus," managed to field two hundred thousand).

There seemed additional reasons for thinking that the eighties would usher in a period of heightened progress for gay people. By 1980, the National Gay Task Force's annual budget hit a new high of $260,000, and the Human Rights Campaign Fund in Los Angeles was raising fifty thousand dollars at a single fund-raising event. The road ahead still looked plenty bumpy, as the continuing string of local and state defeats of gay rights bills attested. Yet those defeats seemed somehow overbalanced by the presence at the 1980 Democratic National Convention of seventy-seven openly lesbian and gay delegates (by far the largest number ever) *and* the passage of a plank in the party platform that called for the protection of "all groups from discrimination." Few of us were under the illusion that Jimmy Carter and Walter Mondale could realistically be thought of as gallant crusaders (or even moderate enthusiasts) for gay rights. But most of us instinctively felt that we stood a far better chance of making gains in their administration than in a Reagan-Bush one.

Thus the Reagan landslide came as a major blow. I went to a friend's election party, and watched the returns kill off one liberal senator after another. Americans are notorious ticket-splitters, and when they *don't*, when they machine-gun down progressives on local, state, and federal levels alike, something more frightening is involved than sending a Carter back to Plains. Something more, even, than anger over an inflationary economy. Something like an encompassing Carrie Nation fury at the "decay of moral values."

The right wing had succeeded in tying together a bundle of scapegoat issues—from abortion to busing to ERA to gay rights—and had persuaded the electorate that *those,* and not corporate greed, were the chief villains in American life. The size of Reagan's victory, and the Republican capture of the Senate, had given the right wing every reason to claim a "mandate" to push back the barbarians at the gate, to hold the line on "traditional family values."

About all that lightened the gloom was the realization that Washington's "permanent government" of bureaucrats and middle managers, who were more centrist than right-wing, would likely impede or dilute a full-scale conservative repression; that nearly fifty percent of the eligible populace hadn't voted, and did not necessarily approve nineteenth-century morality, nor measures to solidify the already entrenched privileges of the economic elite—and might now move from inertia to protest; that the organized resistance already in place—

from NOW to the Democratic Socialist Organizing Committee to remnants of labor union liberalism to African-American and Latino organizations (and to the pitifully small lesbian and gay ones)—would prove strong enough to hold onto *some* ground, and might finally be wise enough to seek long-overdue mutual aid and alliance. "Perhaps our best hope," I wrote in my diary, "is that given the way things are these days, if Reagan does push the button, it won't work."

THREE WEEKS AFTER THE ELECTION, having learned that the rent on my Village apartment of ten years was about to be more than doubled, I put down a deposit on a co-op apartment on West Twenty-second Street, in Manhattan's Chelsea district. Then I had to try and raise the needed cash. I sold almost everything I owned of value—from rugs to paintings to archival materials to two thirds of my library—got a high mortgage, and made the closing payment by a hair.

"At last!" I wrote exultantly in my diary. "I'll be getting out of this damned place, closing a literal door on the seventies, starting over. It's going to be a tight squeeze all the way, with some long-overdue belt-tightening. But it's going to be well worth it." I spent the next two months cleaning out piles of detritus from closets, mooning over old letters, giving away periodicals, clothing, and furniture. And I felt the standard mixed bag of emotions, from sadness at the flood of recollections, to exhilaration at putting them aside.

The transition was bruising and disorienting, but by early February 1981, I had resettled in the new place, the shift back to life completed. As I wrote in my diary, "I've gone from a rented apartment haunted by old griefs to a warm and sunlit home with the chance, anyway, for quieter, deeper pleasures, less luxuriant miseries."

I was well aware that in my head, at fifty, I still clung tenaciously to the insatiable fantasy needs and emotional strategies of a young man starting out. But I *knew* better, having had more than a glimpse of opportunities curtailed, energies diminished. And knew, too, that I wasn't entirely uneducable.

POSTSCRIPT

Digging on my terrace one day, happily debating whether impatiens or dahlias would look better in the planters, I was interrupted by a phone call from a friend. Had I heard the strange news? The Centers for Disease Control had announced that a handful of young, previously healthy gay men in Los Angeles had been diagnosed with an unusual form of pneumonia called "Pneumocystis."

No, I hadn't heard. But soon other reports came filtering in. An equally rare form of cancer, Kaposi's Sarcoma—which usually attacked only older men of Mediterranean ancestry—was being seen among homosexual men in their twenties and thirties in several large cities.

By the end of 1981, the reports were no longer a handful, and it had become abundantly clear that a devastating new illness was upon us. *The New York Times* didn't think the news worthy of a feature article—though it put a story about the outbreak of a viral illness among the much-beloved Lippizaner horses on the front page.

But Jerry Falwell immediately saw the significance of AIDS—and its usefulness in whipping up antigay hysteria. He called AIDS "the judgment of God," insisted that gay men deserved no sympathy for a plight their own "sick" lifestyle had brought down on them, publicly rejoiced that the disease seemed incurable and "hopeless," and warned all good Americans to stay away from these foul creatures, these "disease carriers," called gay men.

It was a new decade indeed.

INDEX

INDEX